Race and the Early Republic

Racial Consciousness and Nation-Building in the Early Republic

Edited by Michael A. Morrison
and James Brewer Stewart

ROWMAN & LITTLEFIELD PUBLISHERS, INC.
Lanham • Boulder • New York • Oxford

ROWMAN & LITTLEFIELD PUBLISHERS, INC.

Published in the United States of America
by Rowman & Littlefield Publishers, Inc.
4720 Boston Way, Lanham, Maryland 20706
www.rowmanlittlefield.com

12 Hid's Copse Road
Cumnor Hill, Oxford OX2 9JJ, England

Introduction copyright © 2002 by Rowman & Littlefield Publishers, Inc.

Originally published in *Journal of the Early Republic,* Winter 1999, vol. 19, no. 4.
Copyright © 1999 by the Society for Historians of the Early American Republic.
Reprinted with permission of the Society.

British Library Cataloguing in Publication Information Available

Library of Congress Cataloging-in-Publication Data

Race and the early republic: racial consciousness and nation-building in the early
republic / edited by Michael A. Morrison and James Brewer Stewart.
    p. cm
  Includes bibliographical references and index.
  ISBN 0-7425-2130-3 (alk. paper)—ISBN 0-7425-2131-1 (pbk. : alk. paper)
    1.United States—Politics and government—1775–1783. 2. United States—Politics and
government—1783–1865. 3. United States—Race relations—Political aspects—History. 4.
African Americans—Civil rights—History—18th century. 5. African Americans—Civil
rights—History—19th century. 6. Indians of North America—Civil rights—History—18th
century. 7. Indians of North America—Civil rights—History—19th century. 8. Political
culture—United States—History—18th century. 9. Political culture—United
States—History—19th century. 10. Racism—Political aspects—United States—History. I.
Morrison, Michael A. 1948– II. Stewart, James Brewer.

E302.1 .R33 2002
323.1'73'09—dc21

                                                                          2001048274

⊗™ The paper used in this publication meets the minimum requirements of American
National Standard for Information Sciences—Permanence of Paper for Printed Library
Materials, ANSI/NISO Z39.48-1992.

Contents

Introduction

Michael A. Morrison and
James Brewer Stewart

By 1840, political institutions and political culture in the United States had evolved far in the direction of white supremacy—a system that historians have variously characterized as "*herrenvolk* democracy," "*herrenvolk* republicanism," or, simply, as the "white republic."[1] Whatever their differences in meaning, each of these terms emphasizes that the emergence of the United States as a mass-participation political system in the 1820s and 1830s rested on a terrible paradox: As personal freedom and political equality for men of European backgrounds and ancestries became ever more widely shared, this same process became ever more deeply involved in the isolation and degradation of people of African and American Indian descent. The essays presented in this volume, when read together, offer a rich account of how this process of racialized state-building developed from the time of the emerging republic of the 1770s to the age of the two-party electoral democracy of the antebellum era.

In this regard, it is essential to stress to readers the importance of the order in which these essays are presented. Since their sequencing proceeds forward from the Revolution toward the Civil War, their overall content illustrates the long-term evolution of political culture and political institutions in the new Republic toward (1) the national integration and mass participation in politics of white people, men in particular, (2) the ever more systematic subordination of people of color, and (3) the development of new forms of political resistence and adjustment among Indians and African Americans when facing this mounting suppression.

A second feature of this collection is also designed to assist readers in establishing clear understandings of these complex and interwoven developments. In an effort to suggest underlying themes and larger connections, the authors have taken care to indicate clearly how various aspects of their individual contributions might be related to important points developed by other essays in the volume. The purpose, then, is to offer readers opportunities to engage in their own interpretive dialogues with each of the essays, and with the collection as a whole, as they consider the works together in developmental sequences. In this regard the ordering of the individual essays invites the reader to begin the volume through an introductory essay by David R. Roediger and next by considering four essays (by Daniel K. Richter, Lois E. Horton, Joanne Pope Melish, and Jon Gjerde) that analyze the role of race in the shaping of political *cultures* in the transition from a revolutionary republic to a (white) democratic state. Next, three essays (by James Brewer Stewart, Lacy K. Ford Jr., and James Ronda) stress relationships between racialized ideologies and the growth of political *institutions and practices* in the period between 1790 and 1840. The final essay, by David Brion Davis, offers the reader a concluding opportunity for synthesis by presenting a comprehensive meditation on historical relationships between racial subordination and democratic struggle in the history of the early republic that speaks to the contributions of all the other essayists.

To frame and highlight this important transition from *culture* to *institutions and practices*, Roediger's and Davis's essays emphasize and synthesize both aspects of the process. The opening essay, Roediger's " The Pursuit of Whiteness: Property, Terror, and Expansion, 1790–1860," stresses the importance of interdisciplinary endeavors between historians of racial politics and cultural studies analysts of racial identities. After reminding readers of the long-established and ongoing work of historians on problems of race, and after illustrating the value of newer poststructuralist approaches, Roediger then applies both modes of study to an analysis of political culture by concentrating on the racialized content of a very specific moment in a very specific political practice: the 1858 climactic debate over slavery's western expansion between Abraham Lincoln and Stephen A. Douglas.

While also linking political culture to political practices, Davis's concluding essay, "The Culmination of Racial Polarities and Prejudice," meditates expansively on the implications of all the other essays when offering a comprehensive understanding of the nation's overall history as a racialized political system. In so doing, Davis locates the origins of white republican racial bias deep in medieval and renaissance history in order to explain why the period between 1776 and 1830 became such a critical juncture in American history. It was then, he explains, that white Americans' most deeply rooted and ancient prejudices came into violent conflict with the unprecedented possibility that people of color in the new republic might actually be liberated by their oppressors or, more traumatic still, might liberate themselves. These decades thus constituted seismic moments in the reshaping of the republican state, Davis emphasizes, the shock waves from which still reverberate disturbingly into our time.

Between Roediger's opening essay and Davis's concluding statement are seven additional essays, the first four of which explore racial influences in shaping republican political culture in the new nation. In Daniel Richter's "'Believing That Many of the Red People Suffer Much for Want of Food': Hunting, Agriculture and a Quaker Construction of Indiannness in the Early Republic" one finds a telling analysis of why philanthropic gestures by even the most forward-thinking whites toward indigenous Americans so quickly went astray into prejudice and projects of domination. As a complement to Richter's treatment of Indian–white interactions, in "From Class to Race in Early America: Northern Post-Emancipation Racial Reconstruction, Lois E. Horton analyzes the historical processes that transformed northern black people in the eyes of most whites from their traditional positions within the early republic's multiethnic "lower orders" into a "permanently degraded" and distinctly "despicable race." Joanne Pope Melish then elaborates on many of these same themes in "The 'Condition' Debate: Racial Discourse in the Antebellum North," an analysis the counterpoint between white New Englanders' deepening biases against the "condition" of "blackness" and struggles of free African Americans to define themselves as independent and equal people. To conclude the essays on race and the formation of early republic's political culture, Jon Gjerde's "Here in America there is neither king or tyrant: European Encounters with Race, 'Freedom,' and Their European Pasts" extends Melish's work on white identity formation by explaining how European immigrants came to understand relationships between race, slavery, and citizenship embedded in republican political culture, and once so understanding, to claim the privileges of whiteness.

At this juncture in the sequence of essays, the emphasis shifts from analyses of racial influences in the early republic's political culture to analyses of race and the development of political institutions, political practices, and processes of state-building. James Brewer Stewart's "Modernizing Difference: The Political Meanings of Color in the Free States, 1776–1840" explains how Whig and Democrat mass-participation party politics in the 1830s were powerfully shaped by unprecedented forces of white supremacy during a violent crisis in northern race relations that erupted in response to increased African-American activism, a nascent white abolitionist movement, and deeper social tensions generated by rapid urbanization and the expansion of consumer capitalism. Lacy K. Ford Jr.'s "Making 'White Man's Country' White: Race, Slavery, and State-Building in the Jacksonian South" delineates the powerful impact of this same Jacksonian racial crisis on white politics within the slave states, which resulted in wide-ranging political debates among white legislators and the adoption of many new laws and policies to strengthen and perpetuate *herrenvolk* democracy. Read together, the essays by Ford and Stewart demonstrate just how pervasive the impact of the Jacksonian racial crisis actually was, and how powerfully it compelled already racist political systems in the early republic to become all the more repressive in the name of equality for all whites. The final essay addressing political institutions and practices, James P. Ronda's "'We Have a Country': Race, Geography, and the Invention of Indian Territory" continues in this vein by illustrating the the deeply contradictory impact of *herrenvolk* public policy on American Indians in the new republic. For white politicians, policy makers, and explorers, Ronda explains that "Indian country" constituted, first, an innovative, imaginative geographic construct and, next, a politically defined specific location reserved for Indians marked for expulsion by the expanding republic. To Indians, however, this same geographic invention ultimately took on the meaning of "homelands" where they, themselves, possessed the freedom to reconstruct racial politics and political economy on terms exclusively theirs.

Readers will quickly discover while working through these essays that they have all been written in ongoing dialogue with one another. Since contributors all read one another's essays while revising their own drafts, the process of discovering connections between them proved to be obvious, revealing, and, ultimately, the feature of this volume that creates the opportunity of presenting something "greater than the sum of its parts." Consequently, readers are invited not only to follow the inter-essay conversations that proceed throughout the collection, but to extend, modify, and revise them as seems to them most rigorous, revealing, and rewarding. For in the final analysis, the political culture and the political practices of racial consciousness in the early republic were "of a piece," which is why understanding their relationships requires as much critical engagement from readers as it did from the contributors and editors.

NOTE

1. These terms appear respectively in George Fredrickson, *The Black Image in the White Mind: The Debate on Afro-American Character and Destiny* (New York, 1971): David R. Roediger, *The Wages of Whiteness: Race and the Making of the American Working Class* (London, 1997); Alexander Saxton, *The Rise and Fall of the White Republic: Class, Politics and Mass Culture in Nineteenth-Century America* (New York, 1990).

1

The Pursuit of Whiteness: Property, Terror, and Expansion, 1790–1860

David R. Roediger

Paul Gilroy, holding acerbically forth in the collection *Black British Cultural Studies*, warns that attempts to write in an interdisciplinary way about identity "can send the aspirant practitioners of cultural studies scuttling back toward the quieter sanctuaries of their old disciplinary affiliations, where the problems and potential pleasures of thinking through identity are less formidable and engaging." Behavior after the scuttling, he adds, follows disciplinary lines: "Anthropologists utter sighs of relief, psychologists rub their hands together in glee, philosophers relax [and] literary critics look blank and perplexed. Historians remain silent."[1]

In the particular case of the study of white identity and privilege in the United States, historians have been less silent than Gilroy's model implies. The major review essays on what has lamentably been named "whiteness studies" consistently place social history at the center of a burgeoning multidisciplinary literature, citing the work of Alexander Saxton, Theodore Allen, and Noel Ignatiev, among others.[2] Most ambitious accounts of white identity by (in terms of formal departmental affiliations) non-historians, including those of Karen Brodkin, Susan Gubar, Eric Lott, and Michael Rogin, frame their material historically. Moreover, I will argue, a too often "lost" historical literature on American Indians and white identity anticipated many of the insights of more recent work and deserves rereading in the light of cultural studies.[3]

Nonetheless, tensions surround the place of history in investigations of white identity. Much cultural studies work in the area lacks historical grounding and ignores or misconceives the emphasis on class relations common among historians of whiteness. Conversely, not a few historians disdain cultural studies approaches, and even inquiries into race and cultural representation more generally, as ethereal and frivolous. One goal of this essay is therefore to expose an audience of historians to critical insights from those not formally or entirely in the history business. Implicit throughout, that agenda is forwarded explicitly at the outset in a prelude bringing together the writings of the legal analyst and critical race theorist Cheryl Harris and the American Studies scholar Saidiya Hartman around the themes of property, happiness, and terror in the formation of white identity.[4] The main section of the essay will then use a dramatic moment in the Lincoln-Douglas debates as a window through which the strengths, weaknesses, and gaps of recent writings on whiteness, expansion, and terror in the early national and antebellum periods might be surveyed. In arguing that relatively neglected older studies offer promising approaches to deepen understanding of that moment in the Lincoln-Douglas confrontation, the necessity of considering white racial formation in the context of a settler colonial nation, as well as a slaveholding one, will receive emphasis.

WHITE PURSUITS: A PRELUDE

When the Founding Fathers used the wonderful phrase "the pursuit of happiness," political theorists tell us that they may have had in mind largely the pursuit of property. The fascinating connections between property and happiness hinge not only on the vocabulary of Lockean political philosophy but also on the ways in which both property and happiness found meaning in their relationship to whiteness and white privilege.[5] In some ways these relationships are familiar. From Edmund Morgan to the recent work of the political philosopher Charles Mills, it has been clear that ideas of freedom for the mass of white males developed hard by, and against, notions and practices that ensured that those not white could not pursue happiness effectively in political, social, and economic realms.[6] What Mills calls a "racial contract" served as a fundamental part of the bourgeois social contract. "European humanism," Mills wryly observes, all too consistently "meant that only Europeans were human" and rewrote history as a struggle to extend both the property- and happiness-producing rights of Europeans and the hegemony of white "civil" spaces over nonwhite "wild" spaces.[7] The most sophisticated and celebrated bringing together of property and enjoyment as benefits of whiteness remains W. E. B. Du Bois's discussion of the financial as well as the "public and psychological" wages accruing to whites in his *Black Reconstruction*, a study that undergirds much recent scholarship on whiteness.[8]

But even given that they draw on so rich a tradition, Cheryl Harris and Saidiya Hartman sharpen our understanding of whiteness, property, and happiness in startling ways. In her massive *Harvard Law Review* article, "Whiteness as Property," Harris's deeply historical work pushes far beyond the commonplace that whiteness has carried, and still carries, greater access to property in the United States. She argues instead that whiteness has been so tied to the right to own property as to itself come to constitute a legally recognizable, usable, and cherished form of property, *possessed by all whites*. The attempted reduction of Blacks, but not whites, to "objects of property" in slavery and the expropriation of Indian land via legal processes that "established whiteness as prerequisite to the exercise of enforceable property rights," created, in Harris's view, an enduring set of expectations that whiteness had a value as property.[9]

In addition to its ability to ground whiteness both within and beyond binary Black-white dynamics, Harris's approach offers great insight into the complexity of the label "white." Far from denying the existence and import of poverty among whites, Harris establishes the grounds on which poor whites became chained to both their poverty and their anticipations of property benefits as whites—often a bad check but as often the only one they had.[10] Harris specifically notes that whiteness fits legal definitions of property in that those categorized as white enjoyed the "right to use and enjoy" their racial position. She adds tellingly that "As whiteness is simultaneously an aspect of identity and a property interest, it is something that can both be experienced and deployed as a resource,"—that is, it has utility in both the pursuit of happiness and the pursuit of property and forms part of the connective tissue between the two.[11]

Hartman's cultural study originates at a point very near to Harris's legal/historical observations regarding whiteness, property, and enjoyment. Indeed Hartman begins *Scenes of Subjection* with a long section of linked chapters titled "Formations of Terror end Enjoyment." In her specific discussion of "the property of enjoyment," she subtly connects the twinned white pursuits of property and of happiness. Her excerpting of *Black's Law Dictionary* on what it means to "enjoy" drives home her (and Harris's) points dramatically:

> to have, possess, and use with satisfaction; to occupy or have the benefit of . . . the exercise of a right, privilege or incorporeal hereditament. Comfort, consolation, ease, happiness, pleasure and satisfaction.[12]

Holding that white "hereditament" created expectations that relations with Black people would create "delight" as well as wealth, Hartman "re-places" popular culture within economic structures, state policies, and practices of terror. Of blackface minstrelsy and melodrama, she writes, "The punitive pleasures yielded through figurative possession of blackness cannot be disentangled from the bodily politics of chattel slavery." She continues, "The terror of pleasure—that violence that undergirded the comic moment in minstrelsy—and the pleasure of terror—the force of evil that propelled the plot of melodrama and fascinated the spectator—filiated the coffle, the auction block, the popular stage, and plantation amusements in a scandalous equality."[13]

Hartman's study builds on a substantial African-American tradition that regards terror and complicity in terror as the glue binding together those who think that they are white.[14] Hartman's contribution, among much else, is to capture the terror in what she calls "liberal" moments, such as Abraham Lincoln's chilling racialized reflections on what he called the "effect of condition on human happiness." Witnessing twelve slaves on a steamboat, "strung together like so many fish on a trot-line" and being separated from home and kin, Lincoln's attention fell on fiddle-playing, singing, dancing, and joking among the twelve. His conclusion bespeaks the ways in which, as Hartman puts it, "white self-reflection" used the supposed "elasticity of blackness . . . as a vehicle for exploring the human condition," expecting at once to know happiness and to come to terms with misery by looking on Blacks. After his description of the utterly inhuman conditions of the slaves, Lincoln ended by evoking the slaves' mirth and musing that God "renders the worst of the human condition tolerable, while He permits the best to be nothing but tolerable."[15]

If Harris's location of whiteness *within* United Statesian conceptions of property productively complicates attempts to arrive at a materialist account of race and class in the antebellum United States, Hartman's study puts paid to the surprisingly insistent recent attempts to rehabilitate minstrelsy and other racist entertainments. Going far beyond Eric Lott's useful insistence that both "love and theft" were involved in minstrel appropriations of African-American music, David Grimsted and William Lhamon have argued that present-minded scholars have been so eager to brand such entertainments as racist that they have missed the real core of the stagecraft. For Grimsted that core was humor; for Lhamon, it was a subversive lumpenproletarian cultural exchange across the color line, "a racial project more radical even than abolitionism."[16] Hartman elaborates the firm and wise position staked out by Alexander Saxton on this issue a quarter century ago: "The ideological impact of minstrelsy was programmed by its conventional blackface form. There is no possibility of escaping this relationship because the greater the interest, talent, complexity and humanity embodied in its content, the most irresistible was the racist message of its form." *Scenes of Subjection* gives flesh to the reasons for the irony Saxton identifies. At once about pleasure, humor, and property (Minstrel question: "Why is we niggas like a slave ship on de Coast of Africa?" Answer: "Because we both make money by taking off the negroes."), minstrelsy "reiterated racial subjection." The "love" on which blackface bodysnatching traded was, for Hartman, as terrifying as the "theft" its performance implemented. Furthermore, it was utterly inseparable from that theft. Both joined to constitute "the illusory integrity of whiteness." For reasons Kalpana Seshadri-Crooks develops in her recent and rich psychoanalytic account of the dynamics of racial jokes, minstrel scenes of subjection and their punch lines required endless repetition. They could never quite exorcise the threat, subversive to white pleasure and rule, of being laughed at in ways that threatened to expose the lie of whiteness.[17]

CHANTING WHITE MEN

If historical reenactors want to get it just right, reprises of the 1858 Lincoln-Douglas debates will need not only the eloquent starring principals but also a large cast of extras to swell the audience. Among the lines for the Douglas backers were "White men, white men," and the echoing "White, white." These eerie interventions, delivered at the Freeport debate amidst Douglas's denunciations of Lincoln as a race-mixer who allegedly accepted advice from the African-American abolitionist Frederick Douglass, gave voice to the popularity of white identity in the late antebellum United States.[18] In many ways the recent and much celebrated historiography on whiteness between the Revolution and the Civil War effectively positions us to understand that chanting crowd and the ways Douglas (and Lincoln) played to it, especially if we add the insights of Harris and Hartman to those of Allen, Saxton, Ignatiev, and others. Democratic Party demographics, in Illinois and in the national arena where Douglas's larger ambitions lay, depended on the incorporation of Irish and other immigrants as white voters. Ignatiev's *How the Irish Became White* shows why Douglas's insistence on moving beyond an Anglo-Saxon whiteness to posit a pan-white "American race" could resonate dramatically. The homosocial habit of affirming white maleness in public provides the subject matter for recent analyses of minstrelsy that go to the heart of how Douglas's auditors rehearsed their chants and knew their lines. The utility of white identity in forging cross-class alliances and in providing real and psychological payoffs to the more immiserated Douglas Democrats is central to the agenda of studies showing what it meant to be "not a slave" in an increasingly class-divided and proletarianized labor force.[19]

However, the reverberating chants and the debates that they punctuated also signal ways in which "whiteness studies" risks prematurely cutting off historical exchanges, leaving critical dimensions of the working of race, property, and terror unexamined, encouraging classic older studies (and exciting new ones) to go unread when whiteness is investigated. The chants ought immediately to alert us to large gaps in even the best of the "whiteness studies" by historians of the nineteenth century. If cross-class alliances cemented by white consciousness are at issue, our knowledge of working-class motivations for joining such an alliance runs far ahead of what is known, even after James Brewer Stewart's intelligent opening up of the issue about middle-class white identity. Whiteness among midwesterners, and among rural populations generally, is so understudied as to give pause regarding generalizations about Douglas's backers. As well as the process by which the Irish "became white" is understood—and even here some amendments are likely to be required in light of Catherine Eagan's forthcoming revisionist analysis of awareness of race in nineteenth-century Ireland and fascinating recent work on Irish immigrant men and women who in some ways resisted becoming white—studies of other immigrant groups remain lacking.[20] German Americans are the largest and most interesting such group. Bruce Levine's able investigations of radical immigrant Germans and the growth of "black Dutch" participation in the antislavery cause heads a slim body of scholarship. German immigrants also surely found their ways into the ranks of Douglas's militantly white Democrats.[21] That religious fissures conditioned differing stances among Germans only reminds us of another large gap, the absence of discussion by historians of whiteness of religious faith, particularly among antebellum Protestants.[22]

As Dana Frank has eloquently shown, the new literature on white identity, especially among workers, overwhelmingly focuses on white male identity. Though this emphasis might superficially seem an apt one as we try to understand chanting white men, it leaves so much out as to imperil understanding even of the gender on which it concentrates. The chanters in Freeport responded specifically to Douglas's charge that the city had recently been sullied by Frederick Douglass's appearance in a "magnificent" carriage on which a "beautiful young [white] lady" sat while her mother "reclined" with Douglass inside. Although some opponents of Douglas in the crowd shouted, "What of it," Lincoln took such appeals to white purity seriously. He fended them off by attempting to capture the racemixing issue as his own, arguing that it was the spread of slavery that threatened to bring whites and Blacks together sexually in the Midwest. As my recent research on affinities and differences between the antebellum feminist metaphor of "sex slavery" and the (white) labor movement's metaphor of "wage slavery" shows, consideration of white women's identity throws relations between masculinity and property into new relief. Dana Nelson's *National Manhood: Capitalist Citizenship and the Imagined Fraternity of White Men*, discussed at the conclusion of this essay, squarely focuses on the study of white masculinity, but its subtle analysis crosses and recrosses gender lines, making it also the best account yet of white womanhood in antebellum United States.[23]

Nonetheless, the need for gendered accounts that make white womanhood their central subject remains acute, especially since women's history of the early national and antebellum periods brilliantly links gender, property, and citizenship in ways that cry out for both comparison with and connection to the property, of whiteness. Indeed Nancy Isenberg grounds her *Sex and Citizenship in Antebellum America* in the idea of a "disinvestment" of women's rights to property and liberty. Jeanne Boydston's remarkable *Home and Work* reminds us that whiteness became a much more common male public performance precisely in the context of a widening and deeply gendered ideological split between the private and the public. Moreover, this split denied the fact that white women's labor was critically and increasingly tied to the market economy. Even as white masculine identity could be used to paper over contradictions between free labor ideals of economic independence and increasing proletarianization, white true womanhood could shore up perceptions of isolation from the world of power and money. I have long enjoined every student who reads *Wages of Whiteness* to also read *Home and Work*, but the crying need is for studies that discuss race, gender, and the market together, accounting for the ways in which exceptional women performed and challenged whiteness in public and for the ways in which white female identity was (re)made in private spaces.[24]

Superb recent studies of slavery and white womanhood in the South by Martha Hodes, Ariela Gross, Nell Painter, and others suggest that we are poised for exactly such a sweeping new interpretation, which will also usefully draw on Karen Sanchez-Eppler's important *Touching Liberty*. The latter study includes telling observations on terror, arguing that antebellum women's rights advocates used narratives regarding slave women's bodies as a means both to broach and evade the ways in which sexual violence touched their own bodies. Appropriately enough, Cheryl Harris has initiated the synthetic investigations so badly needed by considering whiteness and gender within both systems of production and reproduction in her recent and provocative "Finding Sojourner's Truth."[25]

WHITE RACE, POWER, AND REPRESENTATION

A fascinating dimension of Douglas's own performance suggested especially critical issues much in need of debate by historians of whiteness who wish to emphasize questions of property and terror. He characterized the overwhelmingly white and avowedly white supremacist state of Illinois in terms of a racial spectrum. The Lincoln-Douglas debates toured the state, whose political/racial geography Douglas summed up thusly: ". . . pretty black in the north end of the state, about the center it is pretty good mulatto and it is almost white when you get down to Egypt [Southern Illinois]."[26] In his positing of an imperiled "white politics" (and of black deviations from it) even in areas almost all white, Douglas takes us to a particularly vexed issue, that of the extent to which white identity grew in face-to-face contact with people of color (crudely, in the realm of social history) or in the context of representation and symbolism (crudely, in the realm of cultural theory and history). Reviewers of *Wages of Whiteness* rightly criticized its tilt toward the latter emphasis. Since property and terror so closely imply power relationships, it is tempting to think that sites where such power was exercised, or resisted, most immediately ought to be the focus of the research. The richness of accounts that attend more closely to the labor process and to race relations in neighborhoods underline the force of calls for finely grained social history of whiteness. Studies, such as those by James Brewer Stewart, Lois E. Horton, and Joanne Pope Melish in this collection, which are well-grounded in the histories of free Blacks in the North, likewise demonstrate the value of textured scholarship that crosses the color line. So too do fine recent inquiries, including Lacy K. Ford's essay in this volume, regarding race and whiteness in the South, an oddly underemphasized site of white racial formation where opportunities for face-to-face transracial contacts were most extensive.[27]

Given the excellence of such scholarship and the common sense association of property and of terror with direct social experience, the flat assumption that white identity is always best studied as the local product of immediate social relations across racial lines has its appeals. However, such an assumption can generate quite naive positions that neglect Saidiya Hartman's reminders regarding the "filiation" of slavery, discrimination, and cultural representations of race. As Douglas and his chorus of supporters demonstrate, white racial identity could function, largely in the absence of people of color, to position white voters in national, partly race-based political coalitions, to shore up exclusionary efforts in the face of real and perceived threats of in-migration of those not categorized as white, and to produce pleasure as well as unity. As Stuart Hall has forcefully shown, posing representations of race as outside of and opposed to concrete lived experience clarifies little. If starkly and consistently contradicted by day-to-day direct experiences, racist representations could not in the end survive intact. But in the shorter run there was ample space for patterns of representation to structure how such interactions would unfold and would be understood.[28]

Two very recent works make especially noteworthy and materially grounded assaults on questions involving race, representation, and day-to-day interactions. Joanne Pope Melish's *Disowning Slavery: Gradual Emancipation and "Race" in New England, 1780–1860* argues against locating white identity in the region mainly in the context of Yankees' contemplation of the slave South. The New England experience of slaveholding, and of a gradual, oppressive emancipation designed to serve interests of order and property among whites, mattered greatly in racial formation, according to Melish. However, in restoring this social experience to the important position it deserves in white racial formation in the Northeast, Melish evokes great complexity. She shows that it was not just the dynamics and end of New England slavery that influenced white identity but also the process by which slavery was forgotten ("disowned") and a vision of a "free white republic" without significant African-American presence was propagated in various cultural forms and political forums. Melish's apt discussion of the fascination with the terror accompanying the supposed enslavement of whites in the Barbary States in the 1780s and 1790s details an important chapter in the prehistory of ideas about "white slavery" but one based on direct social experience of a relatively small number of victims.[29]

John Kuo Wei Tchen's monumental *New York Before Chinatown: Orientalism and the Shaping of American Culture, 1776–1882* also serves as a model of a healthy refusal to imagine a choice between experience and representation in accounting for white racial formation. In his early chapters Tchen fleshes out a United Statesian orientalism honed in the presence of very few Asian people but out of highly property-inflected relationships to Asian commodities such as porcelain and tea. However, later sections place Chinese migrants squarely in the wildly diverse and freewheeling "port culture" of New York City, where they worked with, worked for, sold to, cohabited with, and (representation never being absent) performed before white New Yorkers.[30]

EXPANDING PURSUITS OF WHITENESS

Another of Douglas's arresting appeals went out to white-thinking Mexican War veterans. They could, Douglas argued, corroborate his views on the need to defend "white blood" against threats of racial "amalgamation." In the war, they had seen the results of mixing "white men, Indians and negroes" in the faces and the degradation of the Mexican population. Douglas explicitly defined white manhood as superior to both African-American and Indian others. At another juncture, Douglas took the debate further abroad. When Lincoln held that the Declaration of Independence applied to African Americans, Douglas fretted that, if such arguments were countenanced, white men would be reduced to a parity with Fiji Islanders.[31]

Douglas's expansion of the racial terrain far beyond a Black-white binary identifies an area of weakness in recent histories of white racial formation. Almost all the most-cited historians of whiteness are writers whose earlier writings are in labor history and, or whose analyses are much-influenced by

Marxism, usually both. This materialist bent remains a rather well-kept secret, and the study of whiteness is sometimes criticized as if it emanated entirely from the most airy expanses of cultural studies. But materialist influences characterize the work of Alexander Saxton, George Lipsitz, Noel Ignatiev, Theodore Allen, Dana Frank, and myself.[32] The focus, not too surprisingly, has often fallen on labor systems and property, with slavery looming large as a race-making response to class conflict, as a barrier to working-class unity, and as a counterpoint against which notions of free labor and white identity took form. Whatever its successes, this line of thought has clearly contributed to the tendency to see racial formation in Black and white.

In the case of *Wages of Whiteness*, an emphasis on the history of the white worker made it especially tempting to oversimplify matters. Important as they were, so the argument went, Indian-white relations were about land and not labor and, in any case, Indians were seen as disappearing, not as an ongoing other against which whiteness could be defined and mobilized. (Minstrel pun: "The Indian's race is almost run.") The result was that *Wages of Whiteness* relegated settler colonialism and the terror attending it to the "prehistory" of white racial formation among workers, repeating an error made in even some of the best accounts of race in the colonial period. Even on their own terms, these particular arguments in *Wages of Whiteness* collapse utterly. Early and mid-nineteenth-century labor politics often hinged precisely on land. Waged Indian labor, as excellent recent studies show, was significant and widespread. In parts of the antebellum North there thrived a wishful pretense that African Americans, and not just Indians, were disappearing. Moreover, as Lora Romero's and Jean O'Brien's superb investigations show, the very act of "disappearing" still-existing Indian populations mattered greatly in the formation of local, national, and racial consciousness in antebellum New England, even as the region also "disowned" its slaveholding past.[33]

Very recent work, and neglected older studies, move us decisively beyond a Black-white binary and towards consideration of settler colonialism in structuring Douglas's expansive commentary on Indians, Mexicans, and Fiji Islanders. Philip Deloria's impressive *Playing Indian*, for example, uses the history of Indian impersonation to enter broad questions of race and nation. Deloria writes, "Blackness, in a range of cultural guises, has been an essential precondition for American whiteness . . . the figure of 'the Indian' holds an equally critical position in American culture." Susan Scheckel, in her *The Insistence of the Indian*, makes similar arguments where connections between race and nation are drawn. Darlene Wilson and Patricia Beaver cause the ignored history of ethnically mixed "Melungeon" people in Appalachia to speak to large questions of Native-American identity, coercion, gender, whiteness, and property in that region and the nation.[34] Paul Foos's ambitious

1997 Yale dissertation, "Mexican Wars: Soldiers and Society in an Age of Expansion," provides a sophisticated study of the social history of "the phenomenon of [white] working class manifest destiny" in war and politics. Despite a certain overeagerness to transcend race, Foos illuminates the position of Douglas and that of the chanters, and even the possible tension between their positions.[35] Recent books on race in California and the Southwest before and during the nineteenth century, especially those by Tomás Almaguer, Ramón Gutiérrez, and Lisbeth Haas, bear strongly on questions regarding who became categorized as white and what it meant to assume white identities. Strongly attentive to questions of property as well as to religion, gender, and racial ideas within subordinated groups, these studies signal rising sophistication and provide models for future work. More broadly, the "new western history" has encouraged that study of white settlers in relationship to a varied and continuing presence of people of color and has insisted, at its best, on historicizing white racial ideologies. Likewise important for studies of whiteness and of race generally are the friendly challenges by leading Asian Americanists to the tendency of some marxists to assume that categories like "labor" or "reserve army" of the unemployed are abstract and raceless except in particular instances when race obtrudes.[36]

As impressive as this emerging scholarship is proving to be, it is perhaps the rereading of older classic studies of race, nation, and U.S. expansion that hold the greatest promise in moving the study of whiteness beyond a Black-white axis and in ensuring that the experience of settler colonialism will not be seen as unrelated to the history of white identity. The most exciting such contributions include Richard Drinnon's *Facing West*, Michael Rogin's *Fathers and Children*, Reginald Horsman's *Race and Manifest Destiny*, Richard Slotkin's *The Fatal Environment,* and, more broadly pitched, Ronald Takaki's *Iron Cages*.[37] These books, most of them written as investigations of racism and nationalism in the context or the wake of antiwar and anti-imperialist movements of the Vietnam period, offer especially apt points of departure for historical reflections, placing questions regarding when and why white identity came to be embraced within the context of anti-Indian violence, capitalist expansion, and nationalism. With some exceptions, these American Studies-influenced works do suffer from a focus, however critical, on conquest, on the conquerors, and on sources generated by victors. Not only is the agency of Indian people, well-invoked in James P. Ronda's and Daniel K. Richter's contributions to this volume, underplayed, but so too are Indians' critical reflections on race and whiteness, topics beginning to be charted in the fine works of Nancy Shoemaker and R. Keith Basso. In probing what Herman Melville called "the metaphysics of Indian hating," Drinnon, Slotkin, and others often greatly emphasize cultural over social history and develop class differences in racial ideology hesitantly.[38] All that said, however, the freshness and force of this older literature remains nothing short of remarkable on several counts when it is read as part of the history of whiteness.

The work of Rogin, Takaki, and others illuminates reasons why direct social experience with "others" cannot be the only focus of research on the generation of white identity. When Douglas debated Lincoln, much of the crowd likely had not encountered Indians, but they knew something of Lincoln's record of soldiering, the folklore of conquest, and arguments regarding the relationship of free labor and "free" land. Some may have been Mexican War veterans; many more heard the stories of those veterans. (Hard-by its discussion of "the metaphysics of Indian-hating," Melville's *The Confidence-Man* adds another ambiguity, drawing a masterful portrait of a "soldier of fortune" who begs as a disabled Mexican War veteran but whose misfortunes likely grew out of class and political conflicts in New York City).[39]

The older literature, centered largely on the ways that the "civilized" white American took the "savage" Indian as his or her counterpoint, deserves attention for several additional reasons. The first involves the considerable extent to which these studies concentrate on matters of importance in shaping property relations far beyond the confines of the (shifting) frontier. In Chapter 31 of *Capital*, Marx's account of the "dawn" of capitalism in processes of "so-called primitive" accumulation of capital emphasized "the extirpation, enslavement and entombment in mines of the aboriginal population" of the Americas as one key to such accumulation. He made this point, however, in a chapter titled "Genesis of the Industrial Capitalist," refusing to imagine separate histories for metropoles and peripheries.[40]

In doing justice to Marx's insight, Slotkin, Rogin, and Takaki have probed white identity not just in zones of contact and conquest but also far more generally. Slotkin subtitles *The Fatal Environment* with *The Myth of the Frontier in the Age of Industrialization*. He lays the ground for his postbellum discussions of convergences between anti-Indian and anti-(white) labor radical stereotypes with a close treatment of how antebellum thinkers as different as Theodore Parker and George Fitzhugh developed "a racialist reading of social class" among whites by drawing on American-Indian as well as African-American counterpoints. Most astoundingly, in terms of Douglas and the chants of "White men," Slotkin offers a surprising reminder that the Kansas-Nebraska conflict—the linchpin of Douglas's career and a set of events almost always discussed in terms of freedom and slavery—also included insistent charges that Douglas's Democratic Party had attempted to create and manipulate an "Indian vote" in Kansas. They brought "savages" to the polls there, so the charges went, even as they rallied racially and religiously suspect Irish voters in urban areas.[41] In a key early chapter of *Iron Cages*, Takaki gracefully moves "Beyond Primitive Accumulation," making the treatment and imagination of Indians by whites central in shaping individualism, asceticism, enterprise, and acceptance of alienation nationally.[42] Rogin, who begins *Fathers and Children* with long sections explicitly titled "Whites" and "Whites and Indians," develops dialectical relationships among primitive accumulation, liberal capitalism, and the "market revolution" patiently. He further elaborates and historicizes an argument on the role of projection of desires onto Indians and into "wild" spaces by whites uneasily internalizing new disciplines. His views strikingly parallel George Rawick's seminal insights regarding the ways in which white bourgeois anxieties were projected onto Africans and African Americans. Rogin writes:

> Disastrously for the liberal self-conception, however, its distance from primitive man was not secure. At the heart of ambitious expansionism lay the regressive impulse itself. Indians were in harmony with nature; lonely, independent liberal men were separated from it. Liberalism generated a forbidden nostalgia for childhood—for the nurturing, blissful, primitively violent connection to nature that white Americans had to leave behind.[43]

Noteworthy too is the great extent to which the older literature foregrounds questions of gender and terror. This is true not only within Rogin's explicitly family-centered and psychoanalytic framework but also, for example, in Takaki's brilliant commentary on just why Melville took care to have a "western" character describe his model Indian-hater, Colonel John Moredock, as "no cold husband or cold father" but a warm, patriarchal protector whose anti-Indian rage allegedly never moved to other realms. (*The Confidence-Man*, published just as the Lincoln-Douglas debates were taking shape, remembers Moredock as being so beloved popularly that he "was pressed to become candidate for governor" of [note well!] Illinois, an honor he declined as possibly "incompatible" with his Indian-hating).[44] In conjunction with more recent work regarding the social history of race and gender in the early Old Northwest and West and regarding the cultural meaning of widely circulating "captivity narratives" describing life among Indians, the older literature challenges assumptions that contemplation of African Americans was *the* central process shaping ideas concerning white gender roles.[45]

It is the very expansiveness of the consideration of race, class, and expansion in the works written in the 1970s and early 1980s that offers the greatest food for thought. These writers were, for example, far more likely to move beyond Black/white binary approaches to white racial formation than have been recent practitioners of "whiteness studies." Drinnon's *Facing West* follows expansion from colonial Indian removals to Indochina, riding the "Occident Express" and tracing its contributions to racism and bureaucracy. His chapter on the South Carolina writer William G. Simms joins anti-Indian and anti-Black racism in especially destructive counterpoint.[46] Takaki's *Iron Cages* is as expansive and alternates chapters on Indians and Blacks. It demonstrates, for example, how Richard Henry Dana's whiteness, so central to his celebrated indictment of the "slavelike" treatment of white sailors, was inflected by experiences with Mexican and Kanaka (Hawaiian) others and how Hinton Rowan Helper's whites-only attack on slavery partook of his earlier distress at living alongside Chinese workers in California, where he came to fear and to hate the "motley crowd [including] the tattooed islanderr, the solemn Chinaman and the slovenly Chilian [*sic*]."[47] Horsman's *Race and Manifest Destiny* ranges widely in time and place. He develops the history of the drawing of a vital distinction between an invigorated "mixed" white "American" race (e.g., Douglas told his listeners, "Our ancestors were not all of English origin . . . , we inherit from every branch of the Caucasian race.") and nonwhite "mongrel" offspring, especially in the wake of the Mexican War. It is not an accident, given his spanning of older and newer studies, that Alexander Saxton's *Rise and Fall of the White Republic* so thoroughly surpasses other recently published accounts in its encompassing narrative and its ability to address questions of whiteness, property, and national political power.[48]

Perhaps the greatest and most instructive tribute that can be paid to this older body of scholarship is to observe that the very best of the newest work on racial identity stands on it shoulders in ways that reveal the potential of wider appreciation of its insights. Dana Nelson's stunning *National Manhood: Capitalist Citizenship and the Imagined Fraternity of White Men* sets a new standard for the synthetic treatment of white racial formation in the early national and antebellum periods. Nelson describes and dramatizes a series of failed attempts to create fellowship among white men who were set in fierce competition by capitalist expansion, who feared women's work and sexuality, and who worried over the possibilities of democracy. She shows, in analyses of subjects ranging from gynecology to Egyptology, how African Americans, women, Indians, and "primitives" functioned as the "others" necessary to forge white masculinities that were as powerful as they were "melancholy," which promised fraternity but delivered atomized racial identities.[49] No book better positions us to understand the chants from Douglas's supporters.

For all of its insights from postcolonial theory, from critical race theory, from recent interventions in feminist psychology, and from Jeanne Boydston's history of gender and work, *National Manhood* resonates equally with the work of Rogin, Takaki, and others of their cohort. It frames events within capitalist transformation, alienation, and needs unfilled within liberal obsessions with individual gain. It moves deftly from "Inindianation" as a key to white national symbolism to antiblack racist science, from the explorations of Lewis and

Clark, to the abolitionism of Lydia Maria Child. Herman Melville moves through Nelson's pages, as he does through Rogin's and Drinnon's. Above all, the emphasis on the production of white manhood in private as well as in public is sure. Indeed what is perhaps Nelson's most vigorous exposition of her position comes precisely in her effort to supplement Rogin's use of "a psychoanalytic model of 'regression'—a forbidden nostalgia for childhood—to explain the energy at the heart of the United States' westward expansion and its murderous consequences." Nelson writes of the need to locate white masculinity within "that ideological fiction of the 'peaceful competitiveness' of early U.S. capitalism (the providentially soothing logic of the 'invisible hand') versus its experientially anxious, potentially vicious cultural and material results." She continues, in ways that as much complement as contest Rogin, by arguing that newer formations of manhood, tied complexly to national ideals and emerging capitalist practices, effectively and ideologically isolated men, setting them at a long remove from the "thick network of obligation and duty within family and community" that had characterized older masculine ideals. White identity, she shows, perpetually promised to build a bridge (back) to the eighteenth-century ideals of mutuality and fraternity but succeeded only in supplementing the fictions of the liberal marketplace with its own lies.[50]

The existing literature does not contain final answers to the riddles of white racial formation. But it does demonstrate that in addressing Gesa Mackenthun's call to "add empire" to the study of history, we build on substantial foundations where racial identity is concerned.[51] Moreover, looking back to fine older works ought to alert us to the fact that many themes addressed in recent scholarship are not exotic concerns driven by cultural studies, but longstanding concerns of historians. Nelson's insights, and those of the scholars on whom she draws, position us to see, with Melville, the extent to which white racial identity partook of interactions with African Americans, South Sea Islanders, American Indians, Mexicans, Cape Verdeans, and others. Such work will connect us to critical literatures on race, property, empire, and nation beyond the United States and to studies on the role of the astonishingly diverse international maritime proletariat in spreading and challenging ideas about race. These connections will help us immeasurably in identifying what is exceptional about white identity in the United States and what is shared with a larger white world.[52] Those of us who believe, with Theodore Allen, that whiteness in the United States is a "peculiar institution," formed in a unique conjuncture of anticolonial/bourgeois revolution, industrial takeoff and continuing slavery can only make the case for such peculiarity if these dramas are discussed along with the scenes of subjection, racializations of property, and pursuits of white happiness which accompanied U.S. expansion.[53]

NOTES

1. Paul Gilroy, "Black British Cultural Studies and the Pitfalls of Identity," in *Black British Cultural Studies: A Reader*, ed. Houston A. Baker Jr., Manthia Diawara, and Ruth H. Lindeborg (Chicago and London, 1996), 224. Thank you to Steven Garabedian for research assistance and to John Howe and Jean O'Brien for important suggestions.

2. Alexander Saxton, *The Rise and Fall of the White Republic: Class Politics and Mass Culture in Nineteenth Century America* (New York and London, 1990); Theodore W. Allen, *The Invention of the White Race:* Volume One: *Racial Oppression and Social Control* (London and New York, 1994); and *The Invention of the White Race,* Volume Two: *The Origins of Racial Oppression in Anglo-America* (London and New York, 1997); Noel Ignatiev, *How the Irish Became White* (New York and London, 1995); David R. Roediger, *The Wages of Whiteness: Race and the Making of the American Working Class* (London and New York, 1991). See also Michael Goldfield, *The Color of Politics: Race and the Mainsprings of American Politics* (New York, 1997), 74–112. Among the review essays, see esp., David Stowe, "Uncolored People: The Rise of Whiteness Studies," *Lingua Franca*, 4 (Sept.-Oct. 1996), 68–77; George Lipsitz, "Swing Low Sweet Cadillac: White Supremacy, Antiblack Racism and the New Historicism," *American Literary History*, 7 (Winter 1995), 700–25; and Judith Levine, "The Heart of Whiteness," *Voice of Literary Supplement* (Sept. 1994), 11–16. The term "whiteness studies" is a misguided one as it wrenches the critical study of white identity from its necessary embeddedness in the consideration of cultural and social relations among races. Would anyone say that James Baldwin and Toni Morrison, the two leading students of whiteness in my lifetime, engage in "whiteness studies?"

3. Karen Brodkin, "How Did Jews Become White Folks?" in *Race*, ed. Roger Sanjek and Steven Gregory (New Brunswick, NJ, 1996), 78–102; Eric Lott, *Love and Theft: Blackface Minstrelsy and the American Working Class* (Oxford and New York, 1993); Michael Rogin, *Blackface, White Noise: Jewish Immigrants in the Hollywood Melting Pot* (Berkeley, Los Angeles, and London, 1996); Susan Gubar, *Racechanges: White Skin, Black Face in American Culture* (New York, 1997); Richard Drinnon, *Facing West: The Metaphysics of Indian-Hating and Empire-Building* (New York and London, 1980); Michael Paul Rogin, *Fathers and Children: Andrew Jackson and the Subjection of the American Indian* (New York, 1975); Reginald Horsman, *Race and Manifest Destiny: The Origins of American Racial Anglo-Saxonism* (Cambridge, MA, and London, 1981); Richard Slotkin, *The Fatal Environment: The Myth of the Frontier in the Age of Industrialization, 1800–1890* (New York, 1985); Ronald Takaki, *Iron Cages: Race and Culture in Nineteenth Century America* (New York and Oxford, 1990). See also Robert F. Berkhofer Jr., *The White Man's Indian: Images of the American Indian from Columbus to the Present* (New York, 1979); and Roy Harvey Pearce, *The Savages of America: A Study of the Indian and the Idea of Civilization* (Baltimore, 1953).

4. Matt Wray and Annalee Newitz, ed., *White Trash: Race and Class in America* (New York and London, 1997). For a burlesque treatment of "whiteness studies" that rests on a caricature of the influence of cultural studies, see Margaret Talbot, "Getting Credit for Being White," *New York Times Magazine* (Nov. 30, 1997), 116–19; Pat Jennings and Meredith Redlin, "Constituting White Identities: *disClosure* Interviews David Roediger," *disClosure*, 7 (1998), 133–35, on history, cultural studies, and race; Cheryl Harris, "Whiteness as Property," *Harvard Law Review*, 106 (June 1993), 1709–91; Saidiya Hart-

man, *Scenes of Subjection: Terror, Slavery, and Self-Making in Nineteenth Century America* (New York and Oxford, 1997).

5. For a discussion of the older scholarly contention that the Declaration of Independence was Lockean at its core, with Jefferson more or less inexplicably or magically substituting "pursuit of happiness" for Locke's emphasis on the right to property, see Garry Wills, *Inventing America: Jefferson's Declaration of Independence* (Garden City, NY, 1978), 229–55. Wills sharply and successfully challenges this view insofar as Jefferson's political philosophy is concerned. However, property and happiness were certainly paired in significant ways, in and beyond Locke. See also Herbert L. Ganter, "Jefferson's 'Pursuit of Happiness' and Some Forgotten Men," *William and Mary Quarterly*, 16 (July 1936), 422–34.

6. Edmund Morgan, *American Slavery, American Freedom: The Ordeal of Colonial Virginia* (New York, 1975); Orlando Patterson, *Freedom, Volume One, Freedom in the Making of Western Culture* (New York, 1991); Charles Mills, *The Racial Contract* (Ithaca and London, 1997).

7. Mills, *The Racial Contract*, 41–53, 27 (quote).

8. W. E. B. Du Bois, *Black Reconstruction in the United States, 1860–1880* (New York, 1977, originally 1935), 700–701, 727; Stowe, "Uncolored People," 71.

9. Harris, "Whiteness as Property," 1721, 1724.

10. Harris, "Whiteness as Property," 1734–36, 1759–61, esp. 1760, n. 226; the discussion of whiteness, property, and "reputation" in Harris opens onto critical connections among race, masculinity, and honor in the South. Cf. Ariela J. Gross, "'Like Master, Like Man': Constructing Whiteness in the Commercial Law of Slavery, 1800–61," *Cardozo Law Review*, 18 (Nov. 1996), 265–66, 298.

11. Harris, "Whiteness as Property," 1734.

12. Hartman, *Scenes of Subjection*, 23.

13. *Ibid.,* 17–112 and esp. 32. Elsewhere (26) Hartman probes more deeply into property's links to minstrel happiness: "The fungibility of the commodity, specifically its abstractness and immateriality, enabled the black body or blackface mask to serve as the vehicle of white self-exploration, renunciation, and enjoyment."

14. Regarding African-American thought on terror and whiteness, see David R. Roediger, ed., *Black on White: Black Writers on What It Means to Be White* (New York, 1998), 14–17, 317–49.

15. Hartman, 34–35. Cf. Robyn C. Wiegman, *American Anatomies: Theorizing Race and Gender* (Durham and London, 1995), 193–201.

16. Lott, *Love and Theft*; W. T. Lhamon Jr., *Raising Cain: Blackface Performance from Jim Crow to Hip Hop* (Cambridge, MA, London, 1998); Grimsted, "Review of Bluford Adam's *E Pluribus Barnum*," *American Historical Review*, 103 (June 1998), 974–75. The overwrought comparison of blackface and abolitionism is found, incredibly enough, in the Spring-Summer, 1998 catalogue of Harvard University Press, advertising *Raising Cain*. See also William J. Mahar's *Behind the Burnt Cork Mask: Early Blackface Minstrelsy and Antebellum American Popular Culture* (Urbana, 1999).

17. Alexander Saxton, "Blackface Minstrelsy and Jacksonian Ideology," *American Quarterly*, 27 (Mar. 1975), 27; Roediger, *Wages of Whiteness*, 119; Hartman, *Scenes of Subjection*, 32; Kalpana Seshadri-Crooks, "The Comedy of Domination: Psychoanalysis and the Conceit of Whiteness," *Discourse*, 19 (Winter 1997), 152–56; see also Saxton's insightful revisiting of these questions in his "Blackface Minstrelsy, Vernacular Comics, and

the Politics of Slavery in the North," in *The Meaning of Slavery in the North*, ed. David Roediger and Martin H. Blatt (New York and London, 1998), 157–75.

18. Paul M. Angle, ed., *Created Equal?: The Complete Lincoln-Douglas Debates of 1858* (Chicago, 1958), 156. For emphases I have added in this version of this article, I am indebted to the apt published remarks of David Brion Davis. Davis suggests that at Freeport the shout "White, white" was repeated while "White men, white men" was the isolated utterance of one person. The text reproduced in Angle is less than fully clear on this point, however. See Davis, "The Culmination of Racial Polarities and Prejudice," *Journal of the Early Republic*, 19 (Winter, 1999), 774–75.

19. Ignatiev, *How the Irish Became White*; Lott, *Love and Theft*; Hartman, *Scenes of Subjection*; Roediger, *Wages of Whiteness;* Saxton, *White Republic*; see also Barry Goldberg, "Wage Slaves and White 'Niggers'," *New Politics*, Second Series, 3 (Summer 1991), 64–83.

20. James Brewer Stewart, "The Emergence of Racial Modernity and the Rise of the White North, 1790–1840," *Journal of the Early Republic*, 18 (Spring 1998), 181–217; Mary Cathryn Cain's forthcoming Emory University dissertation, tentatively titled "The Whiteness of White Women: Gender and the Use of Race Privilege in the Urban Northeast, 1820–1870," promises to make a most substantial contribution to the history of middle-class whiteness; on the Irish and whitness, see Catherine Eagan, "When Did the Irish Become White?" (unpublished paper, American Studies Association, Washington, DC, 1997); on resistant Irish Americans see Leslie M. Harris, "'Rulers of the Five Points': Irish and Black Workers in New York City," in her *In the Shadow of Slavery: African Americans, Class, Community and Political Activism in New York City, 1626*–1863, forthcoming; Graham Russell Hodges, *Slavery, Freedom, and Culture Among Early American Workers* (Armonk, NY, and London, 1998), 122–44; John Kuo Wei Tchen, *New York Before Chinatown: Orientalism and the Shaping of American Culture, 1776–1882*, forthcoming from Johns Hopkins University Press; Michael Hogan, *The Irish Soldiers of Mexico* (Guadalajara, 1997).

21. Bruce Levine, "'Against All Slavery, White or Black': German Americans and the Irrepressible Conflict," in *Crosscurrents: African Americans, African and Germany in the Modern World*, ed. David McBride, Leroy Hopkins, and C. Aisha Blackshire-Belay (Columbia, SC, 1998), 53–64; and *The Spirit of 1848: German Immigrants, Labor Conflict, and the Coming of the Civil War* (Urbana, 1992); see also Darlene Wilson, "'Black Dutch' — A Polite Euphemism?" at http://www.clinch.edu/appalachia/melungeon/dw_dutch.html; Gjerde, "'Here in America There Is Neither King Nor Tyrant': European Encounters with Race, Freedom and Their European Pasts," in this collection; Maria Diedrich, *Love Across Color Lines: Ottile Assing and Frederick Douglass* (New York, 1999), and new material in Matthew Jacobson's superb recent study, *Whiteness of a Different Color* (Cambridge, MA, 1998), 46–48.

22. Richard Dyer's important overarching discussion of whiteness and Christianity in his *White* (London and New York, 1997), esp. 14–18, makes specific studies for the United States still more urgent; see also Mason Stokes, "Someone's in the Garden with Eve: Race, Religion and the American Fall," *American Quarterly*, 50 (Dec. 1998), 719–25.

23. Dana Frank, "White Working Class Women and the Race Question," *International Labor and Working Class History*, 54 (Fall 1998), 80–102; Angle, ed., *Created Equal?*, 156; David Roediger, "Race, Labor and Gender in the Languages of Antebellum Social

Protest," in Stanley L. Engerman, ed., *Terms of Labor: Slavery, Serfdom and Free Labor* (Stanford, CA, 1999), 168–87; Dana D. Nelson, *National Manhood: Capitalist Citizenship and the Imagined Fraternity of White Men* (Durham and London, 1998), 395–415; Maggie Montesinos Sale, *The Slumbering Volcano: American Slave Revolts and the Production of Rebellious Masculinity* (Durham, 1997). On Lincoln, See George Fredrickson, "A Man But Not a Brother: Abraham Lincoln and Racial Equality," in *The Arrogance of Race: Historical Perspectives on Slavery, Racism and Social Inequality* (Middletown, 1988), 54–72. Davis, "Culmination," 774–75, raises this dimension of the Freeport debate sharply.

24. Nancy Isenberg, *Sex and Citizenship in Antebellum America* (Chapel Hill and London, 1998), esp. 27–29, 33–36, 122–27; Jeanne Boydston, *Home and Work: Housework, Wages and Ideology in the Early Republic* (New York and Oxford, 1990). See also Amy Kaplan, "Manifest Domesticity," *American Literature*, 70 (Sept. 1998) 581–606. For promising new work combining insights regarding gender and regarding whiteness, see Cain, "The Whiteness of White Women," forthcoming, and Lori Askeland, "Remodeling the Model Home in *Uncle Tom's Cabin* and *Beloved*," in Michael Moon and Cathy N. Davidson, eds., *Subjects and Citizens: Nation, Race and Gender From Oroonoko to Anita Hill* (Durham, 1995), 395–415. Particularly impressive for its insistence on whiteness as performance, and on the gendered nature of such performance, is Ariela J. Gross, "Litigating Whiteness: Trials of Racial Determination in the Nineteenth Century South," *The Yale Law Journal*, 198 (Oct. 1998), 109–88.

25. Martha Hodes, *White Women, Black Men: Illicit Sex in the Nineteenth Century South* (New Haven, 1997); Nell Irvin Painter, "Soul Murder and Slavery: Towards a Fully Loaded Cost Accounting," in Linda Kerber, Alice Kessler-Harris, and Kathryn Kish Sklar, eds., *U.S. History as Women's History* (Chapel Hill and London, 1995), 125–46; Victoria E. Bynum, *Unruly Women: The Politics of Social and Sexual Control in the Old South* (Chapel Hill, 1992), esp. 35–38; Elizabeth Fox-Genovese, *Within the Plantation Household: Black and White Women in the Old South* (Chapel Hill, 1988); Karen Sanchez-Eppler, *Touching Liberty: Abolition, Feminism and the Politics of the Body* (Berkeley and Los Angeles, 1993); Russ Castronovo, "Incidents in the Life of a White Woman: Economics of Race and Gender in the Antebellum Nation," *America Literary History*, 10 (Summer 1998), 239–65; Gillian Brown, *Domestic Individualism: Imagining Self in Nineteenth Century America* (Berkeley, 1990), 3–38; Cheryl Harris, "Finding Sojourner's Truth: Race, Gender and the Institution of Slavery," *Cardozo Law Review*, 18 (Nov. 1998), 309–410.

26. Douglas as quoted in Robert W. Johannsen, *Stephen A. Douglas* (New York, 1973), 726. On the efforts successful in Illinois in 1853 of Midwestern states to exclude African-American migrants, see Eugene Berwanger, *The Frontier Against Slavery: Western Anti-Negro Prejudice and the Slavery Extension Controversy* (Urbana, 1967), 44–59.

27. See, e.g., Joe Trotter's review of *Wages of Whiteness*, *Journal of Social History*, 25 (Spring 1992), 674–76. For rich studies of specific social histories of race, see Ignatiev, *How the Irish Became White*; Hodges, *Slavery, Freedom and Culture Among Early American Workers*; John Kuo Wei Tchen, "Quimbo Appo's Fear of Fenians: Chinese-Irish-Anglo Relations in New York City," in *The New York Irish*, ed. Ronald H. Bayor and Timothy J. Meagher (Baltimore and London, 1996), 123–52; on free Blacks in the North, see Stewart, "The Political Meaning of Color in the Free States," in this collection; Horton "From Class to Race in Early America: Northern Post-Emancipation Social Reconstruction," in this book; Melish, "The 'Condition' Debate and Racial Discourse in the

Antebellum North," in this collection; on the South, see Hodes, "*White Women, Black Men*; Ford, "Making the 'White Man's Country' White: Race, Slavery, and State-Building in the Jacksonian South," in this book.

28. For a vigorous endorsement of the clear superiority of local approaches, see Eric Arnesen's "Up from Exclusion: Black and White Workers, Race, and the State of Labor History," *Reviews in American History*, 26 (1998), 162–67; Stuart Hall, "What Is This 'Black' in Black Popular Culture?" *Social Justice*, 20 (Spring-Summer 1993), 111; John Kuo Wei Tchen, "Believing Is Seeing: Transforming Orientalism and the Occidental Gaze," in *Asia/America: Identities in Contemporary Asian American Art*, ed. Margo Machida (New York, 1994), 12–25.

29. Joanne Pope Melish, *Disowning Slavery: Gradual Emancipation and "Race" in New England, 1780–1860* (Ithaca and London, 1998), 5, 151–62 (Barbary slavery), 210 ("free white republic") and *passim*. See also Paul Baepler, ed., *White Slaves, African Masters: An Anthology of American Captivity Narratives* (Chicago and London, 1999).

30. Tchen, *New York Before Chinatown*.

31. Angle, ed., *Created Equal?*, 201.

32. In addition to the works cited in notes 2 and 22 above, see George Lipsitz, *The Possessive Investment in Whiteness* (Philadelphia, 1998).

33. Roediger, *Wages of Whiteness*, 21–23; Frank Dumont, *Burnt Cork; or, The Amateur Minstrel* (New York, 1881), 45; Martha Knack and Alice Littlefield, ed., *Native Americans and Wage Labor: Ethnohistorical Perspectives* (Norman, OK, 1996); Jean M. O'Brien, "'Vanishing' Indians in Nineteenth-Century New England: Local Historians' Erasure of Still-Present Indian Peoples" (Unpublished paper in possession of author, 1998); Lora Romero, "Vanishing Americans: Gender, Empire and the New Historicism," *Subjects and Citizens*, 87–105. For the colonial studies, see *American Slavery* and Kathleen M. Brown, *Good Wives, Nasty Wenches and Anxious Patriarchs: Gender, Race and Power in Colonial Virginia* (Chapel Hill and London, 1998).

34. Philip Deloria, *Playing Indian* (New Haven and London, 1998), 5; Susan Scheckel, *The Insistence of the Indian: Race and Nation in Nineteenth Century American Culture*, (Princeton, 1998); Darlene Wilson and Patricia Beaver, "Embracing the Male Off-Shore Other: The Ubiquitous Native Grandmother in America's Cultural Memory," forthcoming in Barbara Smith, ed., *Links of Iron, Links of Gold: The Social Relations of Southern Women*. Cf. Neal Salisbury, "The Best Poor Man's Country as Middle Ground: Mainstreaming Indians in Early American Studies," *Reviews in American History*, 26 (1998), 497–503.

35. On the Mexican War, see Paul W. Foos, "Mexican Wars: Soldiers and Society in an Age of Expansion, 1835–1855" (unpublished Ph.D. diss., Yale University, 1997), 6.

36. Tomás Almaguer, *Racial Fault Lines: The Historical Origins of White Supremacy in California* (Berkeley, Los Angeles, and London, 1994); Lisbeth Haas, *Conquests and Historical Identities in California, 1769–1936* (Berkeley, 1995); Ramón A. Gutiérrez, *When Jesus Came, the Corn Mothers Went Away: Marriage, Sexuality and Power in New Mexico, 1500–1846* (Stanford, 1991), 193–206, 338–39. See also David Montejano, *Anglos and Mexicans in the Making of Texas, 1836–1986* (Austin, 1987); and Amoldo De León, *They Called Them Greasers: Anglo American Attitudes Toward Mexicans in Texas* (Austin, 1983). On marxism and race categories, see Lisa Lowe, *Immigrant Acts: On Asian American Cultural Politics* (Durham, 1996), 24–28. Ronald Takaki, *Strangers from a Different Shore: A History of Asian Americans* (New York and London, 1989), 30–31. See also Patricia Nelson

Limerick, *The Legacy of Conquest: The Unbroken Past of the American West* (New York, 1987), esp. 179–292; Richard White, *"It's Your Misfortune and None of My Own": A History of the American West* (Norman, OK, 1991); Quintard Taylor, *In Search of the Racial Frontier: African Americans in the American West, 1528–1900* (New York, 1998), esp. 27–102.

37. Drinnon, *Facing West*; Rogin, *Fathers and Children*; Horsman, *Race and Manifest Destiny*; Slotkin, *The Fatal Environment*; Takaki, *Iron Cages*; Berkhofer, *The White Man's Indian;* and Pearce, *The Savages of America.*

38. Ronda, "'We Have a Country': Race, Geography, and the Invention of Indian Territory," in this book; Richter, "'Believing That Many of the Red People Suffer Much for the Want of Food': Hunting, Agrculture, and the Quaker Constructions of Indianness in the Early Republic," in this book; Nancy Shoemaker, "How Indians Got to Be Red," *American Historical Review*, 102 (June 1997), 625–44; R. Keith Basso, *Portraits of "The Whiteman": Linguistic Play and Cultural Symbols Among the Western Apache* (Cambridge, MA, 1979); Herman Melville, *The Confidence-Man: His Masquerade*, ed. Bruce Franklin (Indianapolis, 1967, originally 1857), 203.

39. Drinnon, *Facing West*, 198–99; Melville, *Confidence-Man*, 129–39; Eric Foner, *Free Soil, Free Labor, Free Men: The Ideology of the Republican Party Before the Civil War* (New York, 1970).

40. Karl Marx, *Capital: A Critique of Political Economy* (Volume One, Ben Fowkes, trans., London, 1976, originally, 1967), 914–26, 915 (quote); on this point I am indebted to Peter Linebaugh, "Review of Robin Blackburn's *The Making of New World Slavery*," *Historical Materialism*, 1 (Autum 1997), 185–96, esp. 190.

41. Slotkin, *Fatal Environment*, 235 (quote), 226–41, 266–68. See also 117 for the link to Marx's point.

42. Takaki, *Iron Cages*, viii-x, 69–79, 125–28.

43. Rogin, *Fathers and Children*, 19–279, 8 (quote). George Rawick, *From Sundown to Sunup: The Making of the Black Community* (Westport, CT, 1972), 125–49, esp. 132–33.

44. Takaki, *Iron Cages*, 83, 90, 139–42; Melville, *Confidence-Man*, 219.

45. Quintard Taylor, *In Search of the Racial Frontier: African Americans in the American West, 1528–1990* (New York, 1998); Bruce M. White, "The Power of Whiteness, or the Life and Times of Joseph Roletter, Jr.," *Minnesota History*, 56 (Winter 1998), 178–201; Sylvia Van Kirk, *'Many Tender Ties': Women in Fur-Trade Society, 1670–1870* (Norman, OK, 1983); Richard White, *The Middle Ground: Indian Empires and Republics in the Great Lakes Region, 1650–1815* (Cambridge, UK, and New York, 1991); June Namias, *White Captives: Gender and Ethnicity on the American Frontier* (Chapel Hill, 1993).

46. Drinnon, *Facing West*, 131–46, 355 (quote).

47. Takaki, *Iron Cages*, 156–61, 215–16; Helper, as quoted in Robert Lee, *Orientals: Asian Americans in Popular Culture* (Philadelphia, 1999), 26.

48. Horsman, *Race and Manifest Destiny*, 208–71, (quoting Douglas at 251); and Saxton, *White Republic*. For an expansive and important new study that extends questions broached by Horsman, see Jacobson, *Whiteness of a Different Color.*

49. Nelson, *National Manhood*; *passim.*

50. Nelson, *National Manhood*, 62.

51. Gesa Mackenthun, "Adding Empire to the Study of American Culture," *Journal of American Studies*, 30 (1998), 263.

52. See, for example, Ann Laura Stoler, *Race and the Education of Desire: Foucault's 'History of Sexuality' and the Colonial Order* (Durham, 1995); George Mosse, *Nationalism and Sexuality* (Madison, 1985); Homi Bhabha, "The Other Question: The Stereotype and Colonial Discourse," *Screen*, 24 (Nov.-Dec. 1983), 18–36; Frantz Fanon, *The Wretched of the Earth* (New York, 1963); W. Jeffrey Bolster, *Black Jacks: African American Seamen in the Age of Sail* (Cambridge, MA, and London, 1997); Peter Linebaugh and Marcus Rediker, "The Many-Headed Hydra: Sailors, Slaves, and the Atlantic Working Class in the Eighteenth Century," *Journal of Historical Sociology*, 3 (Sept. 1990), 225–52. On Melville, see Leonard Cassuto, *The Inhuman Race: The Racial Grotesque in American Literature and Culture* (New York, 1997), 170–79, 203–15; Carolyn Karcher, *Shadow Over the Promised Land: Slavery, Race and Violence in Melville's America* (Baton Rouge and London, 1980); Sterling Stuckey, "The Death of Benito Cereno: A Reading of Herman Melville on Slavery," *Going Through the Storm: The Influence of African American Art in History* (New York and Oxford, 1994), 158–69; Robert J. C. Young, *Colonial Desire: Hybridity in Theory, Culture and Race* (London and New York, 1995), 118–41.

53. Allen, *Invention of the White Race*, I:1.

BIBLIOGRAPHY

Almaguer, Tomás. *Racial Fault Lines: The Historical Origins of White Supremacy in California*. Berkeley: University of California Press, 1994.

Baepler, Paul, ed. *White Slaves, African Masters: An Anthology of American Captivity Narratives*. Chicago: University of Chicago Press, 1999.

Boydston, Jeanne. *Home and Work: Housework, Wages and Ideology in the Early Republic*. New York: Oxford University Press, 1990.

Deloria, Philip. *Playing Indian*. New Haven: Yale University Press, 1998.

Harris, Cheryl. "Whiteness as Property." *Harvard Law Review,* 106 (June 1993), 1709–91.

Lee, Robert. *Orientals: Asian Americans in Popular Culture*. Philadelphia: Temple University Press, 1999.

Otter, Samuel. "Race in *Typee* and *White-Jacket*." Robert S. Levine, ed. *The Cambridge Companion to Herman Melville*. Cambridge: Cambridge University Press, 1998.

Saxton, Alexander. *The Rise and Fall of the White Republic: Class, Politics and Mass Culture in Nineteenth-Century America*. New York: Verso, 1990.

Scheckel, Susan. *The Insistence of the Indian: Race and Nation in Nineteenth-Century American Culture*. Princeton: Princeton University Press, 1998.

Tchen, John Kuo Wei. *New York Before Chinatown: Orientalism and the Shaping of American Culture, 1776–1882*. Baltimore: Johns Hopkins University Press, 1999.

Wiegman, Robyn. *American Anatomies: Theorizing Race and Gender*. Durham: Duke University Press, 1995.

2

"Believing That Many of the Red People Suffer Much for the Want of Food": Hunting, Agriculture, and a Quaker Construction of Indianness in the Early Republic

Daniel K. Richter

In the spring of 1804, Gerard T. Hopkins travelled from Baltimore to Fort Wayne, in Indian country. As secretary of the Baltimore Yearly Meeting of Friends and a member of its Committee on Indian Affairs, he carefully kept a journal, which he later edited to "convey inteligibly, both the route we took and the various circumstances attendant upon our Journey"; his traveling companions were fellow committee member George Ellicott and a young man named Phillip Dennis, who had been employed by the Baltimore Quakers to live with the Indians and "instruct them in Agriculture & other useful knowledge." Hopkins's journal records that when the three travelers reached Fort Wayne, they appeared before a council of chiefs convened by Miami leader Little Turtle. Speaking with the assistance of resident federal agent and interpreter William Wells, they announced that, "in coming into the Country of our Red brethren, we have come with our eyes open and . . . are affected with sorrow in believing that Many of the red people suffer much for the want of food and for the want of Clothing." If only the Miamis would "adopt our mode of Cultivating the earth and of raising useful animals," they would, the Quakers assured them, "find it to be a mode of living not only far more plentif[ul] and much less fatiguing but also much more Certain . . . than is now attendant upon hunting."[1]

Eyes may have been open, but brains apparently were not processing much of what was seen. For Hopkins also noted that a few days before the Quakers delivered their speech, one of those supposedly starving Native women—Wells's wife and Little Turtle's daughter, Sweet Breeze—treated them to "an excellant dinner" featuring "a very large well roasted wild Turkey [and] also a wild Turkey boiled," both accompanied by "a large supply of Cramberry Sauce." Later, the Marylanders visited a camp where Miami women and their

27

"very fat and healthy looking children" dressed in "very costly silver ornaments" were producing maple sugar for Euro-American markets.[2] Hopkins
did not know it, but it is likely that the Indians engaged in that commercial
activity because it was early April and not yet time to plant the corn, beans,
and squash that their agriculturalist ancestors had known how to grow for at
least eight hundred years before Dennis was born. To insist that these people
were ill-fed and ill-clad was a remarkable triumph of ideological construction
over visual and gastronomical evidence.

As Hopkins tried to "convey inteligibly" his experiences, he relied less on
what he had actually seen than on what he thought he knew before he began his
journey. An easterner whose knowledge of Native people came largely from
eighteenth-century books—most of them published by European authors who
themselves had not even visited North America—he deployed a powerfully
wrong-headed analysis of who Indians were and what kind of problems they
faced as the new republic assumed control of the continent. Despite a maize of
evidence, this analysis insisted that Indians were not really farmers. Despite the
economic importance of the trade in fur and hides (and, at Fort Wayne, maple
sugar), it similarly insisted that they did not participate in the modern commercial economy in any significant way, except to purchase rotgut liquor and other
self-destructive luxuries. Supposedly hunters living hand-to-mouth in a world
where game lands were rapidly shrinking, these imagined Indians *had* to be facing starvation because their way of life was doomed by the presence on the continent of an allegedly more advanced society based, unlike theirs, on agriculture
and commerce. Their only earthly salvation was to take up the plough that Hopkins and his companions offered them.

The *belief* "that Many of the red people suffer[ed] much for the want of
food"—and that such abstract categories as "red people" and "hunters" provided in themselves sufficient explanation for the economic and social distress of Indians whose particular circumstances need not be considered—
proved almost impervious to contradictory evidence, in part because it so
conveniently justified Euro-American expropriation of Indian land and resources. But for Hopkins and his fellow turn-of-the-nineteenth-century Quakers, the noble work of turning starving hunters into sturdy subsistence farmers held greater appeal because it addressed their own unease with the
emerging economy of the new republic, an economy in which commercial activity in particular threatened to undermine morality. Thus blinded to the possibility that ploughs may not have been the answer, they could not translate
their genuinely humanitarian impulses into any kind of meaningful assistance
for Native people who sought not mere subsistence but to preserve a place for
themselves in the expanding market economy of early nineteenth-century
North America.

The background and results of Hopkins's trip to Fort Wayne can quickly be summarized. The Indian Affairs Committee of the Baltimore Yearly Meeting first convened in 1795, at much the same time as a similar group took shape in Philadelphia and as urban Friends throughout the United States were beginning to concentrate on the agricultural transformation of Native Americans. The two committees agreed on a division of labor: the Philadelphians would concentrate on Indian communities in New York State and the Marylanders on those of the Old Northwest, a responsibility the latter exercised until the Ohio Yearly Meeting took over in 1813. Small-scale as it was, the effort to establish a model farm at Fort Wayne was by far the most ambitious project the Baltimore organization attempted in its less than two decades of existence.[3]

The mission had its origins in the visit by Little Turtle, the Potawatomi chief Five Medals, and several other leaders of their two nations to Washington, DC, in December and January 1801–1802. En route, the delegation stopped in Baltimore, where it met with members of the Indian committee. A year later, the Friends sent "a considerable number of implements of husbandry; such as *Ploughs, Hoes, Axes*, &c. &c." to Fort Wayne for distribution to the two nations.[4] In February 1804, the committee received a letter of thanks that Little Turtle and Five Medals had sent the previous September. "It is our wish that the Great Spirit will enable you to render your red Brethren that service which you appear to be so desirous of doing them and their women and children are so much in need of," the Native leaders said. "We will try to use the Articles you have sent us and if we should want more we will let You know it," but "we are sorry to say that the minds of our people are not so much inclined towards the cultivation of the earth as we could wish them." Nonetheless, Little Turtle and Five Medals expressed a "hope that the Great Spirit will permit some of you to come and see us when you will be Able to know whether you can do any thing for us or not." On the basis of that ambiguous invitation, the committee appointed Dennis and asked Hopkins and Ellicott, along with two other Friends who declined the call, to see that he got safely to Fort Wayne.[5]

The spot Miami leaders chose for Dennis to set up operations was not, as the Quakers had hoped, at an established village, but at an uninhabited, though fertile, riverside locale eighteen miles from the nearest Indian town. After Hopkins and Ellicott returned to Maryland, Dennis went about his work of clearing, ploughing, and fencing twenty acres of ground, from which he said he reaped "about 400 bushels of corn, besides a quantity of turnips, potatoes, cucumbers, water melons, pumpkins, beans, parsnips and other garden vegetables." When he returned to Maryland in the fall, he left the fruits of his harvest, along with perhaps two dozen hogs and a log house, with the few Miamis who had agreed to work with him. Neither Dennis nor anyone else in the Baltimore Yearly Meeting could be induced to resume the mission the next year, although agent Wells reported that ten Miami families had moved in and were raising bumper crops on the land. (He was vague about whether they used ploughs or more traditional Indian methods to do so.) In 1806, the Baltimore committee employed a man named William Kirk, who, though a Friend, was not a member of their Yearly Meeting, to take over the work Dennis began. The newcomer promptly alienated Wells by refusing to take his advice, and Little Turtle and other Miamis by appearing to pocket funds meant for them. By 1808 he had moved on to start an agricultural mission among the Shawnees at Wapakoneta, Ohio, which continued to receive support from Baltimore and Ohio friends after the War of 1812.[6]

The tactless Kirk and the sorry end he brought to the feckless efforts of a well-meaning group of eastern humanitarians tells us something about the problems facing those who tried to bridge the increasingly wide racial divide of turn-of-the-nineteenth-century America. But the language and imagery through which Hopkins composed his narrative of those efforts reveals much more about the evolution of racial categories during that crucial period. In his journal, Hopkins stressed not only his pity for the Indians' supposedly starving present, but also his awareness of a very different Indian past he believed to be irrevocably doomed by a great, ongoing historical transition. Repeatedly in his travels, he noted reminders of bygone epochs. A stone fish weir that spanned the Monongahela River caught his attention because it was so old "that the Indians who resided upon this River at the time of its discovery by the whites had no knowledge even traditional of the making of these Fish Pots nor of the erection of the fortification."[7] Similarly Hopkins was fascinated by the mystery of the ancient Indian mounds of the Ohio valley; his journal includes several detailed sketches of those near Chillicothe.[8]

More recent material reminders of Native people also conveyed an image of a country emptied of its former inhabitants and rapidly refilling with Euro-American newcomers. "We have Observed hunting Camps erected by the Indians but no Indians in them," he wrote as the party reached the Great Miami River. The absent hunters had also left behind "many curious & to us uninteligeble Indian Hieroglyphics cut upon the trees . . . & painted in various colours upon the wood after Cutting away the Bark."[9] Perhaps because of his Quaker pacifism, Hopkins also remarked on physical reminders of fortifications and battles during the war between the United States and the Western Confederacy that had ended nine years earlier with the Treaty of Greenville. Most notably, where Fort Wayne now stood, fragments of the soldiers' skeletons could still be seen "scattered upon the surface of the Earth," as testimony to the great victory of Little Turtle's forces over General Josiah Harmar's army in 1790. Hopkins was "told that the route by which his army made their escape can be readily traced for the distance of 5 or 6 miles by the bones of those who were slain by the Indians." With his own eyes he saw "Skulls which had marks of the scalping knife and of the Tommahawk." But the battles were over, and an Indian town that had "contained upwards of One thousand Warriors" was gone, replaced by Fort Wayne and its sleepy contingent of "about 40 officers & Soldiers."[10]

For Hopkins, the Indian cemeteries that travelers frequently passed perhaps most fully evoked the end of an era for Native people—and the beginning of one for the white farmers who were replacing them. Near Fort Wayne he "viewed the remains of Old Indian houses also of the fields in which they cultivated corn" and "also observed large numbers of Indian Graves . . . discoverable at present only by the sunken Cavities in the surface of the earth." Reiterating that, elsewhere in their travels, the Friends had "seen many of the Graves of the Indians of more recent date," Hopkins was inspired by "the many circumstantial evidances which have fallen under our Observation of the former vast Population of this western world . . . to adopt the expression of a pious author," the poet Edward Young:

Where is the dust that hath not been alive?
The spade the plough disturb our Ancestors.
From human mould we reap our daily Bread.[11]

To describe the kind of transition that the plough represented, in their speech to the Miami council, Hopkins and his fellows evoked a fanciful vision of their own ethnic past. "The time was when the forefathers of your brothers the White people lived beyond the Great waters in the same manner that our red brethren now lived," the Quakers declared. "The Winters can yet be counted when they went almost naked when they procured their living by fishing and by the bow and arrow in hunting and when they lived in houses no better than yours." Fortunately, the ancient Britons "were encouraged by some who came from toward the sun-rising and lived amongst them to change their mode of living." After this beneficent conquest by the Roman Empire, Britons "cultivated the earth and we are sure the change was a happy one."[12] In this context, one wonders whether Hopkins contemplated some additional lines from Young's *Night Thoughts*, which appear in the next stanza after the passage evoked by his visit to the Native graveyard:

Nor man alone; his breathing bust expires,
    His tomb is mortal; empires die: where, now,
    The Roman? Greek? they stalk, an empty name!
    Yet few regard them in this useful light;
    Tho' half our learning is their epitaph.[13]

In his linkage of ancient European history with the contemporary situation of North American Indians, Hopkins tapped a rich eighteenth-century vein of cultural images promulgated alike by the French *philosophes* and the Scottish Common Sense theorists whose influence was omnipresent in the intellectual life of the early republic. Enlightenment thinkers of various stripes disagreed on the details, but most postulated a lineal "conjectural history" of humanity comprised of four developmental stages—"hunting," "pasturage," "agriculture," and "commerce"—each defined by its increasingly sophisticated mode of subsistence. The pursuit of game, and perhaps of fish, sustained the most primitive state of humankind, which many authors labeled "savagery"—a term they claimed to use with technical precision rather than as an insult. The presumed precariousness of this mode of subsistence led many popular writers to posit starvation as virtually its normal condition. The more advanced level of development often called "barbarism" rested on the more secure food supplies allowed by the nomadic herding of flocks. Finally, when people settled down to grow crops and to tend fully domesticated barnyard animals, they became "civilized"; this was the great gift Hopkins believed the Romans had brought to Albion. The final commercial stage, characterized by a complex division of labor and sophisticated mechanisms of exchange and finance, was clearly "civilized" too and, in the eighteenth century, it was certainly regarded as the wave of the future if not a description of the present.[14]

Whether that was a good thing was a matter of considerable controversy, however. Commerce either produced refined achievements that were the crowning glory of civilization or it fostered the corrupted self-indulgence, the fall from manly virtue, that eighteenth-century thinkers called "luxury"; more likely, the result was a troubling mixture of both. As historians Drew McCoy and Joyce Chaplin point out, the effects of commercial development were nowhere more hotly debated than in the United States from the 1780s through the first decade of the 1800s.[15] The famous contrast between Alexander Hamilton's Federalist insistence on "the necessity of enlarging the sphere of our domestic commerce" by encouraging the division of labor and of Thomas Jefferson's Republican vision of an agricultural republic populated by "those who labour in the earth"—although often overdrawn—nonetheless symbolizes the conflicting ways in which the age of commerce could be evaluated.[16]

However much they may have differed on whether the republic they were building was, or should be, agricultural or commercial, white Americans at the turn of the nineteenth century almost unanimously agreed on one thing: Indians still lived in the primitive hunter stage. As Roy Harvey Pearce concluded in his classic study of the ideology of savagery, Euro-Americans' "intellectual and cultural traditions, their idea of order, so informed their thoughts and their actions that they could see and conceive of nothing but the

Indian who hunted."[17] Indeed, when Enlightenment figures wrote about "hunters" and the conjectural history of humankind, they almost always drew their main examples from American Indians—or rather from their fanciful library stereotypes about Native people—making the terms *hunter* and *Indian* became virtually synonymous. "In the Beginning," John Locke famously said, "all the World was *America*."[18]

Almost all authors who explored conjectural history agreed that any society's progress from one stage to another rested on a simple ratio of population to resources. In the "age of hunters," Adam Smith postulated, "in process of time, as their numbers multiplied, they would find the chase too precarious for their support" and "be necessitated to contrive" a pastoral mode of subsistence that would suit them until renewed population growth made them "naturally turn themselves to the cultivation of land and the raising of such plants and trees as produced nourishment fit for them."[19] The problem was that, whether Indians were ready or not, the age of hunters was past in North America. For good or ill, the expansion of Euro-American agriculturalists would deprive Native people of the land resources necessary to support their hunting mode of subsistence. White public figures who professed any humanitarian concerns at all agreed that if Indians were to avoid extinction, they had to skip the pasturage stage and leap, almost overnight, to the agricultural level of development.[20]

In practical terms, therefore, few differences separated the Indian policies advocated by Federalists in the 1790s from those pursued by Republicans in the first decade of the 1800s. A "civilization" program, begun by Henry Knox in the Washington administration and elaborated with yeoman-farmer themes under Jeffersonian leadership, sought to teach Indian men to farm, and to farm lands held as private property. In their speeches to Native leaders, federal officials wrapped the project in humanitarian rhetoric and promises of concrete aid in the form of ploughs and tools. But in practice they engaged in a relentless effort to deprive Indians of the "excess" land that made their extravagant hunting lifestyle possible—an effort that, as James P. Ronda's contribution to this collection shows, was assuming new rigor at the very moment Hopkins traveled west.[21]

Whatever Baltimore Quakers thought of the more coercive elements of the Jeffersonian program, they saw themselves as great allies of the president in bringing the plough to savage hunters. "We are . . . bound to acknowledge those philanthropic exertions, which have been used to ameliorate the condition of the Indian natives, by introducing amongst them a knowledge of agriculture, and some of the mechanic arts," Hopkins wrote to Jefferson on behalf of the Yearly Meeting in 1807. The president in turn praised the Friends' "judicious direction toward producing among those people habits of industry, comfortable subsistence, and civilized urges."[22] As English Quakers who had contributed funds to support the Baltimore Friends' efforts approvingly stated, the lofty aim of all good people was to hasten along "the advancement of our Indian brethren in the scale of civil life."[23]

However appealing the ideal of raising Indians from the hunter to the agricultural state may have seemed—and quite apart from any general logical fallacies inherent in the four-stage theory of human development—the basic assumptions of the Baltimore Friends, like those of nearly all white Americans, rested on four basic errors about the role of hunting in the eastern Indian cultures of their day. First and most obvious was the inconvenient fact that the Miamis and their neighbors, like virtually all other Native peoples east of the Mississippi, already *were* farmers, and their food supply traditionally rested far less on the chase than on the Indian horticultural trinity of corn, beans, and squash.

The stereotype of improvident hunters was particularly ill-suited to the Miamis, and when the Quakers proposed to teach them how to grow crops, it must have required all of interpreter Wells's ingenuity to phrase the offer in a way that did not provoke laughter. In the eighteenth century, as the Miamis' most comprehensive historian concludes, they enjoyed a "stable and provident village life" and were renowned for a distinctive soft white maize that was considered far superior to the run-of-the-mill flint corn grown by their neighbors. Families typically stored a surplus of five bushels of this crop to get through the winter.[24] In late March and early April, when the Baltimore Quakers arrived at Fort Wayne, those supplies would have been largely exhausted, but their impact on the health of the local population should nonetheless have been clear. The sugaring camp Hopkins visited, for example, apparently had no corn, but it was "well supplied with Jerk-Venison, Dryed Racoon, Sturgeon &c." More importantly, the "very fat and healthy looking children" he saw there hardly looked like they had eked their way through the winter on meager hunter's fare.[25]

The second conceptual error about Indian hunting was an apparent failure to recognize—or rather to legitimize—the gendered division of labor in Native societies. Everywhere in eastern North America, agriculture was primarily women's work. Men assisted in clearing new fields, and they cultivated the ritually important tobacco plant. But women were in charge of corn, beans, and squash, and so—no small matter—they controlled the staple food supply. At least a few late eighteenth-century Euro-American social theorists recognized that Indian women grew corn, but they invariably dismissed the phenomenon to irrelevance. As no less influential an intellectual figure than Smith put it, "their women plant a few stalks of Indian corn at the back of their huts. But this can hardly be called agriculture" because "it does not make any considerable part of their food" and "serves only as a seasoning or something to give a relish to their common food; the flesh of those animalls they have caught in the chase." Similarly, New England writer William Douglass asserted that Indians did "not cultivate the Earth by planting or grazing: Excepting a very inconsiderable Quantity of *Mays* or *Indian Corn*, and of *Kidney-Beans* . . . which some of their *Squaas* or Women plant."[26]

The pronouns are important: "Their women" may have sown a few trifling crops, but Indian men—the people who mattered—were by definition hunters, and thus their societies by definition remained at the hunter stage. When whites said they wanted to teach Indians to farm, then, what they really meant was that they wanted to teach Indian *men* to become farmers, and to reduce Indian women to their proper position indoors behind a spinning wheel. "Your brothers the white people," the Quaker's prepared speech to the Miamis explained, "in order to get their land cultivated find it necessary that their young men should be employed in it and not their women. Women are less than men. They are not as strong as men. They are not as able to endure fatigue and toil as men."[27] These may seem strange words from a member of an Anglo-American religious community that had long idealized courageous women who traveled the world to preach and be persecuted for the faith, yet turn-of-the-nineteenth-century Quaker men nonetheless embraced a model of domesticity in which the gendered division of labor remained very clear. Women inspired by the spirit might preach to reap a spiritual harvest, but the crops of this world were to be watered with the sweat of male brows.[28]

And so a third error related not just to gender roles but to Indian labor patterns more generally. Instead of the heavy ploughs and neat monoculture that made European agriculture so laborious, Native women used a few simple tools—a digging stick and perhaps a European-manufactured hoe—to plant fields where corn, beans, and squash jumbled together in the same hills so that the maize derived some natural fertilizer from the nitrogen-fixing roots of the legumes and both profited from the natural weed control of spreading squash vines. Once the process was well started and beans started curling around their symbiotic cornstalk poles, fields needed hardly any tending until the crops became ripe enough to attract hungry birds. In Euro-American eyes, these "few stalks of Indian corn at the back of their huts" (even if, as in the Miami country, they typically stretched a mile or more outside a village) simply did not require enough hard work. The sight of Indian men who refused even the minimal requirements of such effortless horticulture only further reinforced a reputation for improvidence and laziness.[29] Thus in 1798 another Quaker missionary had condemned "the oppressive labour which the Senecas imposed upon their women, in getting and bringing home fire-wood, and similar employments, whilst the men and boys were amusing themselves with shooting arrows, and in other diversions." Instead, he "recommended" that they "take their boys out to hoe and work in the fields."[30]

Which points to the final, and perhaps most important, error embedded in the image of the Male Indian Hunter. Far from a matter of "amusing themselves with shooting arrows," hunting was serious labor to the region's Native men. In that, the gender and developmental stereotype was correct. The primary purpose of the work of hunting, however, was *not* to obtain food. Dietary benefits (meat more often provided the "relish" for corn soup than vice versa) were secondary to the need to acquire furs and hides to be traded for European manufactured goods. By 1804, Great Lakes Indians had relied on trade with Euro-Americans for well over a century. In exchange for furs, hides, and other commodities, they purchased cloth, tools, cooking and eating utensils, weapons, liquor, and countless other items not just enriching but crucial for everyday life. As Anthony F. C. Wallace observes, "professional huntsmen . . . were used to traveling hundreds of miles in search of the game needed in the trade." In this economy, "skins and furs were the traditional cash crop that procured hardware, cloth, and other necessities for Indian families."[31]

Hopkins's journal contains multiple unanalyzed glimpses of the complex ways in which the region's Indian men—and women—participated in the market economy that was supposedly characteristic of only the most advanced stage of human development. A couple of days before they reached Fort Wayne, Hopkins's party crossed the St. Mary's River in a canoe operated by an English-speaking Delaware ferryman named Stephen, who gave the Quakers a seventy-five percent discount on the usual dollar fare. (Alas, his previous customers—white traders who evidently paid their toll with liquor— left Stephen so drunk he fell out of the canoe halfway across and had to be rescued by Dennis.[32]) At Fort Wayne, the Baltimoreans were shown the grave of Little Turtle's son, which, like that of most high-status eighteenth-century eastern Indians, contained not only the corpse but "his Rifle hunting Apparatus his best clothing all his Ornaments, Trinkets &c &c &c." The value of these trade goods, his market-oriented hosts told him, was "not less than 300 Dollars."[33] Fort Wayne itself was notable to Hopkins not only for its government factory—"a large store of goods Established by the United states for the purpose of supplying the Indians"—but also for the "Several Cannadian Traders" who "reside[d] here who exchange goods with the Indians for furs & skins." These men had "generally intermarried with the Indians and some of them have resided here for more than 30 Years." Native men were, Hopkins said, "daily arriving here with Peltry[;] some of them exchange it for goods and others require money." Women, meanwhile, traded maple sugar, which was "generally very completely Packed in a Square Box made of bark containing about 50 pound[s]."[34]

On the return trip to Baltimore as well, the travelers saw repeated evidence of how market-oriented the region's Native people were, and of how important resident Canadian traders were to their societies. On the Auglaize River at the site of what, in the Fallen Timbers campaign of 1794, had been General Anthony Wayne's Fort Defiance (and before that a settlement of British traders based at Fort Miami), at least one "Cannadian Trader" had gone back into business, in an area thickly settled with Shawnee and Ottawa towns, to which hunters were returning from their winter's work. As a result, houses in these villages were well "stocked with peltry, also Jerk venison Dryed Raccoon &c &c." Meanwhile, women were "mostly employed in knitting bags belts &c and making mockasins," some of which no doubt were intended for sale to whites or Natives from other communities. "A considerable number of Indians" clogged "the River in bark canoes loaded with Peltry" on its way to market. Similarly, in the neighborhood of the former British post at Fort Miami, "many Indian Villages" lined "both shores of the [Maumee] River" with "many Cannadian Traders . . . residing amongst them." The Canadians—most of them ethnically French—had "generally intermarried with the Indians and . . . adopted their manners." That "some of the Indian Houses" were "built of small round logs" rather than the traditional poles and bark, however, might have suggested to Hopkins that the exchange of "manners" went both ways. Like nearly all Anglo-Americans of the period, though, he placed the Creole French and the métis culture they and their wives and children were creating in the same category of doomed nonagricultural hunters in which he classed the Miamis and Potawatomis.[35]

Yet the Indian communities Hopkins and his compatriots visited were populated by anything but the primitive subsistence hunters of Anglo-American imaginations. Indeed, it would make more sense to describe the region's Native people as producers and consumers in a global market economy. Quaker schemes to "advance" them to a subsistence agricultural economy thus asked them not only to withdraw from the markets in which they had been enmeshed for generations but actually threatened to *lower* the standard of living they had enjoyed for most of the eighteenth century. In this context, the Friends' insistence that Indian women cease their agricultural labors and learn to spin yarn becomes even more ironic than their notion that the males' reliance on hunting threatened Native people with starvation. In precisely the same era when white women were beginning to banish their spinning wheels to the attic in favor of cheap store-bought cotton cloth—and in the process to liberate themselves from the mind-numbing work of turning raw flax into crude homemade cloth—Indian women were being urged to abandon purchased textiles in favor of homespun.[36]

Within the terms of the four-stage theory of human progress, then, the Miamis and their Native neighbors should have been considered to be on the cusp of the transition from agriculture to commerce—just as were the whites who considered themselves destined to take the continent from them. The Baltimore Quakers' own unease with their own transition might thus explain their curious blindness to the Indians' situation. For if the tendency of commerce to encourage vicious luxury was a general concern in the early republic, the dilemma was particularly acute for urban Friends. As one religious historian concludes, "perhaps the leading trait" of American Quakerism at the turn of the nineteenth century "was its increased devotion to simplicity." The ideal was to shun "the enjoyment of wealth as well as power in favor of a standard of living attainable by any industrious self-supporting man."[37] Yet many prominent Baltimore Quakers were prosperous and would-be prosperous merchants for whom such an ideal was fraught with personal tension—and no one more than Hopkins, who ran one of the city's most successful provision stores, and his traveling companion Ellicott, whose family ran its most prominent flour mill. Significantly, both dealt in foodstuffs, and thus found themselves at precisely the point where commerce intersected agricultural self-sufficiency. As the Baltimore Yearly Meeting's published book *Disciplinel*—revised only two years after the journey to Fort Wayne—put it, "the inordinate love and pursuit of the things of this world, hath prevailed with too many amongst us, and produced the fruits of pride and ambition."[38]

To complicate matters further, tensions between simplicity and luxury joined broader contradictions among Quakers torn between an inward-turning impulse to maintain a separate identity in an increasingly complicated American religious landscape and an outward-focused emphasis on humanitarian reforms that set an example of Christian benevolence. All developed against the backdrop of the loss of political power—indeed the political ostracism—that the Quakers' pacifism had earned them during the generation between the Seven Years War and the American Revolution. To some degree, projects targeted at Native Americans—like those designed to aid African Americans, prisoners, and other social outcasts—can be understood as uneasy resolutions of these tensions, melding the self-sacrifice of distinctively Quaker unpopular causes with exemplary assaults on worldly problems that had material as well as spiritual dimensions. But this solution exposed additional fault lines in the realm of gender roles. In reclaiming their public influence through humanitarianism, Quaker men asserted themselves in areas that might otherwise have fallen within the female sphere of domesticity; women, pointedly, were not members of such bodies as committees on Indian affairs, although they participated creatively across a range of new humanitarian activities, including Indian missions sponsored by the Baltimoreans' Philadelphia counterparts.[39]

In light of their own varied problems in reconciling gender identity, economic behavior, political activism, and religious belief, it is no wonder that the Baltimore Quakers saw little virtue in Indians' gender roles and commercial activity, even when they recognized them—or that they attempted to impose an idealized model of virtuous simplicity upon the targets of their benevolence. The *Discipline* admonished Baltimore Friends to "be careful not to venture upon business they do not understand; nor to launch in trade beyond their abilities, and at the risk of others."[40] How much more must that advice have applied to Indians alleged to be in the hunter state and who, unlike those in the more advanced agrarian and commercial stages of human development, could not possibly fathom the dangers of the marketplace?

Moreover, in the Baltimore Friends' eyes, the most visible impact of trade on Indians had been "the baneful effects of spiritous liquors . . . they being at that time supplied with it in almost every village, by Canadian traders, residing amongst them."[41] The authors of the Baltimore *Discipline* would not have been surprised. Drunkenness being a symptom of the more general spiritual disease of "baneful excess," it became "incumbent on all, both by example and affectionate entreaty, to caution and dissuade all our members, against either the importation, distillation, or vending of" alcohol.[42] That Hopkins in particular took this message to heart, is suggested by the quarrel he had with his nephew Johns Hopkins, in 1819. The younger Hopkins, who saw nothing wrong with letting customers use whiskey to pay for their goods, left the elder's firm to go into business with his brothers and begin the fortune that funded his later philanthropies.[43]

On the moral and economic dangers of the commerce in liquor, Indian leaders of the southern Great Lakes region agreed with Gerard T. Hopkins. Its disastrous economic, social, and medical effects were, of course, nothing new to them. But the issue assumed particular urgency after the Greenville Treaty of 1795, as political demoralization among the defeated remnants of the Western Indian Confederacy combined with the movement of villages and refugees to new homes and a wide-open trading environment.[44] In what one Friend called "a very pathetic and impressive speech" delivered during his Baltimore visit in 1801, Little Turtle lamented that liquor had left "more of us dead since the treaty of Greenville, than we lost by the six years war before."[45] Partly in response to this oration—which Baltimore Friends rushed into print in order to press its message on the Jefferson administration before the Indian delegation left Washington—under the terms of the revised Indian Trade Intercourse Act of 1802, the War Department established the federal agency at Fort Wayne, to which Wells was appointed. Soon thereafter, the trade factory opened there. One aim of both innovations was to suppress the commerce in liquor by licensing traders and putting much of the area's economy under government

control. As the Baltimore Friends saw it, these reforms "in some measure provided a remedy for the evil" and removed "the principal obstruction to the introduction of agriculture amongst the Indians."[46] Little Turtle and Five
Medals agreed that, when Jefferson endorsed these measures, "it was the best
thing he could do for his red children."[47]

If the Baltimore Quakers had very real reasons for stressing the horrors of
the liquor trade—and thus found support for their ideological fears of the per-
nicious effects of market commerce on Native people—we might also suspect
they had some empirical basis for concluding that Indians really did "suffer
much for the want of food." Indeed, the first group of Indians described in
Hopkins's journal actually were male hunters rather than female farmers, and
they really were desperately short of basic supplies. Their story, although it
came to Hopkins secondhand, apparently made a major impact on him, for it
seemingly confirmed his assumption that the hunting mode of subsistence
doomed Indians to starvation.

At Redstone (present-day Brownsville, Pennsylvania), the Baltimoreans
attended the local Quarterly Meeting and discussed with some Ohio Friends
two messages the latter had recently received from the Wyandot leader Tarhe,
who, with perhaps a hundred of his people, had gotten trapped by a blizzard
while hunting bear on Mahoning Creek. "My Dear Brothers Quakers listen to
what I now say to You," his first letter began. "You always called us Indians
your brothers and now dear white brothers I am in distress and all my young
men who are with me[.] Brothers Will you Please to help me to fill my Ket-
tles and my horses trough, for I am afraid my horses will not be able to carry
me home again?" Before the Monthly Meeting could respond, Quakers who
lived nearer the stranded hunters contributed enough food to ease the crisis.
Tarhe then sent the Friends a second letter. "Brothers Quakers," he began,

> I want you should all know what distress I am in.
>   Brothers
> I want you to know I have got help from some of my near neighbour[s].
> Brothers
> I would be glad to know what you will do for me if it is but a little.
> Brothers
> If you cannot come soon it will do by & by for my belly is now full.
> Brothers
> I hope you have not forgotten our great fathers when they first met it was in
> friendship we are of the same race.

In response, the Ohio Quakers sent "a considerable quantity of provisions
. . . to these Indians for which they expres[sed] great tha[n]k-fulness." Hopkins noted that "Tahhee himself divi'd the presents between man & man making no difference for distinction in rank."[48]

Surely if any "red people" were starving, they were these Wyandot hunters. Yet several things have to be considered before we can accept the story on the terms Hopkins apparently understood it. First, though of course the Wyandots, trapped as they were by "a fall of Snow 3 feet in depth," faced a dire predicament, it was a freak emergency that said nothing about the everyday ability of agricultural Great Lakes Indian economies to feed their populations. Second, Tarhe ("the Crane"), whom Hopkins's journal describes only as "a Wyandot of Great distinction," was not just any unfortunate Native American; he was one of the most important figures in Great Lakes politics and diplomacy at the turn of the nineteenth century. At the Greenville Treaty, he had mediated disputes among the Native participants and—particularly over the objections of Little Turtle—had helped to ensure that they would leave convinced that they genuinely negotiated, rather than simply acquiesced, to Wayne's terms. "Have done trifling: let us conclude this great Work," Tarhe had then proclaimed to his wartime Indian allies; "let us sign our names to the Treaty now proposed and finish our business."[49] Later, as headman of the Upper Sandusky (Cranetown) Wyandots, he was one of the most consistent pro-United States figures in the Great Lakes region. Throughout the period of the War of 1812, he—like the Miami Little Turtle and the Potawatomi Five Medals —would consistently oppose the efforts of the Shawnees Tecumseh and Tenskwatawa ("the Prophet") to build a new religiously based anti-United States confederacy.[50]

Nor was Tarhe previously unknown to the Baltimore Quakers. When the Ohio Friends delivered their gifts to Tarhe, he complained "that Several years ago he had sent a Talk to Indian committee at Baltimore accompanied by a Belt of Wampum worth fifty Dollars & that he had been long waiting for an Answer but had not received one."[51] As was often the case in intercultural diplomacy, however, things were not so simple as a costly message sent by a trusting Indian and rudely snubbed by insensitive whites. The earliest contact between the Baltimore committee and Tarhe occurred less than two years after the group's founding. In the spring of 1797, three committee members journeyed to the country of the Wyandots and Delawares in present-day north-central Ohio "for the purpose of obtaining a more satisfactory knowledge respecting them." This voyage evidently had helped to fix the image of starving Natives in Baltimore Quaker minds. According to the published record of the committee, "Having passed by a number of their hunting camps, and several of their towns," the Baltimoreans "had large opportunity of discovering their situation, often exposed to the inclemency of the seasons, with a very precarious, and often a very scanty supply of food and cloathing." The Wyandots and Delawares, the Friends concluded, "suffered all the miseries of extreme poverty, in a country, which, from its great fertility, would, with but a little cultivation, abundantly supply them with all the necessaries of life."[52]

The published account does not tell us exactly where the Quakers went or how much time they spent trying to understand conditions in Indian country. If they merely "passed by" towns and hunting camps, their knowledge must have been superficial. Still, the Indians probably were in considerable distress. It was, after all, early spring, a time of year when stores of food would have been exhausted and when people would have appeared most heavily reliant on hunting and gathering, if only to escape the winter tedium of parched corn and dried beans. And it was not only early spring, but early spring of 1797, a little over a year after two diplomatic earthquakes had redrawn the map and economic relationships of their part of North America. The Greenville Treaty had deprived the Delawares of most of their lands on the Muskingum River in present-day eastern Ohio, and the majority of that nation were in the process of establishing new homes on the White River in present-day Indiana. Those who remained in the East clung to villages just north of the treaty line and were no doubt entertaining large numbers of refugees in search of new homes. Meantime, Jay's Treaty between the United States and Great Britain, which mandated the withdrawal of British posts from the area by June 1796, caused additional turmoil, even for the Wyandots, whose possessions on the Sandusky and upper Great Miami rivers were somewhat more securely beyond the Greenville boundary. Fort Miami, on the Maumee River, ceased to exist, and the next closest post, Detroit, became a United States garrison. Neither any longer supplied the subsidies of food, materials, and weapons available during the wars of the early 1790s, and trade routes and supply lines had not yet stabilized under the new regime. The disruption of vital commercial links, rather than any deficiency in the ability of Native people to feed themselves, was what really threatened impoverishment.[53]

Seemingly oblivious to these complexities, the 1797 Quaker delegation met "some of the chiefs and hunters of the *Wyandot* and *Delaware* nations." The Native leaders listened politely to a speech about "the advantages they would derive, from permitting to be introduced amongst their people, a knowledge of agriculture, and some of the most useful mechanic arts" and "promised to lay the matter before their grand council." More than a year passed before Tarhe responded on behalf of that council in a speech and wampum belt delivered at Detroit. Five more months elapsed before his message got to Baltimore in February 1799. It said nothing specific about the Friends' proposal to teach the agricultural Wyandots how to farm, but instead invited the Quakers to come to Tarhe's home at Sandusky. From thence he promised to escort them to a grand council of his nation's leaders to renew the old alliance between Friends and Indians—"a chain of silver, that would never get rusty" and "would bind us in brotherly affection forever." He looked forward to the chance to "talk of those things that were done between our GOOD GRAND-FATHERS, when they first met upon our lands—upon this great island!"[54]

Tarhe's rhetoric of a covenant chain, of grandfathers, of the legend of peaceful beneficence epitomized by the Quaker founder William Penn, were part of the ritualized vocabulary of eighteenth-century intercultural diplomacy. To one attuned to their meaning, such phrases conveyed a desire for something quite different than chasing women out of the fields so men could take up the plough. The language evoked the kinds of connections that, before the American Revolution, Indian leaders repeatedly articulated with European imperial governments. The Covenant Chain was a metaphor for the relationship Indians allied to the British had with their "brethren"; in the Great Lakes region a generation earlier, a more common usage would be to speak of filial obligations to the French "father." In both instances, the fundamental concept was that Natives—without diminishing their political autonomy—placed themselves under the protection of more powerful Europeans. In exchange for their allegiance, they expected their "father" or "brethren" to keep the peace among Indians in the alliance and to provide military protection and economic benefits, the latter in the form of both diplomatic gifts and a secure trading environment.[55] "Listen to your children, here assembled; be strong, now, and take care of all your little ones," Tarhe instructed Wayne at the Greenville Treaty. "Should any of your children come to you crying, and in distress, have pity on them, and relieve their wants."[56]

In the 1790s and 1800s, as Great Lakes Indians faced an aggressive, expansive Unites States government that acted like anything but a fatherly protector, Native leaders repeatedly requested that Quaker observers be present at treaty conferences to provide a moral check on government negotiators and in other ways to mediate between them and authorities in the federal and state capitals. Tarhe, it seems likely, hoped that the Baltimore Quakers would go still farther to protect their interests and provide economic (not just narrowly agricultural) assistance—to take up the Covenant Chain broken when the British withdrew from Indian country. Reflective of just how quaint these eighteenth-century concepts of diplomatic protection and economic alliance had become in the United States-dominated world after the Greenville and Jay treaties, however, is the tragic comedy of errors that followed Tarhe's invitation. The translator at Detroit had gotten the date of the upcoming Wyandot grand council wrong, and so a delegation from Baltimore showed up at Tarhe's Sandusky village several weeks early. Rather than wait, the Friends held a hastily arranged conference with their host, who again promised to "communicate fully" to the council the Quakers' proposals and to send "a written speech of their conclusion thereon." That speech—probably the one accompanied by Tarhe's fifty-dollar wampum belt—never reached the shores of the Chesapeake. Having thus heard nothing, the Baltimoreans sent a inquiring letter to Sandusky, "but the person to whose care it was directed . . . not being at home, it was returned to the committee."[57] Meanwhile, the more promising invitation from Little Turtle and Five Medals had encouraged the Baltimore Friends to shift their humanitarian efforts away from the Wyandots toward the apparently more receptive Miamis and Potawatomis.

Hopkins's journal betrays not the slightest acknowledgment of the complicated history behind Tarhe's complaint nor the eagerness with which he had earlier sought a protective alliance with the Baltimore Friends. Nor, for that matter, does it seem to make much of a distinction among Wyandots, Miamis, and other "red people." But the importance the Wyandot leader placed on establishing that alliance provides a final explanation for the pathetic rhetoric in which he phrased his temporarily snowbound condition—and his plea to Wayne at Greenville in 1795. As anthropologist Mary Black-Rogers points out, when Great Lakes Algonquian-speakers said they were "starving," in "distress," or in other ways presented themselves as objects of pity, they were often using a coded social vocabulary that really was not about economic privation at all. Instead, it was about the etiquette of social and political alliance. Especially in relationships between parties of unequal status, it was important for everyone to behave in ways that did not imply a pride in his own power or, especially, an overt attempt to control other persons. (Such coercion was the definition of sorcery.) As a result, a host, in a position of superiority, must display generosity by lavishly feeding his guest, but he must not offer food unless asked, lest he betray too much pride in his own possessions and humiliate a person of lesser power. A visitor, by the same token, was supposed to ask for food in what Euro-Americans would consider an excessively self-deprecatory fashion, using language that translated into English as begging for pity on one's starving condition. "I'm poor, I'm poor in food—I'm starving," moans a traditional Ojibwa song. "Have pity," Tarhe said at Greenville. Such words were not to be taken literally. They encoded, explains Black-Rogers, "the approved way of behaving as a visitor, the host having avoided being coercive by politely allowing a guest to decide whether he wished to receive food" while allowing the guest to display an appropriate lack of pride in power and material possessions. Tarhe's rhetorical cries of distress, then—especially in his second message, when real starvation no longer threatened—spoke more about the nature of the relationship he perceived between his people and the Baltimore Quakers than about his hunting party's short-term woes.[58]

The Baltimore Quakers were not at all mistaken, then, when they believed that at least some Great Lakes Indian leaders were eager for their assistance. It was the complexities of the *kind* of assistance—and the diplomatic and political difficulties involved with gaining Native acceptance of their aid—that they failed to appreciate. At Fort Wayne, Five Medals lodged almost the same complaint on account of his Potawatomis that Tarhe had earlier made with regard to the Wyandots: the Quakers in their haste to leave were missing a vital opportunity to make a personal appearance before a council of his nation's chiefs and establish political support for a productive diplomatic relationship. "Our young men are out hunting and our women and children are now at work at their sugar Camps," he told Hopkins. "The time is far off when th[e]y will return to our towns and when it is usual for us to meet together" and he begged the Quakers' patience to "allow us time to Collect our people generally." When the Friends said they really could only stay a few days and asked the Potawatami leader simply "to get together some of your people" to hear their presentation, Five Medals "Observ'd that in the time proposed they could easily convene a considerable number of their Indolent people who were too Lazy to hunt or make sugar but such they did not wish us to see."[59] Both activities, it should be stressed, produced marketable commodities.

Thus, just as the Baltimore Quakers misunderstood the political needs of their Indian hosts, so too they misinterpreted Native economic expectations. When Five Medals and Little Turtle visited Baltimore in 1801, Hopkins's colleague on the Indian committee, Evan Thomas, reported that the Miami leader "appeared to be much rejoiced at" the Friends' proposal to instruct his people in Euro-American methods of agriculture, "for although the game was not so scarce, but that they could get enough to eat, yet they were sensible it was daily diminishing, and that the time was not far distant, when they would be compelled to take hold of such tools as they saw in the hands of the white people." Despite his apparently genuine advocacy of a controversial policy that faced considerable opposition at home, however, Little Turtle had not brought up the subject of agriculture. Moreover, he emphatically did not propose to renounce commerce more generally in favor of the subsistence farming that Friends had in mind. "Brothers fetch us useful things—bring goods that will cloth us, our women and our children, and not this evil *liquor* that destroys our reason; that destroys our health; that destroys our lives," he said he had repeatedly told the traders who lived in his people's villages.[60]

Similar themes echo in most of the requests the Miamis, Potawatomis, Delawares, and Wyandots—and Senecas and Oneidas and others—sent to Quakers in the East at the turn of the nineteenth century. Indian leaders who expressed interest in the "civilization" program sought not help with agriculture *per se* but with the broader dilemma of how to ensure safe and secure trade and the survival of the productive resources necessary to obtain imported goods. Indeed, as anthropologist Diane Rothenberg has shown, Quakers' and other white reformers' only hope of succeeding in their efforts to

introduce plough agriculture and domestic animals came when they also contributed such market-oriented improvements as water-powered grain and
lumber mills that would provide cash income for Native communities. More
typically, as Rothenberg concludes of the Philadelphia Friends who worked
with Seneca Iroquois in this period, "the Quakers had no clear markets in
mind for the sale of the products resulting from the more intensive farming
methods that they advocated. Without such a system of distribution to supply
the cash needed by the community to purchase items essential to them that
they could not themselves manufacture, attempts to divert a male population
from cash deriving activities to non-cash deriving activities were doomed to
failure."[61]

"It must be a prospect truly gladdening to the enlightened christian mind,
to survey the hastening of that day, when this part of the human family,
weaned from savage habits, and allured by the superior advantages of civilized life, shall exchange the tomahawk and scalping knife for the plough and
the hoe," the Baltimore Indian committee proclaimed in a published account
of the work Dennis had begun in Indian country.[62] Yet the Miamis whom the
Quakers hoped to save from starvation and extinction lived, not in the hunter
state of Euro-American imaginations, but in a complicated, multicultural,
market-oriented economy. That economy—while rooted in ancient patterns—
was superbly adapted to the eighteenth-century imperial world in which it
evolved. Whether it would be equally suited to nineteenth-century conditions
of United States domination and the relentless pressure of westward migrat-
ing white settlers was very much in doubt—but not because the "red people"
were somehow locked in ancient patterns of behavior, showed an inexplica-
ble fondness for the wild, free ways of the hunting life, or were unable to
adapt to changing circumstances. (No Native people who survived the demographic, military, and economic carnage of the seventeenth and eighteenth
centuries could be accused of the latter flaw.) If starvation loomed, it would
not literally be for lack of food. Instead it would be because the Jeffersonian
design of systematically expropriating Indian hunting territories deprived
them of the opportunity to produce marketable products to exchange for manufactured goods or cash.

In retrospect, the future of something else in the complex market economy
of the southern Great Lakes was just as profoundly in doubt as that of hunting: the coexistence of whites and Indians, the intermarriage of traders and
Native women, the resulting métis population—the very blurring of ethnic
and cultural lines that was so utterly incompatible with the ever-hardening
racial categories of the nineteenth century. Even so well-meaning a folk as the
Baltimore Quakers could only categorize the targets of their humanitarianism
by the stereotypical labels of "red people" and "hunters," rather than as hu-

man participants in a complicated milieu in which people both hunted animals and produced sugar for market in neatly weighed bundles, carved "hieroglyphics" on trees and wrote letters on paper, charged cash for ferrying customers and buried costly items with their dead, dressed mostly in tattoos rather than clothes, and lived in log cabins. There was no room in the emerging constructions of whiteness and redness for such complications.

"The passion of the red man for the hunter life has proved to be a principle too deeply inwrought, to be controlled by efforts of legislation," wrote anthropologist Lewis Henry Morgan a generation after Hopkins composed his journal. "The effect of this powerful principle has been to enchain the tribes of North America to their primitive state," and so, he concluded, "we have here the true reason why the red race has never risen, or can rise above its present level."[63] The "powerful principle" was indeed the key factor—not because it accurately described Native realities but because it utterly dominated white analyses of what they were coming to describe as the "Indian Problem." Morgan, like the Quakers before him, considered himself to be on the Indians' side. That even the defenders of Native rights could not escape the overwhelming power of racial categories—could only see Indians as primitive hunters doomed to pitiable extinction—reveals just how bleak the future was for Indians in a white man's republic.

NOTES

1. Gerard T. Hopkins, Journal, 1804–05 (unpaginated) (Historical Society of Pennsylvania, Philadelphia), quotations from introductory paragraph, extract from Baltimore Indian committee minutes, Feb. 6, 1804, and entry for Apr. 10, 1804. According to a late-nineteenth-century New York local historian, Hopkins's journal "was published as a pamphlet" shortly after it was completed. Frank H. Severance, "Visit of Gerard T. Hopkins, A Quaker Ambassador to the Indians who Visited Buffalo in 1804," *Publications of the Buffalo Historical Society*, 6 (1903), 217–22. No such work, however, is listed in Ralph R. Shaw and Richard H. Shoemaker, *American Bibliography, a Preliminary Checklist, 1801 to 1819* (22 vols., New York, 1958–66). A version was printed by Ellicott's daughter Martha Tyson in 1862, with an appendix based on her own recollections and on papers of the Baltimore Yearly Meeting; Gerard T. Hopkins, *A Mission to the Indians, from the Indian Committee of Baltimore Yearly Meeting to Fort Wayne, in 1804* (Philadelphia, 1862). Tyson's text—much abridged and with a number of inaccuracies in transcription—forms the bulk of William H. Love, "A Quaker Pilgrimage: A Mission to the Indians from the Indian Committee of the Baltimore Yearly Meeting, to Fort Wayne, 1804," *Maryland Historical Magazine*, 4 (Mar. 1909), 1–24. An accurate modern addition of major portions of the document appears in Joseph E. Walker, ed., "Plowshares and Pruning Hooks for the Miami and Potawatomi: The Journal of Gerard T. Hopkins, 1804," *Ohio History*, 88 (Autumn 1979), 361–407.

2. Hopkins, Journal, *s.v.* Apr. 2, 15, 1804.

3. Love, "A Quaker Pilgrimage," 19–24; Bliss Forbush, *A History of Baltimore Yearly Meeting of Friends: Three Hundred Years of Quakerism in Maryland, Virginia, the District of Columbia, and Central Pennsylvania* (Sandy Spring, MD, 1972), 60; Sydney V. James, *A People among Peoples: Quaker Benevolence in Eighteenth-Century America* (Cambridge, MA, 1963), 298–311; Diane Brodatz Rothenberg, "Friends Like These: An Ethnohistorical Analysis of the Interaction between Allegany Senecas and Quakers, 1798–1823" (Ph.D. diss., City University of New York, 1976), 124–41.

4. *A Brief Account of the Proceedings of the Committee, Appointed by the Yearly Meeting of Friends, Held in Baltimore, for Promoting the Improvement and Civilization of the Indian Natives* (Baltimore, 1805), 15–20 (quotation at 20).

5. Little Turtle and Five Medals to Evan Thomas *et al.*, Sept. 18, 1803, in Hopkins, Journal; Indian committee minutes, Feb. 6, 1804, *ibid.*

6. *Brief Account of the Proceedings*, 39–45, 45n–46n (quotations at 40); *The Report of a Sub-Committee to the General Committees on Indian Concerns, Appointed by the Yearly Meetings of Baltimore and Ohio* (Mount Pleasant, OH, 1816); Harvey Lewis Carter, *The Life and Times of Little Turtle: First Sagamore of the Wabash* (Urbana, 1987), 197–208.

7. Hopkins, Journal, *s.v.* Mar. 9, 1804.

8. *Ibid.*, *s.v.* Mar. 10–19, 1804.

9. *Ibid.*, *s.v.* Mar. 27, 1804.

10. *Ibid.*, *s.v.* Mar. 31, Apr. 5, 1804; see also *ibid.*, *s.v.* Mar. 26, Apr. 7, 1804. On Harmar's defeat, see Wiley Sword, *President Washington's Indian War: The Struggle for the Old Northwest, 1790–1795* (Norman, OK, 1985), 96–122.

11. Hopkins, Journal, *s.v.* Apr. 4, 1804. Hopkins quotes here one of the most widely read poems of his era, Edward Young's, *The Complaint: Or, Night-thoughts on Life, Death, and Immortality* (1742; rep., Edinburgh, 1774), 272. The passage from "Night the Ninth and Last: Consolation"—which Hopkins, omitting the poet's name, attributes only to "Nights Thoughts"—continues as follows:

Where is the dust that has not been alive?
The spade, the plough, disturb our ancestors;
From human mould we reap our daily bread.
The globe around earth's hollow surface shakes,
And is the ceiling of her sleeping sons.
O'er devastation we blind revels keep:
Whole buried towns support the dancer's heel
The *moist* of human frame the Sun exhales,
Winds scatter, thro' the mighty void, the *dry;*
Each repossesses part of what she gave;
And the freed spirit mounts on wings of fire;
Each element partakes our scatter'd spoils;
As nature, wide, our ruins spread: man's *death*
Inhabits all things, but the thought of man.

For other remarks on Indian cemeteries, see Hopkins, Journal, *s.v.* Mar. 10, 14, and 31, 1804.

12. Hopkins, Journal, *s.v.* Apr. 10, 1804. The parallel between the Roman conquest of Britain and the English conquest of peoples they considered culturally less developed was a commonplace drawn at least since the sixteenth century. See Nicholas P. Canny, "The Ideology of English Colonization: From Ireland to America," *William and Mary Quarterly*, 30 (Oct. 1973), 585–93.

13. Young, *The Complaint*, 272.

14. Roy Harvey Pearce, *Savagism and Civilization: A Study of the Indian and the American Mind* (1953; rep., Berkeley, 1988), 82–91; Ronald L. Meek, *Social Science and the Ignoble Savage* (Cambridge, UK, 1976), *passim*; Theda Perdue, *Cherokee Women: Gender and Culture Change, 1700–1835* (Lincoln, NE, 1998), 110; Elizabeth Vibert, *Traders' Tales: Narratives of Cultural Encounters in the Columbia Plateau, 1807–1846* (Norman, 1997), esp. 162–204.

15. Drew R. McCoy, *The Elusive Republic: Political Economy in Jeffersonian Virginia* (Chapel Hill, 1980), 13–47; Joyce E. Chaplin, *An Anxious Pursuit: Agricultural Innovation and Modernity in the Lower South, 1730–1815* (Chapel Hill, 1993), 23–65.

16. Thomas Jefferson, *Notes on the State of Virginia* (1781; rep., New York, 1964), 157; *The Papers of Alexander Hamilton*, ed. Harold C. Syrett (27 vols., New York, 1961–87), X, 230; Joyce Appleby, "Commercial Farming and the 'Agrarian Myth' in the Early Republic," *Journal of American History*, 68 (Mar. 1982), 833–49; Charles Sellers, *The Market Revolution: Jacksonian America, 1815–1846* (New York, 1991), 3–40; James Henretta, "The 'Market' in the Early Republic," *Journal of the Early Republic*, 18 (Spring 1998), 289–304.

17. Pearce, *Savagism and Civilization*, 66.

18. Meek, *Social Science and the Ignoble Savage*, 37–67.

19. Quoted *ibid.*, 117–18.

20. Robert F. Berkhofer Jr., *The White Man's Indian: Images of the American Indian from Columbus to the Present* (New York, 1978), 134–53.

21. Bernard W. Sheehan, *Seeds of Extinction: Jeffersonian Philanthropy and the American Indian* (Chapel Hill, 1973), 148–81; James P. Ronda, "'We Have a Country': Race, Geography, and the Invention of Indian Territory," in this volume.

22. Society of Friends, Baltimore Yearly Meeting, *An Address of the Yearly Meeting of Friends . . . to Thomas Jefferson, President of the United States, and His Reply* ([Baltimore], 1807).

23. *The Epistle from the Yearly Meeting, Held in London, by Adjournment, from the 20th to the 29th of the Fifth Month, 1807, inclusive, to the Quarterly and Monthly Meetings of Friends in Great Britain, Ireland, and Elsewhere* (Baltimore, [1807]), 2.

24. Bert Anson, *The Miami Indians* (Norman, 1970), 20–22 (quotation at 22); Carter, *Life and Times of Little Turtle*, 15–16.

25. Hopkins, Journal, *s.v.* Apr. 15, 1804. Hopkins was not completely ignorant of Native agricultural traditions and settled living arrangements, although he seemed to place them in the past rather than the present. "Their corn hills," he noted, were "still discernable" near the cemetery that inspired his poetic lament on the triumph of the plough; *ibid.*, *s.v.* Apr. 4, 1804.

26. Quoted in Meek, *Social Science and the Ignoble Savage*, 117–18, 137.

27. Hopkins, Journal, *s.v.* Apr. 10, 1804.

28. J. William Frost, *The Quaker Family in Colonial America: A Portrait of the Society of Friends* (New York, 1973), 183; Barry Levy, *Quakers and the American Family:*

British Settlement in the Delaware Valley (New York, 1988), 193–230; Rebecca Larson, *Daughters of Light: Quaker Women Preaching and Prophesying in the Colonies and Abroad, 1700–1775* (New York, 1999), 133–71.

29. Richard White, *The Middle Ground: Indians, Empires, and Republics in the Great Lakes Region, 1650–1815* (Cambridge, UK, 1991), 41–43; James Axtell, *The European and the Indian: Essays in the Ethnohistory of Colonial North America* (New York, 1981), 46–53. For a brief introduction to traditional eastern Native-American agricultural practices, see Carolyn Merchant, *Ecological Revolutions: Nature, Gender, and Science in New England* (Chapel Hill, 1989), 74–81.

30. [Religious Society of Friends, London Yearly Meeting] Aborigines Committee of the Meeting for Sufferings, *Some Account of the Conduct of the Religious Society of Friends towards the Indian Tribes in the Settlement of the Colonies of East and West Jersey and Pennsylvania: With a Brief Narrative of their Labours for the Civilization and Christian Instruction of the Indians, from the Time of their Settlement in America, to the Year 1843* (London, UK, 1844), 122.

31. Charles Callender, "Miami," in William C. Sturtevant, gen. ed., *Handbook of North American Indians*, Vol. XV: *Northeast*, ed. Bruce G. Trigger (Washington, DC, 1978), 682; James Axtell, *Beyond 1492: Encounters in Colonial North America* (New York, 1992), 125–51; Anthony F. C. Wallace, *Jefferson and the Indians: The Tragic Fate of the First Americans* (Cambridge, MA, 1999), 297–98 (quotation).

32. Hopkins, Journal, *s.v.* Mar. 29, 1804.

33. *Ibid.*, *s.v.* Mar. 31, 1804.

34. *Ibid., s.v.* Apr. 3, 1804. See also *ibid., s.v.* Apr. 7, 15, 1804.

35. *Ibid.*, *s.v.* Apr. 17, 19, 1804 (quotations); Helen Hornbeck Tanner, ed., *Atlas of Great Lakes Indian History* (Norman, 1987), 90; R. David Edmunds, "'Unacquainted with the Laws of the Civilized World': American Attitudes toward the Métis in the Old Northwest," in Jacqueline Peterson and Jennifer S. H. Brown, eds., *The New Peoples: Being and Becoming Métis in North America* (Lincoln, 1985), 185–93. On the Canadian traders and the origins of métis communities south of the Great Lakes, see Jacqueline Peterson, "Many Roads to Red River: Métis Genesis in the Great Lakes Region, 1680–1815," *ibid.*, 37–71; and Susan Sleeper-Smith, "Silent Tongues, Black Robes: Potawatomi, Europeans, and Settlers in the Southern Great Lakes, 1640–1850" (Ph.D. diss., University of Michigan, 1994).

36. For an evocative description of the impact of machine-made cloth on white women's domestic work in the early nineteenth century, see Jack Larkin, *The Reshaping of Everyday Life, 1790–1840* (New York, 1988), 25–27, 50, 187–91.

37. James, *People among Peoples*, 271–72.

38. Forbush, *History of Baltimore Yearly Meeting*, 48–49, 57; Society of Friends, Baltimore Yearly Meeting, *Discipline of the Yearly Meeting of Friends, Held in Baltimore, Printed by Direction of the Meeting, Held in the Year 1806* (Baltimore, [1807]), 71–72 (quotation). On the tensions within Quakerism in the late eighteenth and early nineteenth centuries, see Jean R. Soderlund, *Quakers and Slavery: A Divided Spirit* (Princeton, 1985); Jack Marietta, *The Reformation of American Quakerism, 1748–1783* (Philadelphia, 1984); Thomas D. Hamm, *The Transformation of American Quakerism: Orthodox Friends, 1800–1907* (Bloomington, IN, 1999); and H. Larry Ingle, *Quakers in Conflict: The Hicksite Reformation* (Knoxville, TN, 1986).

39. Mary Maples Dunn, "Women of Light," in Carol Ruth Berkin and Mary Beth Norton, eds., *Women of America: A History* (Boston, 1979), 131–32; Margaret Hope Bacon, *Mothers of Feminism: The Story of Quaker Women in America* (San Francisco, 1986), 80–81; Margaret Morris Haviland, "Beyond Women's Sphere: Young Quaker Women and the Veil of Charity in Philadelphia, 1790–1810," *William and Mary Quarterly*, 51 (July 1994), 418–46; Bruce Dorsey, "Friends Becoming Enemies: Philadelphia Benevolence and the Neglected Era of America Quaker History," *Journal of the Early Republic*, 18 (Fall 1998), 395–428.

40. Baltimore Yearly Meeting, *Discipline*, 107. One of the "Nine Queries" to be answered annually in every Preparative or Monthly Meeting was whether members were "careful to live within the bounds of their circumstances, and to avoid involving themselves in business beyond their ability to manage"; *ibid.*, 95.

41. *Brief Account of the Proceedings*, 12–14.

42. Baltimore Yearly Meeting, *Discipline*, 72–73.

43. Dumas Malone, ed., *Dictionary of American Biography* (New York, 1932), *s.v.* "Hopkins, Johns."

44. *Brief Account of the Proceedings*, 16. For a carefully researched overview of this sensitive subject, see Peter C. Mancall, *Deadly Medicine: Indians and Alcohol in Early America* (Ithaca, 1995).

45. *Memorial of Evan Thomas, and Others, A Committee Appointed for Indian Affairs, By the Yearly Meeting of the People Called Friends, Held in Baltimore, 7th January, 1802* (1802), 6–8.

46. Anson, *Miami Indians*, 144; Carter, *Life and Times of Little Turtle*, 161–63; Wallace, *Jefferson and the Indians*, 211–12; *Brief Account of the Proceedings*, 19–20 (quotations). From 1797 until the establishment of Indiana Territory in 1800, Wells had been deputy agent at Fort Wayne, which lacked full agency status during the period of his appointment and had no official Indian Department presence from 1800 to 1802.

47. Little Turtle and Five Medals to Evan Thomas *et al.*, Sept. 18, 1803, in Hopkins, Journal.

48. *Ibid.*, s.v. Mar. 1–8, 1804.

49. "Minutes of a treaty with the tribes of Indians called the Wyandots, Delawares, Shawanoes, Ottawas, Chipewas, Putawatimes, Miamis, Eel River, Kickapoos, Piankashaws, and Kaskaskias; begun at Greene Ville on the 16th day of June, and ended on the 10th day of August 1795," Indian Treaties, 1778–1795, fol. 293r, Anthony Wayne Papers, 1765–1890 (Historical Society of Pennsylvania) (quotation); Anson, *Miami Indians*, 135–36; Andrew R. L. Cayton, "'Noble Actors' upon 'the Theatre of Honour': Power and Civility in the Treaty of Greenville," in Andrew R. L. Cayton and Fredrika J. Teute, eds., *Contact Points: American Frontiers from the Mohawk Valley to the Mississippi, 1750–1830* (Chapel Hill, 1998), 252–67.

50. Sword, *President Washington's Indian War*, 328–36; R. David Edmunds, *Tecumseh and the Quest for Indian Leadership* (Boston, 1984), 118–19; Tanner, ed., *Atlas*, 117; Gregory Evans Dowd, *A Spirited Resistance: The North American Indian Struggle for Unity, 1745–1815* (Baltimore, 1992), 123–47.

51. Hopkins, Journal, s.v. Mar. 1–8, 1804.

52. *Brief Account of the Proceedings*, 6–8.

53. Tanner, ed., *Atlas*, 98–102.

54. *Brief Account of the Proceedings*, 7–12.

55. William N. Fenton, "Structure, Continuity, and Change in the Process of Iroquois Treaty Making," in Francis Jennings *et al.*, eds., *The History and Culture of Iroquois Diplomacy: An Interdisciplinary Guide to the Treaties of the Six Nations and Their League* (Syracuse, 1985), 10–14, 21–22; White, *Middle Ground*, 84–85; Daniel K. Richter, "Onas, the Long Knife: Pennsylvanians and Indians, 1783–1794," in Frederick Hoxie, Ronald Hoffman, and Peter Albert, *eds., Native Americans and the Early Republic* (Charlottesville, 1999), 125–30.

56. Quoted in Cayton, "'Noble Actors' upon 'The Theatre of Honour,'" 265.

57. *Brief Account of the Proceedings*, 12–15.

58. Mary Black-Rogers, "Varieties of 'Starving': Semantics and Survival in the Subarctic Fur Trade, 1750–1850," *Ethnohistory*, 33 (Fall 1986), 353–83 (quotations at 370); Bruce White, "'Give Us a Little Milk': The Social and Cultural Meaning of Gift-Giving in the Lake Superior Fur Trade," *Minnesota History*, 48 (Summer 1982), 60–71.

59. Hopkins, Journal, *s.v.* Apr. 2, 1804.

60. *Memorial of Evan Thomas*, 6. On Little Turtle's and Wells's attitudes toward the Jeffersonian "civilization" program, see Carter, *Life and Times of Little Turtle*, 197–208. On Miami opposition to Little Turtle, see Rob Mann, "The Silenced Miami: Archaeological and Ethnohistorical Evidence for Miami-British Relations, 1795–1812," *Ethnohistory*, 46 (Summer 1999), 399–427.

61. Rothenberg, "Friends Like These," 144–48.

62. *Brief Account of the Proceedings*, 47.

63. Lewis H. Morgan, *League of the Ho-dé-no-sau-nee, Iroquois* (1851; rep., New York, 1962), 57.

BIBLIOGRAPHY

Anson, Bert. *The Miami Indians.* Norman: University of Oklahoma Press, 1970.

Berkhofer, Robert F., Jr. *The White Man's Indian: Images of the American Indian from Columbus to the Present.* New York: Knopf, 1978.

Black-Rogers, Mary. "Varieties of 'Starving': Semantics and Survival in the Subarctic Fur Trade, 1750–1850." *Ethnohistory* 33 (Fall 1986): 353–83.

Carter, Harvey Lewis. *The Life and Time of Little Turtle: First Sagamore of the Wabash.* Urbana: University of Illinois Press, 1987.

Hamm, Thomas D. *The Transformation of American Quakerism: Orthodox Friends, 1800–1907.* Bloomington: Indiana University Press, 1999.

James, Sydney V. *A People among Peoples: Quaker Benevolence in Eighteenth-Century America.* Cambridge: Cambridge University Press, 1963.

Meek, Ronald L. *Social Science and the Ignoble Savage.* Cambridge: Cambridge University Press, 1976.

Pearce, Roy Harvey. *Savagism and Civilization: A Study of the Indian and the American Mind.* Berkeley: University of California Press, 1988.

Rothenberg, Diane Brodatz. "Friends Like These: An Ethnohistorical Analysis of the Interaction between Allegany Senecas and Quakers, 1798–1823." Ph.D. diss. City University of New York, 1976.

Sheehan, Bernard W. *Seeds of Extinction: Jeffersonian Philanthropy and the American Indian.* Chapel Hill: University of North Carolina Press, 1973.

Tanner, Helen Hornbeck, ed. *Atlas of Great Lakes Indian History.* Norman: University of Oklahoma Press, 1987.

White, Richard. *The Middle Ground: Indians, Empires, and Republics in the Great Lakes Region, 1650–1815.* Cambridge: Cambridge University Press, 1991.

3

From Class to Race in Early America: Northern Post-Emancipation Racial Reconstruction

Lois E. Horton

The American Revolution created an immediate break from England's political and economic control. It also marked the beginning of internal evolutionary changes in America. The Revolution began the abolition of slavery in the North, transforming the operation and meaning of class and race. Gradual emancipation strategies preserved unfree black labor just when indentures for European-American workers were disappearing, and this had important consequences for the relationship between poor blacks and poor whites. They were less likely thereafter to share a common condition and, from the perspective of white workers, were more likely to be in competition. Racial tensions were undoubtedly exacerbated as the nation moved toward its first labor surplus in the 1820s with many northern blacks occupying a middle ground of labor, neither slave nor free. A growing racial divide at the bottom of society can be traced through the institution of racially defined political statuses, violent racial conflicts, labor competition, the systematic exclusion of blacks from certain occupations, and the development of an ideology of racial inferiority. Analysis of these changes can deepen our understanding of the role of race and racism in the early republic and of the transformation of race and class.

Part of the postrevolution story of race is well known. With abolition measures in the North and slavery's retention in the South, the country was split, and that fracture would lead to civil war. The complicated social, political, and economic changes that marked the evolution from a slaveholding to a free society in the North are less familiar. Indeed, it is only with a growing literature on northern black thought and activism, and with recent works on the phenomenon of race and color, that we have begun to understand these changes.[1] From the earliest European settlement in America, both race and

55

class were important organizing principles. In fact, racial differentiation was the hallmark of American slavery. Typically, Native Americans and Africans were enslaved while white Europeans served defined terms as indentured servants. Additionally, colonial officials instituted policies designed to maintain racial lines. In 1656, Massachusetts removed Indians and Africans from the militia and by 1707 required them to perform alternative service. In the mid-1600s and early 1700s, Maryland, Virginia, and Massachusetts banned interracial sexual relations and marriage. Under a 1726 Pennsylvania law, a free black person could be sold into slavery for marrying a white person, while no punishment was provided for the white partner.[2]

Laws separating the races demonstrate official perceptions and concerns, but the perceived necessity for them also indicates the multiracial character of early America and the prevalence of the relationships they regulated. As historian Edmund Morgan concluded for colonial Virginia, it was not unusual for "servants and slaves to run away together, steal hogs together, get drunk together . . . [and] not uncommon for them to make love together." Material conditions created common bonds, as the every-day lives and working conditions of unfree workers were comparable, especially in the urban North. Slaves and indentured servants generally received similar food and clothing. The disdain of the privileged classes, who characterized them as "mean and vile" or the "lower sort," also united them. In this elite view, God placed poor whites and blacks at the bottom of the social order, "Ordain[ing] different degrees and orders of men, some to be high and Honorable, some to be Low and Despicable." In colonial eighteenth-century New York City, weekly auctions sold both black slaves and the indentures of white servants. There were crucial differences, since slavery was without term, and owners also confiscated a slave's children. But both slaves and indentured servants stood on the auction block, and indentured servants often perceived themselves to be in comparable circumstances. Soul drivers carried unsold white indentured servants into the countryside in search of buyers, according to one servant, "exposing [them] for sale in all public fairs and markets as brute beasts." Another reported to correspondents in Britain that the servant in America was sold "for a slave at public sale."[3]

Plantation agriculture, North and South, and especially the more common household slavery in the North, black workers and white workers intermingled in shared tasks and commonly experienced punishments. Such other occupations as seafaring and work as craftsmen and artisans brought blacks and whites together on a relatively equal footing. Work at sea was difficult and dangerous, and the status and working conditions of common sailors were only marginally better than those of plantation slaves. In fact, most black mariners in the seventeenth and much of the eighteenth century were slaves.

All sailors suffered confinement, poor diet, and harsh punishments including whipping, but black sailors were likely to find a greater measure of geographical and social freedom at sea than on shore. By the early nineteenth century, African Americans constituted about twenty percent of American sailors, with much higher proportions working in river and coastal shipping. Black sailors faced racism in job assignments and in general treatment, but facing the isolation and dangers of the sea together fostered a camaraderie that carried over into interracial associations in integrated boarding houses, bars, and other shoreside facilities and activities.[4]

Although labor provided the most continuous interracial contacts in colonial America, there were many other occasions when people joined across racial lines. Local festivals and celebrations often had an interracial character. The Dutch-initiated spring holiday of Pinkster in New York and New Jersey was identified as an African-American celebration by the late eighteenth century, but people of all races and ethnicities participated. Music and dance of African origin dominated festivities that included performers, animals, Native-American craft vendors, and booths selling food and drink. At Pinkster celebrations in Albany, New York, in the early nineteenth century, "King Charles," an elderly colorfully-costumed Angolan, presided over the multitudes. Astride his horse, Charles led the procession and collected a monetary tribute from each booth. Africans and African Americans, Native Americans, European indentured servants, and other whites also congregated for such festive occasions in colonial America as general election days and local militia muster days. In 1760, one poet described election day participants:

> Of black and white, and every sort
>   of high, low, rich and poor;
>   Squaws, negroes, deputies in scores . . .
>   A motley crew
>   Of Whites & Blacks & Indians too.[5]

Not all broadly inclusive gatherings were raucous occasions. As religious enthusiasm caught fire after 1730 in the Great Awakening, thousands of ordinary people were swept up in the call for spiritual rebirth. South and North, urban and rural, bound and free, black, white, and Indian, men and women participated as worshippers and as preachers. In emotional services of song and exhortation, they espoused an evangelical gospel of personal liberty with intonations of equality that many of the elite believed threatened public order. African Americans' religious sensibilities and musical styles brought a thrilling fervor to these multiracial gatherings. In the North, ministers like Rhode Island's Samuel Hopkins, inspired by the groundswell of religious sentiment, used the revival's broad participation as an object lesson. Revivalists made the social and political message explicit by creating a religiously based antislavery doctrine.[6]

Other racially integrated activities were for less laudatory purposes. In New York City, poor whites and free blacks ran informal unregulated drinking establishments in their homes, much to the consternation of officials who believed them "destructive to the morals of servants and slaves." In fact, saloons in the mid-eighteenth century were often sites for prostitution, the exchange or sale of stolen goods, and gambling. Two of the most notorious saloons in colonial New York were run by white business partners, John Romme and John Hughson, who handled stolen goods. Romme and Hughson had ties to black gangs and plans to develop interracial gangs, hoping eventually to organize and control vice throughout the city.[7]

Hughson's establishment was a popular gathering place for Sunday dinner, and many slaves came there after church for goose, mutton, and fresh-baked bread, as well as for the music and dancing. However, neither this more respectable cover nor the secret oaths and rituals of their criminal underground protected Hughson, Romme, or their conspirators from discovery and arrest. In 1741, authorities suspected that a series of fires was connected to a rebellion by the blacks and whites who met at Hughson's saloon. After a swift trial, the punishment meted out was severe: thirteen blacks were burned at the stake, sixteen were hanged, and over seventy were banished from Britain's colonies; four whites, including Hughson, were hanged, and seven were banished.[8]

Harsh punishment may have been influenced by memories of a slave/servant revolt about a generation earlier during which conspirators had also burned several buildings. In 1712, blacks, whites, and Indians seeking revenge against their masters had ambushed fire fighters. They wounded six people and killed nine before local citizens routed them. Six of the leaders committed suicide, but the militia eventually apprehended the escaped rebels. Authorities arrested seventy blacks in a general sweep of the region and put nineteen to death. The torture and execution of blacks and Native Americans included death by breaking on the wheel, starvation, burning at the stake, and hanging.[9]

Throughout the colonial period, there were interracial actions with even more directly political purposes. Many were led by sailors protesting British impressment. There were impressment riots in Boston in 1745 and 1747 and in New York, Newport, Rhode Island, Casco Bay, Maine, and Norfolk, Virginia, in the 1760s. Several thousand people attacked the governor's house in Boston after troops attempted to quell one such mob action there in the 1740s. In 1765, five hundred men and boys rioted after five weeks of impressments in Newport. One investigation made clear that participants represented a dangerous combination, accusing them of being a "riotous, tumultuous assembly of foreign seamen, servants, Negroes and other persons of mean and vile condition."[10]

In the colonies, political participation by nonelite unpropertied colonists was in the informal public sphere of outdoor politics. Mob actions were quasi-legitimate expressions of public discontent that exerted pressure on the government; when they escalated to full-scale riots, they were put down by military force. Thus, for example, during the late 1730s in Boston, inflation and high unemployment sparked riots by "young People, Servants and Negroes," riots that eventually forced changes in the way goods were marketed. Similarly, economic depression following the French and Indian War in 1763 brought mobs of laborers and sailors to the streets to protest such British regulations as the Stamp Act. Even more established workers and a few prosperous people joined to express these complaints against the crown. Revolutionary leaders recognized the power and usefulness of the interracial mobs. A tavern in New York City run by a West Indian mulatto called Black Sam Fraunces served as headquarters for violent opposition to the Stamp Act. By 1770, another Boston interracial mob action expressing revolutionary discontent became enshrined as the "Boston Massacre." John Adams, expressing no surprise, identified Crispus Attucks, a sailor and fugitive from slavery in Massachusetts, as the leader. Attucks, one of the three Americans killed, became celebrated as the first martyr in the struggle for independence.[11]

As revolutionary actions moved from urban disorder to armed confrontation, blacks and whites continued to stand together. Among the minutemen who faced the British in Lexington in April 1775 was Peter Salem, freed from slavery to serve in the militia. A number of other African Americans in that battle included those whose names, Pompy, Prince, and Cato, indicated their former enslavement. Other blacks were among those who engaged the British at the Battle of Bunker Hill, and one, Salem Poor, was recognized for his heroism. Southerners, however, objected to the inclusion of African-American soldiers in the Continental army, believing their participation expressed a dangerous equality. Equally ominous, no doubt, was the prospect of an organized interracial military force in areas with large numbers of slaves. Efforts to discharge blacks already serving failed, but initially, southern protestations managed to prevent enlisting any others.[12]

Lord Dunmore, royal governor of Virginia, understood southerners' views and believed that a defeat by black troops would humiliate them, and so he began recruiting blacks in 1775. His promise of freedom to slaves and servants willing to fight with the British Ethiopian Regiment was highly successful. It also encouraged many women and children to seek refuge with British forces, depriving the South of thousands of laborers. Historians have estimated that as many as 100,000 left southern plantations for British protection, but most did not obtain their freedom. Over 1,000 blacks served the British army, and the approximately 800 African Americans who fought in Dunmore's regiment earned their freedom.[13]

Difficulties recruiting troops, short-term militia enlistments for white soldiers, the length of the war, and Dunmore's embarrassing strategy combined to force the Continental Congress to reconsider African-American recruitment. In 1776, New York slaveowners began to place slaves in the state militia to serve in their stead. Attempting to fill quotas, other states soon followed. Jack Anthony, a slave in Connecticut, enlisted in 1777 and earned his freedom by serving for the duration of the war in the place of his owner Nathan Dibble and his son Eli. London Hazard, a slave from Rhode Island, served for his owner and several of his owner's relatives. Rhode Island's William Wanton earned his freedom by serving from 1777 until the end of the war, replacing a number of white townsmen.[14]

Except for South Carolina and Georgia, even southern states enlisted African Americans. Throughout the Continental army, however, blacks were more likely to be placed as laborers, servants, cooks, wagon drivers, or drummers. Like southerners, many northern officers were disturbed by black soldiers and white soldiers serving together in apparent equality. Yet, there were many accounts of black soldiers and sailors serving with bravery and distinction. They served mainly in integrated units but also in three black regiments commanded by white officers. More than 5,000 African Americans fought with the Continental army and navy during the Revolution. Some gained freedom by agreements with masters, some in return for extended service, and some as an initial condition of their service. Ironically, a few black veterans returned to slavery after helping win America's freedom.[15]

African Americans believed that service in the Revolution had earned them the right to freedom in the new nation. They also felt entitled to equal citizenship under the principles of liberty and natural rights that formed the nation's philosophical foundation. Blacks, they argued, had been invaluable to America's development, were part of its cultural and religious life, and had worked side-by-side with whites. Though profoundly handicapped by enslavement, many had achieved freedom and had proven themselves to be productive workers. Most remained in a subordinate status, but their ranks included a few of remarkable achievement: successful entrepreneurs, preachers of great spiritual gifts, musicians of recognized ability, a published poet, a noted mathematician and astronomer. As they had agitated for political change before the war, they began to petition the new government for slavery's abolition and for full citizenship rights.

African Americans had few illusions about their prospects. Despite revolutionary rhetoric, they knew that opinion among America's leaders was divided. In 1765, Bostonian James Otis had argued that all colonists, "black and white, born here, are free born British Subjects, and entitled to all the essential civil rights of such." Thomas Jefferson, on the other hand, expressed doubts about blacks' capabilities, feared their vengeance, and believed, if freed, they could not be settled in America. Blacks remembered years of slave petitions that had met with no response. In 1773, Peter Bestes, Sambo Freeman, Felix Holbrook, and Chester Joie, representing Massachusetts slaves, modestly proposed that they be allowed one day a week to work to earn money to purchase their own freedom. They had noted that even the Spanish, who lacked the Americans' lofty principles, allowed their slaves this privilege. These petitioners even accepted the idea of special regulations applying only to freed slaves until they were able to leave the country, but they received no satisfaction. In 1774, another group of petitioners had called upon the principles of the Revolution in a "free and christian country," declared their religious convictions, and appealed to the authorities' reverence for marriage and family. Prince Whipple, who had fought alongside General George Washington in 1776, joined eighteen others in Portsmouth, New Hampshire, in 1779 to petition for freedom "for the sake of justice, humanity, and the rights of mankind." They eloquently declared that "the God of nature gave them life and freedom, upon the terms of the most perfect equality with other men; That freedom is an inherent right of the human species, not to be surrendered but by consent."[16]

There was some reason for optimism. Not only was the rhetoric of the patriots replete with condemnations of slavery and assertions of natural God-given rights, but wartime actions in northern states seemed to promise slavery's demise. Vermont's 1777 constitution stated the conviction that "all men [were] born equally free and independent," outlawed slavery, and prohibited servitude past the age of twenty-one for males and eighteen for females. Legislatures in Massachusetts in 1777, New Jersey in 1778, and Rhode Island in 1779 discussed abolition. According to early constitutions in northern states, black men who met the property requirements could vote on an equal basis with white men. The ranks of free blacks grew as people gained freedom legally in exchange for military service, effectively as a result of war's dislocations, or privately as masters fighting for liberty heeded their consciences. Quok Walker sued for his freedom, and in 1783 the chief justice of the Massachusetts supreme court declared that slavery was not consistent with the state's constitution. The bill of rights in Massachusetts's 1780 constitution surpassed the Declaration of Independence by declaring that "all men are born free and equal," and assured them "the right of enjoying and defending their lives and liberty." Discussions at the Constitutional Congress indicated that sentiment against slavery even extended to such southern plantation states as Virginia.[17]

African Americans' hopes and fears both were vindicated as it became clear that there would be no clear-cut national victory over slavery. Compromise left the institution's future to state actions while protecting slaveholders' rights to human property. The Congress debated banning slave importations, but they ended by protecting the trade for another twenty years. Yet, northern white artisans, strongly influenced by black craftsmen, generally supported abolition.[18]

Responding to black actions, petitions, and efforts by white abolitionists, freedom marched unsteadily across the North. Although Vermont's constitution had explicitly abolished slavery, and the courts had declared slavery unconstitutional in Massachusetts, there remained uncertainty. As historian Joanne Pope Melish has noted, the status and condition of freed slaves in Massachusetts likely depended on the self-assertion of the former slave and the goodwill of the master for some time after the courts' declaration. By the first census in 1790, however, Massachusetts reported no slaves. In New Hampshire, there was some disagreement about whether or not the state's Declaration of Rights of 1788 outlawed slavery. The number of people recorded as slaves there quickly dwindled from about 150 in 1790 to 8 in 1800.[19]

In other states with larger numbers of slaves, abolition represented a potentially greater economic dislocation, slaveholders wielded greater political power, and freedom was even more ambiguous.

Table 3.1 Slave Populations in the North

	1775	1790	1800	1810
New York	15,000	21,193	20,903	15017
Pennsylvania	1,000	3,707	1,706	795
Delaware	9,000	8,887	6,153	4,177
New Jersey	7,600	11,423	12,422	10,851
Connecticut	5,000	2,648	951	310
Rhode Island	4,373	958	380	108
Massachusetts	3,500	0	0	0
New Hampshire	629	157	8	0
Vermont	NA	0	0	0
Total	55,102	48,973	42,523	31,258

Source: Horton and Horton, *In Hope of Liberty*, 81; *Negro Population in the United States*, 57.

Strong postwar abolitionist sentiment in the 1780s and 1790s forced consideration of the question. Where slaveholders were strongest, debate centered on the issues of compensation for the loss of slave property, the problems of postemancipation dependence, particularly for elderly ex-slaves, potential economic disruption, and threats to the social order. Legislatures refused direct compensation, but Pennsylvania in 1780, Connecticut and Rhode Island in 1784, New York in 1799, and New Jersey in 1804 all developed gradual emancipation plans. These plans minimized disruption to the labor system and did provide a kind of compensation to slaveholders. The laws assured slaveholders the lifetime labor of slaves in their possession. They also guaranteed slaveowners the uncompensated labor of children born to those slaves from the time of the law's effect until their adulthood or beyond. The children's indentures, actually a kind of limited-term slavery, lasted until the age of majority in Rhode Island, age twenty-five in Connecticut, age twenty-eight in Pennsylvania, and age twenty-five for females and twenty-eight for males in New York and New Jersey.[20]

Slaveholders argued that they needed this unpaid labor to allow them to recoup the cost of caring for children born to their slaves. Maintaining slavery for the older slaves, others asserted, would save towns from supporting a large indigent freed slave population. Thus, economic safeguards for slaveowners and their communities allowed northern states to become "free states" while preserving slavery and black unfree labor far into the future. For example, barring any other action (or the Civil War), people born into slavery just before the emancipation laws could have reached age seventy, still in slavery, between 1849 and 1874. Assuming that enslaved women were capable of childbearing up to age fifty, these laws would have assured slaveowners unpaid laborers until 1845 in Rhode Island, 1857 in New York, 1858 in Pennsylvania, 1859 in Connecticut, and 1883 in New Jersey. As historians Gary Nash and Jean Sonderlund observed, such indentures made freedom more like a "limited form of slavery."[21]

As many as one-half to two-thirds of European immigrants to colonial America had come as indentured servants for limited terms, making many white workers part of the unfree colonial labor force. By the period of the Revolution, however, indentured servitude for whites was rare; shortly thereafter long-term African-American indentures were introduced. Thus, in the North during the early republic, free white labor competed with free black labor, slave labor, and black indentured labor. In New York State, for example, in 1800 African Americans constituted less than six percent of the population; but they were concentrated in semiskilled and unskilled jobs, and two-thirds of the black workers competing mainly with lower-level white workers were slaves. By 1820, only 10,088 slaves were listed in the state's population, but many of the nearly 30,000 "free blacks" would have been unfree laborers old enough to compete with wage workers. (By then, they would have been as old as 21 years, the age at which an 1814 law freed both males and females from indentures.) In Pennsylvania, the number of slaves dwindled fairly rapidly, from about 10,000 before emancipation to 3,700 in 1790, 1,700 in 1800, fewer than 800 in 1810, and just over 200 by 1820. Yet, the more than 30,000 free blacks in 1820 would also have included many unpaid servants competing with free wage labor.[22]

Such competition with unpaid labor undoubtedly depressed all workers' wages, and there is some indication that the prospects for advancement for white workers were also adversely affected, at least initially. Although most black indentured workers were engaged in domestic work and manual labor, the proportion of African Americans in urban crafts was highest during and immediately after the Revolution. Historian Shane White traced the reliance of certain occupational groups in New York City on black live-in labor. Although it is impossible to distinguish between indentured servants and others in the "free black" census category, White's figures give some indication of the continued reliance of artisan households in particular on unfree labor. Some would have been domestic servants, but white laborers with ambitions as artisans were likely to have perceived slaves or black indentured servants in artisan households as unfair competition. Thus, it is not surprising that early trade organizations barred blacks from participation, or that the Philadelphia Abolition Society reported that one-third of the black male "mechanics and tradesmen" in that city were not able to work at their trades by 1838.[23]

Table 3.2   Slaves and Free Blacks in White Households in New York City, by Occupation of Male Head of Household

	Merchants			Artisans			Retailers		
	Slave	Free	Total	Slave	Free	Total	Slave	Free	Total
1790	449	82	531	426	61	487	295	25	320
1800	724	398	1122	339	128	467	202	59	261
1810	301	438	739	215	307	522	125	151	276

Source: Shane White, *Somewhat More Independent,* 7, 33, 39.

Although it is clear that New Yorkers' reliance on slave labor declined during these years, the extent to which they turned to free blacks as opposed to freed but indentured black workers is not. By 1817, New York State passed a law outlawing slavery altogether as of 1827. This meant, of course, that even the youngest of the 10,000 slaves freed by this measure had already reached age 28. Immediate, rather than gradual, emancipation also marked the end of forced indentures in the state. White also found a trend in New York City that was a portent for the future of black labor. In the gradual shift from slavery to freedom with metropolitan industrialization, employers and owners eventually relied on black workers less for skilled labor and more for unskilled labor and domestic work.[24]

Important social and political changes also signaled a shift in the consequences of racial identity. Gordon Wood observed that social deference gave
way to greater social equality during the revolutionary era. For African Americans, however, the transformation was somewhat different. The social deference that was the organizing principle of colonial society, and that often had
operated to bring together blacks and whites at the bottom, gave way to stratification based more clearly on race as well as class. For northern blacks, the
Revolution was a progressive force establishing their right to freedom, but the
nature of that freedom and the issue of black social and political equality remained to be determined.[25]

Interracial mobs had advanced independence in colonial America, but
when mobs continued their traditional political participation after the Revolution, the new authorities often saw them as a threat to order. Mobs continued to express popular opinion into the 1780s and 1790s, targeting, for example, grave-robbing doctors and medical students, houses of prostitution,
financial speculators, and people kidnapping or failing to pay sailors. Authorities tolerated many such mob actions, but particularly violent distur-
bances or ones that directly challenged the government were likely to be put
down with force. Authorities raised troops, for example, to quell the rebellion
by Daniel Shays and his followers that threatened to shut down local courts
in western Massachusetts in 1786. Interestingly, Bostonian and revolutionary
war veteran Prince Hall offered the services of 700 black men to put down the
angry mob of Massachusetts farmers, but the government declined their aid.

There were, however, some mobs that were different in both nature and
function from the colonial mobs. As urban black communities grew, African
Americans, their churches, and schools became targets for harassment and attack by white mobs. In the 1790s, Prince Hall decried attacks by ruffians and
mobs of "shameless, low-lived envious spiteful persons" on black people who
ventured onto the Boston Common. In 1807 in New York City, African Americans complained to city officials that young pranksters and white mobs repeatedly disrupted church services. Attacks on black street vendors and black
churches were common in Philadelphia. In the early 1800s, a mob of about
sixty young white butchers, ropemakers, carpenters, plasterers, and bakers disrupted a black church service in Philadelphia, physically attacking members of
the congregation and forcing them to escape through the windows.[26]

White mob attacks on urban black community institutions were part of a
new pattern of rioting apparent after 1812, described by historian Paul Gilje.
These riots pitted members of the community against each other on the basis
of differences in race, ethnicity, or religion, rather than uniting the community around common concerns as had colonial mobs. Attacks on black communities became even more common and larger in scale in the 1820s and

1830s. Joanne Pope Melish and James Stewart have placed this violence in context, greatly enhancing our understanding of its causes and consequences and drawing out its implications for racial identity and abolitionist strategies. Such riots occurred in Philadelphia and Cincinnati in 1829. The riot in Cincinnati reportedly drove hundreds of black people out of the city, many to Canada. There were at least nine race riots in Philadelphia between 1834 and 1838. In 1834, "several hundred young white men" invaded the black community, killed two African Americans, and destroyed two churches and twenty homes. An official report laid the riot to whites' fears that blacks were receiving favored treatment in hiring. Rioters often expressed antiabolitionist sentiments, but complaints that blacks were taking jobs away from whites were commonly voiced motivations for increasingly violent attacks on African Americans. Ironically, restrictions on black voting actually made it less likely that African Americans would get political patronage jobs.[27]

Urban authorities had been concerned, as historian David Roediger noted, that early interracial celebrations brought together lower-class blacks and whites for dissipation and "lewd and lascivious behavior." Yet by the nineteenth century, they promised a different kind of disorder. On July 4, 1804, some young black men in Philadelphia formed an "ad hoc military group," cursed and pushed whites, and threatened rebellion. The following year, white mobs drove blacks from the Independence Day celebrations. In 1811, the Albany Common Council forestalled disorder and interracial socializing by banning Pinkster celebrations. By the late 1820s, blacks had been barred from militia days in New York, Philadelphia, and New England and from Independence Day celebrations and Christmas processions in Philadelphia. In the early 1830s, Massachusetts and Connecticut moved their election days to the winter to discourage ancillary interracial festivities. This ban made racial rapprochement less likely in the era of increasing conflicts. Blacks were still represented, however, by the young working-class white men who performed in blackface at such occasions, playing on racial stereotypes and widening the gulf between themselves and the black working class.[28]

At the same time that African Americans faced exclusion from formerly interracial cultural activities, their prospects for political participation also diminished. In the late eighteenth century, urban workers began to transform their fraternal organizations into political action groups. As they expressed political opinions in this sometimes more decorous manner, legislatures lowered property requirements for voting and office holding, and the number of voters increased in Massachusetts, New Hampshire, New York, and New Jersey. Hoping to discourage the excesses of the political mob, American leaders drew more of the working class into elections. By the mid-1820s, the abolition of property requirements had extended the right to vote to virtually all adult males. The advance of democracy, however, often was racially restricted. As northern slavery ended, the freedom that replaced it ushered many blacks into a newly instituted second-class black citizenship. African Americans lost the vote in 1807 in New Jersey, in 1814 in Connecticut, in 1822 in Rhode Island, and in 1842 in Pennsylvania. In 1821, New York removed property qualifications for white males but maintained residence and property requirements for black men. The debates in New York were passionate, and the votes were close. Advocates of restricting the suffrage to whites won by a vote of 63 to 59 in the constitutional convention. Each time this issue was revisited in the 1840s and 1860s, the vote in New York City, where Tammany Hall held sway and where African Americans were concentrated, was overwhelmingly against equal suffrage. In 1837, the editor of *The Colored American*, observed in protest:

> Foreigners and aliens to the government and laws—strangers to our institutions are permitted to flock to this land, and in a few years are endowed with all the privileges of citizens; but we, native born Americans, the children of the soil, are most of us shut out.[29]

Historian Eric Foner has observed that in the early nineteenth century, freedom and citizenship were considered incompatible with dependence. Politicians argued that African Americans, indentured, enslaved, or identified with slavery, were incapable of independence and therefore not entitled to full citizenship. In this regard, they were classed with women and children whose dependence disqualified them from citizenship and who were represented by husbands and fathers. Though women did vote in New Jersey after the Revolution, they lost this right along with black men in 1807. A 1790 law limited naturalized citizenship to whites, but federal law did not stipulate voter qualifications, and so each state made its own determination.[30]

Scholars of race and class have discussed the rise of minstrel performances that satirized and demeaned African Americans during the 1820s—the same period during which blacks were being excluded from many of the cultural activities of industrializing urban America and from the more democratic politics. Broadsides ridiculed black organizations and activities as inept imitations of white society. Such indications of growing racism and attempts to circumscribe the place of African Americans are striking examples of a shifting ideology that was already visible early in the postrevolutionary period. Thomas Jefferson wrote his influential *Notes on Virginia* in 1782 and first published it privately in France in 1785. In this work, he reached the conclusion that blacks were naturally inferior to white people. David Walker was so enraged that he devoted most of article one of his *Appeal*, published a few years after Jefferson's death, to a discussion of Jefferson's contentions.

Walker exhorted his readers to "remember that we are men as well as [whites]. . . . We have just as much right, in the sight of God, to hold them and their children in slavery and wretchedness, as they have to hold us, and no more." In Jefferson's argument for blacks' natural inferiority we can see the beginning of "racial modernity," that racist ideology based on assumptions of biological inferiority, that James Stewart has argued was common by the late 1830s and to which abolitionists would have to respond. As it developed, the assumption of black dependence becomes part of this supposedly natural inferiority, as Joanne Melish has so expertly shown in her analysis of the "effacement" of the memory of slavery in New England.[31]

Of course, some interracial associations at the bottom of the society remained. Blacks and whites joined together in crime, vice, and disreputable entertainments. Social relationships were common between racial groups limited by poverty to residences in less-desirable neighborhoods, and political alliances remained among sailors. By the 1830s, a different kind of relationship joined people across both racial and class lines in political and social action, as radical white middle-class and upper-class abolitionists joined with middle-class and lower-class blacks in the antislavery movement. As free blacks in the North lost ground occupationally and politically, however, the working classes that had previously formed effective political and social alliances were more likely to be divided by race.

In colonial America and in the early republic, working-class alliances had offered African Americans opportunities for political expression, and free blacks had some promise of occupational advancement. During the nineteenth century, social, political, and economic changes made race an even more important divider and a major determinant of political and economic prospects. Southerners under increasing attack from northern abolitionists developed justifications for slavery that contended blacks were innately inferior and naturally dependent. Many northerners subscribed to these theories and feared that disorder and dependency would accompany emancipation. In some states, these fears, slaveowners' economic interests, and Jacksonian political strategies shaped a gradual and limited black freedom that increased economic competition between unfree black workers and white workers, depressing wages, and exacerbating racial antagonisms.[32]

In a perceptive and sophisticated recent study, cultural historian Kenan Malik traces changes in the meaning of race. He argues that its modern meaning developed from the contradiction between an ideology of equality and the persistence of inequalities. Malik links the contradiction to the inherent conflicts between enlightenment ideals and the imperatives of capitalism that inevitably preserved and created inequality. Under the ideology of equality in a democratic and theoretically classless society, structured inequalities, according to Malik's argument, are typically explained by positing innate differences between groups. Such contradictions between theory and reality clearly existed after the Revolution. Northern states moved closer to the ideal with emancipation and universal white male suffrage. But the economic consequences of slavery, and, in some states, limited black citizenship and a system of unpaid black labor somewhere between slavery and freedom, made it more likely that inequalities would be explained by racial differences believed to be part of a "natural order."[33]

Thus African Americans in the North endured a period of racial reconstruction that confined them to a lesser citizenship, limited and sometimes diminished their economic opportunities, and confronted them with theories contending their innate inferiority. They managed to make new alliances, but in interracial activities that crossed class lines they often endured the indignity of paternalistic treatment and were segregated even in some antislavery meetings. Northern free blacks knew that the enslavement of southern blacks affected their status, but they also knew that the dependent state of the northern African Americans still in slavery and long-term indentures bolstered arguments for excluding them from full citizenship. For them, the fight against slavery, actions to eliminate discrimination and racial distinctions, political organization, efforts for education and occupational training, and moral reform and racial uplift to combat racist ideologies were intertwined.

NOTES

1. See, for example, James Oliver Horton and Lois E. Horton, *In Hope of Liberty: Culture, Community and Protest Among Northern Free Blacks, 1700–1860* (New York, 1997); David Roediger, *The Wages of Whiteness: Race and the Making of the American Working Class* (New York, 1991); Noel Ignatiev, *How the Irish Became White* (New York, 1995); Joanne Pope Melish, *Disowning Slavery: Gradual Emancipation and "Race" in New England, 1780–1860* (Ithaca, 1998); Harry Reed, *Platform for Change: The Foundations of the Northern Free Black Community, 1775–1865* (East Lansing, MI, 1994); Sterling Stuckey, *Going Through the Storm: The Influence of African American Art in History* (New York, 1994); and Rita Jean Roberts, "In Quest of Autonomy: Northern Black Activism Between the Revolution and Civil War" (Ph.D. diss., University of California, Berkeley, 1988).

2. Winthrop D. Jordan, *White Over Black: American Attitudes Toward the Negro, 1550–1812* (Chapel Hill, 1968); Nathaniel B. Shurtleff, ed., *Records of the Governor and Company of Massachusetts Bay* (5 vols., Boston, 1854), III, 397; *Acts and Resolves, Public and Private, of the Province of Massachusetts Bay* (Boston, 1869), I, 606–07, 578–79; Horton and Horton, *In Hope of Liberty*, 39; P. Bradley Nutting, "Racial Boundary Formation in Colonial Massachusetts, 1638–1707: The Origins of Statutory Discrimination," unpublished paper in possession of author; A. Leon Higginbotham Jr., *In the Matter of Color: Race & the American Legal Process: The Colonial Period* (New York, 1978), 286.

3. Edmund S. Morgan, *American Slavery and American Freedom: The Ordeal of Colonial Virginia* (New York, 1975), 327; Gary Nash, *The Urban Crucible: Social Change, Political Consciousness and the Origins of the American Revolution* (Cambridge, MA, 1979), 7; Bernard Bailyn and Barbara DeWolfe, *Voyagers to the West: A Passage in the Peopling of America on the Eve of the Revolution* (New York, 1986), 346; Edgar J. McManus, *Black Bondage in the North* (Syracuse, NY, 1973); Horton and Horton, *In Hope of Liberty*.

4. W. Jeffrey Bolster, *Black Jacks: African American Seamen in the Age of Sail* (Cambridge, MA, 1997), 6; Whittington B. Johnson, "Negro Laboring Classes in Early America, 1750–1820" (Ph.D. diss., University of Georgia, 1970).

5. Samuel E. Morison, "A Poem on Election Day in Massachusetts about 1760," *Proceedings of the Colonial Society of Massachusetts*, 18 (Feb. 1915), 54–61 (quotation at 60–61); Shane White, *Somewhat More Independent: The End of Slavery in New York City, 1770–1810* (Athens, GA, 1991); David Steven Cohen, "In Search of Carolus Africanus Rex: Afro-Dutch Folklore in New York and New Jersey," *Journal of the Afro-American Historical and Genealogical Society*, 5 (Fall and Winter 1984), 149–62. The relationship between Native Americans and African Americans is an important and complicating part of the issue of race in America. See, for example, Daniel R. Mandell, "Shifting Boundaries of Race and Ethnicity: Indian-Black Intermarriage in Southern New England, 1760–1880," *Journal of American History*, 85 (Sept. 1998), 466–501. For European perspectives, see Jon Gjerde, "'Here in America there is neither king nor tyrant': European Encounters with Race, 'Freedom,' and Their European Pasts," and James P. Ronda, "'We Have a Country': Race, Geography, and the Invention of Indian Territory," in this collection.

6. Albert J. Raboteau, *Slave Religion: The Invisible Institution in the Antebellum South* (New York, 1978); Alan Gallay, "Planters and Slaves in the Great Awakening," in John B. Boles, ed., *Masters & Slaves in the House of the Lord: Race and Religion in the American South, 1740–1870* (Lexington, 1988), 19–36; David S. Lovejoy, "Samuel Hopkins: Religion, Slavery, and the Revolution," *The New England Quarterly*, 40 (June 1967), 227–43.

7. Edgar J. McManus, *A History of Negro Slavery in New York* (Syracuse, 1966), 87; Daniel Horsmanden, *The New York Conspiracy*, ed. Thomas J. Davis (Boston, 1971).

8. Thomas J. Davis, *Rumor of Revolt: The Great Negro Conspiracy in Colonial New York* (New York, 1985).

9. Davis, ed., *New York Conspiracy*, xii; McManus, *Slavery in New York*, 128–29; Kenneth Scott, "The Slave Insurrection in New York in 1712," *New York Historical Society Quarterly*, 45 (Jan. 1961), 43–74. Historian Timothy Lockley found similar concerns about illegal interracial activities reflected in laws and criminal prosecutions in low country Georgia during the era of the Revolution and early republic. From these records, he concluded that an extensive trade existed between slaves and white shopkeepers. Timothy J. Lockley, "Partners in Crime: African Americans and Non-slaveholding Whites in Antebellum Georgia," in Matt Wray and Annalee Newitz, eds., *White Trash: Race and Class in America* (New York, 1997), 57–72.

10. Howard Zinn, *A People's History of the United States* (1980; rev. ed., New York, 1995), 51; Jesse Lemisch, "Jack Tar in the Streets: Merchant Seamen in the Politics of Revolutionary America," *William and Mary Quarterly*, 25 (July 1968), 371–407.

11. Benjamin Colman to Mr. Samuel Holden, May 8, 1737, quoted in Horton and Horton, *In Hope of Liberty*, 46, 53; Paul A. Gilje, *The Road to Mobocracy: Popular Disorder in New York City, 1763–1834* (Chapel Hill, 1987).

12. Horton and Horton, *In Hope of Liberty*, 59.

13. *Ibid.*, 60, 62, 71.

14. *Ibid.*, 64–65.

15. *Ibid.*, 65, 71.

16. James Otis, *The Rights of British Colonies Asserted and Proved* (Boston, 1764), 37; Sidney Kaplan, *The Black Presence in the Era of the American Revolution, 1770–1800* (Greenwich, CT, 1973), 13, 27.

17. Horton and Horton, *In Hope of Liberty*, 71; McManus, *Black Bondage*, 164.

18. Particularly high numbers of African Americans worked in urban crafts in the early years of the Republic, about fourteen percent of black males in Philadelphia and thirty-eight percent of free black male household heads in New York, for example. Roediger, *The Wages of Whiteness*, 25; Horton and Horton, *In Hope of Liberty,* 71.

19. Gary B. Nash, *Race and Revolution* (Madison, WI, 1990); Melish, *Disowning Slavery*; Horton and Horton, *In Hope of Liberty*, 72.

20. Arthur Zilversmit, *The First Emancipation: The Abolition of Slavery in the North* (Chicago, 1967); Ira Berlin, *Many Thousands Gone: The First Two Generations of Slavery in North America* (Cambridge, MA, 1998). These statutes were based on the same fear of free-black dependency as the harsh colonial Pennsylvania laws of 1726 that required the children of all free blacks to be indentured until age twenty-one for females and age twenty-four for males. Higginbotham, *Matter of Color*, 285.

21. Higginbotham, *Matter of Color*; Gary B. Nash and Jean R. Soderlund, *Freedom By Degrees: Emancipation in Pennsylvania & Its Aftermath* (New York, 1991), 176. It is difficult to know what to call the labor arrangement of northern gradual emancipation. Since there were no individual contracts (governed instead by state laws), they were not entered into voluntarily, and the period of unfree labor was much longer than was customary for European indentures, it could be considered a kind of state-sponsored slavery. Labor conditions were similar to slavery, but the crucial differences of applying only to one generation and having a time limit seem to make it qualitatively different from slavery. Similar gradual emancipation arrangements later in the British West Indies, though of much shorter duration, were also without individual contracts and are referred to as apprenticeships or indentures (followed by imported contract laborers). For lack of a better term and to emphasize their standing between slavery and freedom, I have opted to call them indentures. For Caribbean black indentures, see Arthur L. Stinchcombe, *Sugar Island Slavery in the Age of Enlightenment: The Political Economy of the Caribbean World* (Princeton, 1995), 269–74; David Brion Davis, *Slavery and Human Progress* (New York, 1984), 122–24; and Claude Levy, *Emancipation, Sugar, and Federalism: Barbados and the West Indies, 1833–1876* (Gainesville, FL, 1980).

22. Russell R. Menard, "Indentured Servitude," in Eric Foner and John A. Garraty, eds., *The Reader's Companion to American History* (Boston, 1991), 542–43; *Negro Population in the United States, 1790–1915* (New York, 1968), 57; Zilversmit, *First Emancipation*, 212.

23. Roediger, *Wages of Whiteness*; White, *Somewhat More Independent*; Ignatiev, *Irish Became White*, 100.

24. Zilversmit, *First Emancipation*, 213; White, *Somewhat More Independent,* 54. Since the law was retroactive, the last blacks to serve such indentures probably finished their service in 1838.

25. Gordon S. Wood, *The Radicalism of the American Revolution* (New York, 1992).

26. Horton and Horton, *In Hope of Liberty*, 163; William Otter, Sen., *History of My Own Time,* in Richard B. Stott, ed., *History of My Own Time/William Otter* (Ithaca,

1995), 114–17; Emma Jones Lapsansky, "Since They Got Those Separate Churches: Afro-Americans and Racism in Jacksonian Philadelphia," *American Quarterly*, 32 (Spring 1980), 54–79.

27. Ignatiev, *Irish Became White*, 125; Paul Gilje, *Rioting in America* (Bloomington, IN, 1996), 60–90; Joanne Pope Melish, "The 'Condition' Debate and Racial Discourse in the Antebellum North," and James Brewer Stewart, "The Political Meanings of Color in the Free States, 1776–1840," both in this book; Horton and Horton, *In Hope of Liberty*; Roediger, *Wages of Whiteness*.

28. Roediger, *Wages of Whiteness*, 103; David Waldstreicher, *In the Midst of Perpetual Fetes: The Making of American Nationalism, 1776–1820* (Chapel Hill, 1997), 328; Gary B. Nash, *Forging Freedom: The Formation of Philadelphia's Black Community, 1720–1840* (Cambridge, MA, 1988); Susan G. Davis, *Parades and Power: Street Theater in Nineteenth-Century Philadelphia* (Philadelphia, 1986); Paul A. Gilje and Howard B. Rock, "'Sweep O! Sweep O!': African-American Chimney Sweeps and Citizenship in the New Nation," *William and Mary Quarterly*, 51 (July 1994), 507–38.

29. *The Colored American*, Mar. 4, 1837; Wood, *American Revolution;* Horton and Horton, *In Hope of Liberty*, 167–69; David N. Gellman, "'Sins of the Fathers': Unraveling Freedom and Slavery in New York's Constitution of 1821," paper presented at the annual meeting of the Society for Historians of the Early American Republic, Lexington, KY, July 17, 1999; David Quigley, "The Jim Crow North: New York City and the Legacies of 1821," paper presented at the annual meeting of the Society for Historians of the Early American Republic, Lexington, KY, July 17, 1999. See also David Nathaniel Gellman, "Inescapable Discourse: The Rhetoric of Slavery and the Politics of Abolition in Early National New York" (Ph.D. diss., Northwestern University, 1997). For a nuanced discussion of debates on free black rights within an entrenched slave system in the Jacksonian South, see Lacy K. Ford Jr., "Making the 'White Man's' Country White: Race, Slavery, and State-Building in the Jacksonian South," in this book. Black suffrage was also eliminated in North Carolina and Tennessee, and blacks were generally excluded from political participation in the new western states.

30. Eric Foner, "Free Labor and Political Ideology," in Melvyn Stokes and Stephen Conway, eds., *The Market Revolution in America: Social, Political, & Religious Expressions, 1800–1880* (Charlottesville, 1996), 99–127; Mary Beth Norton, *Liberty's Daughters: The Revolutionary Experience of American Women, 1750–1800* (Boston, 1980), 191–93; Leon F. Litwack, *North of Slavery: The Negro in the Free States, 1790–1860* (Chicago, 1961), 31. Also see Linda K. Kerber, *No Constitutional Right to Be a Lady: Women & the Obligations of Citizenship* (New York, 1998); and Rosemarie Zagarri, "The Rights of Man and Woman in Post-Revolutionary America," *William and Mary Quarterly*, 55 (Apr. 1998), 203–30.

31. David Walker, *David Walker's Appeal*, with an introduction by Charles M. Wiltse (1829; rep., New York, 1965), 11; Roediger, *Wages of Whiteness*; Alexander Saxton, *The Rise and Fall of the White Republic: Class Politics and Mass Culture in Nineteenth Century America* (London, UK, 1990); Eric Lott, *Love & Theft: Blackface Minstrelsy and the American Working Class* (New York, 1993); Shane White, "'It Was a Proud Day': African Americans, Festivals and Parades in the North, 1741–1834," *Journal of American History*, 81 (June 1994), 13–50; Melish, *Disowning Slavery*; James Brewer Stewart, "The Emergence of Racial Modernity and the Rise of the White North, 1790–1840," *Journal of the Early Republic*, 18 (Spring 1998), 181–217. For an insightful analysis of black leaders'

and white Garrisonians' responses to these changes, see Stewart, "The Political Meanings of Color," in this book.

32. The "effacement" of whites' memory of slavery in the North also contributed to the identification of blacks as a "naturally" dependent population. See Melish, "The 'Condition' Debate," in this book.

33. Kenan Malik, *The Meaning of Race: Race, History, and Culture in Western Society* (New York, 1996).

BIBLIOGRAPHY

Bolster, W. Jeffrey. *Black Jacks: African American Seamen in the Age of Sail.* Cambridge: Harvard University Press, 1997.

Gilje, Paul. *The Road to Mobocracy: Popular Disorder in New York City, 1763–1834.* Chapel Hill: University of North Carolina Press, 1987.

Horton, James Oliver, and Lois E. Horton. *In Hope of Liberty: Culture, Community and Protest among Northern Free Blacks, 1700–1860.* New York: Oxford University Press, 1977.

Ignatiev, Noel. *How the Irish Became White.* New York: Routledge, 1995.

Lott, Eric. *Love & Theft: Black-face Minstrelsy and the American Working Class.* New York: Oxford University Press, 1993.

Malik, Kenan. *The Meaning of Race: Race, History and Culture in Western Society.* New York: New York University Press, 1996.

Melish, Joanne Pope. *Disowning Slavery: Gradual Emancipation and "Race" in New England, 1780–1860.* Ithaca: Cornell University Press, 1998.

Nash, Gary. *The Urban Crucible: Social Change, Political Consciousness, and the Origins of the American Religion.* Cambridge: Harvard University Press, 1979.

Roediger, David. *The Wages of Whiteness: Race and the Making of the American Working Class.* New York: Verso, 1991.

Saxton, Alexander. *The Rise and Fall of the White Republic: Class, Politics and Mass Culture in Nineteenth-Century America.* New York: Verso, 1990.

White, Shane. *Somewhat More Independent: The End of Slavery in New York City, 1770–1860.* Athens: University of Georgia Press, 1991.

Zilversmit, Arthur. *The First Emancipation: The Abolition of Slavery in the North.* Chicago: University of Chicago Press, 1967.

4

The "Condition" Debate and Racial Discourse in the Antebellum North

Joanne Pope Melish

In 1859, George T. Downing, a Newport, Rhode Island, African-American caterer and community leader, told participants at the New England Colored Citizens Convention:

> All of the great principles of the land are brought out and discussed in connection with the Negro. . . . We are the alphabet; upon us, all are constructed. We, the descendants, to a great extent, of those most unjustly held in bondage . . . were the most fit subjects to be selected to work out in perfection the realization of a great principle, the fraternal unity of man. This is AMERICA'S MISSION.[1]

Downing's embrace of "America's mission" at a New England convention, clearly invoking John Winthrop's "City on a Hill," endorsed a vision of New England as the site of the original experiment in liberty and the founding mission of America as fundamentally republican and inclusive. At the very same moment, of course, whites were invoking New England's primacy in the American experiment quite similarly in their growing sectional dispute with the slaveholding South. But Downing's vision was different from theirs in one crucial respect—Downing was insisting upon the historical role of slavery and slaves in New England history as well as the central role of their descendants, free African Americans, in the providential mission of America initiated at Massachusetts Bay.[2] In interpreting America's mission as realizing the "fraternal unity of man," Downing invoked the problem of shifting conceptions of difference, especially racial difference, that had become powerful sources of competing visions of citizenship and nationhood in the years since slavery had slowly ended in New England, beginning in the 1780s. His positioning of national themes within a regional context highlights the importance of considering how the national discourse of race articulated with many regional ones.[3]

Downing's speech is notable in other ways as well. He placed African Americans at the very center not only of God's plans for America but also of the heated debates going on among (white) Americans about free labor, citizenship, eligibility for the franchise, and other "great principles of the land." And by arguing that African Americans had been selected (by God) to "work out . . . the fraternal unity of man," Downing was suggesting that they were not to be merely passive spectators, and victims, of ideological debates, but active participants in them.

By 1859, the history of local slavery had been virtually erased from the memory of most white New Englanders. However, northern racial thinking — a distinctive kind of racism that both blacks and whites commented upon regularly from the 1850s to the present day — was and is its legacy. Enslavement, gradual emancipation, and a kind of constructed amnesia about them provided the context of a discourse of race that emerged between 1780 and 1860, as the focus of attention in the northern states shifted from the problem of slavery in their midst to the "condition" of free people of color.

The word "condition" had plural meanings when used in conjunction with free blacks. It could refer to economic status, mental and moral capacity, social behavior, or "situation" with respect to some combination of these. The "condition" of free people of color was quite commonly summed up as "degraded," as often by blacks themselves as by whites, and throughout the early national and antebellum periods, people of color as well as whites struggled to identify its causes. The discourse of condition effectively became a discourse of race. The first part of this paper briefly considers how gradual emancipation shaped race in the North, focusing on New England. It then turns to the evolving discourse of race after the 1780s and the role of free people of color in shaping that discourse.[4]

Africans and also native peoples were held as slaves throughout New England beginning in the 1630s, and their emancipation was a gradual process nearly everywhere in New England, as Lois Horton describes in greater detail elsewhere in this volume. Emancipation was not gradual in the same way in every state — post-nati gradual emancipation acts providing for the eventual (not immediate) freedom of children born to slaves after 1784 were passed in Connecticut and Rhode Island, while ambiguous interpretations of new constitutions in Massachusetts and New Hampshire drew out the process there — but freedom came gradually everywhere.[5]

In a host of ways, gradual emancipation inscribed the ideology and practices of slavery itself in the free society to which it gave birth. Widespread discussion of schemes for compensated emancipation, ultimately rejected, nonetheless cemented the commodity status of existing slaves and framed the proposed category, "free persons of color," as a class collectively obligated to and dependent upon whites. Proposals to ensure the manageability of newly freed slaves reinforced expectations that, outside slavery, people of color would constitute an element of inherent disorder in need of continuing supervision and control.[6] There is abundant documentary evidence that, once emancipation laws were passed, whites continued to convey title and interest in "free" persons of color as though they continued to be legally enslaved. Children born to slaves after passage of the 1784 post-nati statutes were fraudulently represented as slightly older than they were so that their owners could receive full value for them as slaves for life. As gradual emancipation continued and the inevitability of the eventual demise of slavery became obvious, many masters sold their slaves out of state despite statutes passed to prevent the practice. Kidnapping of people of color for sale out of state became a business; so did the recovery of the kidnapped for a fee.[7] In these and other ways, the state of being free continued to draw its meaning from the state of enslavement that had preceded it. But, although slavery had provided the enslaved with a fixed role and status, however difficult and limited, in the larger community for people of color, the state of being emancipated was essentially an empty category, offering to the children of slaves and former slaves no new social role or meaning to take the place of their former role as slaves.

A half century of slow emancipation, then, enabled whites to transfer a language and a set of practices shaped in the context of slavery to their relations with a slowly emerging population of free people of color. The rhetoric of antislavery supported this transfer, reinforcing assumptions that emancipated slaves would likely be dependent and disorderly and would require moral guidance and firm management. At the same time, by structuring the problem of slavery as one of presence/absence of enslaved Africans (promoting a reduction in the numbers of slaves by ending the slave trade and, in gradualist proposals, by ending new births into slavery), antislavery rhetoric also led whites to anticipate that, after some indeterminate period of "managing" a disorderly and dependent population of ex-slaves, that population would diminish and disappear. An extraordinary range of responses of antebellum whites in New England to issues and events involving people of color can be read as attempts to fulfill this implied promise and to effect the removal of people of color—and also to efface the history of their enslavement in New England. By the eve of the Civil War, New England history had been reenvisioned as a triumphant narrative of free white labor in which free people of color were marooned as permanent, unaccountable strangers—a narrative that undergirded antebellum New England nationalism, placing New England in a position of moral authority in an escalating argument with a slaveholding South.[8]

This process transformed notions of the nature and permanence of difference—in other words, it racialized difference. Prevailing scientific theory in the late eighteenth century predicted that both physical and behavioral characteristics of humans would change—perhaps dramatically—in response to environmental conditions. Thus, environmental theory explained servile demeanor, social condition, and even physical attributes of slaves as potentially mutable environmental effects. Comte de Buffon, Samuel Stanhope Smith, and others suggested that a combination of a temperate climate and a new condition of freedom would slowly eradicate servile characteristics—lack of mental acuity (so claimed), laziness, dependency—and also distinctive African appearance.[9]

This argument gained troubling implications in the postrevolutionary climate of anxiety over the uncertain outcome of social change with respect to entitlement to citizenship. Elsewhere in this volume, Lacy K. Ford Jr. discusses what James Brewer Stewart characterizes as the "ideology of racial modernity"—the notion of the innate and permanent inequality of non-white peoples—suggesting that it emerged out of a reevaluation of how racial differences defined citizenship in this period. But the equation can also be read in reverse: the demands and desires of republican citizenship—full membership in the national family—fostered a reevaluation of the meaning and uses of various kinds of differences and similarities, rendering them "racial"—that is, redefining them as innate and permanent. The dissociation of "slave" and "negro" in the course of gradual emancipation inevitably wrenched apart the previously unchallenged association of "free" and "white" as well. Thus, "white" and "slave," "free" and "negro" emerged as free-floating terms, available as an explanatory and metaphorical language useful for investigating and describing the disruptive political, social, and perhaps biological consequences of republican self-rule as well as emancipation. People of color served as a kind of case study or reference point for such investigations, but their implications addressed the possible transformation of whites as well.

The emergence of an extensive literature of black/white role reversal around 1780 seems clearly linked to whites' interpretation of the emergence of free people of color as a disruptive factor, somehow not merely symptomatic of but actually engendering the disordering of society, with implications for the role, status, and even "nature" of white citizens. One of these literatures concerned cases of albinism and vitiligo—the so-called "strange case of the negro turning white." Literally dozens of stories of such cases were published in the popular literature first, then later in the medical literature; clearly the possibility being anxiously probed (literally) here was, could freedom make black persons white? A second such symptomatic literature was generated by the Algerine captivity—the "enslavement" of Americans and

Europeans on the coast of Africa by the so-called Barbary states of Tunis, Morocco, Tripoli, and especially Algiers. Dozens of narratives by former American captives, and fictional imitations of them, were published and reprinted in the 1790s and early 1800s. Here the question was reversed: Could enslavement in a tropical climate by "dark," "tawny," "dusky," or "swarthy" Moors and Arabs transform Americans into darkened and dependent "slaves?"[10]

In each case, these literatures, especially after 1800, finally answered their respective questions with a resounding "no." White negroes were, after all, negroes, not evidence of transformation but mere freaks; republican whiteness would finally triumph over the sun and enslavement. These accounts ultimately reassured their readers that even seemingly extreme types of transformation of human identity could be understood, controlled, and revealed to be superficial rather than essential. Most important, they served to remap the location of difference, situating it deep within the body, where descent provided the only conclusive marker of innate and essential nature, to which superficial characteristics—skin color, hair texture—might provide significant clues but could not substitute for the marker itself—race, which lay deep within the body and was carried in the blood somehow, an essence. This popular conclusion about the stability of whiteness and blackness paralleled the direction of scientific thought, which increasingly turned away from environmental explanations in the early nineteenth century to argue that race represented biological difference. In other words, we might say that science affirmed what politics demanded.[11]

Thus, even as the practices of everyday relations between whites and free people of color absorbed the character and language of practical relations between whites and slaves, popular and scientific discourses of race served to confirm and undergird those practices and that language. At the same time, the "degraded" condition of the majority of northern free people of color served to support the racial argument and provided its context. Whites insisted that "degraded condition" was a consequence of innate inferiority. By the late 1810s and throughout the 1820s, white racists were rioting against black communities and producing a suffocating stream of propaganda— satirical broadsides, condemnatory sermons and pamphlets—that reflected and reinforced popular assumptions about black inferiority. The words of John Hough, a professor of languages at Middlebury College speaking to an audience of colonizationists, provide an extreme but not atypical example:

> The state of the free colored population of the United States, is one of extreme and remediless degradation, of gross irreligion, of revolting profligacy, and, of course, deplorable wretchedness. Who can doubt the blacks among us are peculiarly addicted to habits of low vice and shameless profligacy? They are found in vast

numbers in the haunts of ruin and dissipation and intemperance where they squan-
der in sin the scanty earnings of their toil, contract habits of grosser iniquity and are
prepared for acts of daring outrage and of enormous guilt.[12]

The new generation of white antislavery activists and reformers who
emerged in the 1830s also participated in the discourse of race. They shared
with other whites, from proslavery advocates to the merely indifferent, a
common vocabulary and a common set of assumptions about the general dependency, incapacity, and need for external control of most people of color.
Hence, while the proposals of colonizationists and "whites only" exclusionists were antithetical to those of radical abolitionists and reformers (both
black and white), nearly all of them described the problem of the degraded
condition of free people of color in similarly essentialist language.

In his article in this volume, James Brewer Stewart points out that these im-
mediatists, William Lloyd Garrison and his associates, reacted to the spectacle
of the rioting and verbal violence of whites against blacks by redirecting their
efforts from encouraging northern blacks to rise into the middle class and
adopt middle-class values, to reforming the bigotry of whites. He emphasizes
the dedication of Garrison and others to the categorical equality of all people
of color and their participation in interracial collaborative efforts. There is no
doubt that these people strenuously supported the causes of education, economic advancement, and other efforts to improve the condition of people of
color. After 1830, while the exclusion and ridicule of people of color by whites
were escalating, abolitionist organizations increasingly welcomed African
Americans as members; many of them in their personal lives, as well as in
their public roles as activists in the cause of antislavery, met socially with people of color and advocated strenuously for their political rights. Certainly policies of inclusion and advocacy differed morally from convictions of social superiority and responses of revulsion and exclusion, and their practical effects
differed even more radically. Nonetheless, many abolitionists continued to see
people of color as projects or wards, and even the most progressive, Garrison
among them, continued to press free people of color to reform themselves and
become moral exemplars in order to overcome prejudice and "earn" full equality, even as they agreed that racial prejudice originated in slavery and prevented free blacks from making the very changes whites advocated. The logic
of this position, whether articulated or not, was that the failure of most free
people of color to rise was a moral defect that lay within themselves.[13]

Now, what of free people of color themselves? They were not simply passive observers and objects of this racializing process. Although, as Lacy K.
Ford, Jr., suggests elsewhere in this volume, the ideology of racial modernity
insisted that whites had "virtually unilateral authority to define the nature of

American race relations," they did not and could not exclude other voices from participation in the process of refashioning the meaning of race itself. In fact, any notion that African Americans stood somehow outside the realm of ideological production—that they were not themselves producers of ideology—would be an inherently racist idea. Instead, it is clear that, at all levels of the economic scale, people of color were active participants in the evolving discourse of race. They struggled mightily to deploy racial ideology and to fashion their own racial identity as strategies of resistance.

In what ways can we see evidence of this struggle? We know the least about the engagement of poor people of color with racial production, but occasionally a record crops up that illustrates such engagement. For example, one John Hammer, appearing before the Hopkinton, Rhode Island, Justice Court in 1795 for debt in response to a warrant designating him a "black man," complained that the warrant was flawed because "I am an Indian man." Hammer, in claiming an "Indian" identity rather than a "Narragansett" one, was asserting to the conflation of distinct tribal identities into "Indian" even as he was resisting the further conflation of "Indian" into "mustee" and then "negroes" or "blacks" that was occurring at the end of the eighteenth century. Many people of color seem to have ignored racial characterizations as part of the overall institutional framework of control that they sought to evade wherever possible. Such evasions constituted a form of resistance to racialization at the very moment, ironically, that this and other refusals to participate in the arbitrary mechanics of so-called good citizenship—e.g., failing to abide by the legal settlement system in choosing their places of residence, failing to adopt European-style marriage customs—were being interpreted as just the sort of disorderly and immoral behavior to be expected of ex-slaves—that is, as "racial" behavior.[14]

Racial, too, was the judgment rendered by whites on behavior they interpreted as dependent, although much of this behavior was viewed quite differently by people of color themselves. A particularly clear example of this phenomenon is the frequent reliance of freed slaves upon the economic support of their former masters. Whites considered such reliance a persistence of servile dependency, the refuge of lazy and shiftless persons who thereby forfeited any claim to independent citizenship. To many people of color, however, support from their former owners was an entitlement rooted in tradition established by the earlier colonial laws that had required owners to remain accountable for slaves they emancipated individually and had been enforced by town governments. Although most of these laws had been rescinded in the course of postrevolutionary emancipation, transferring liability for the consequences of enslavement—former slaves' financial need—from the private to the public purse (town charity), many former slaves continued to hold their former owners both financially and morally accountable for their dependent condition. This behavior, too, can be understood as a form of resistance to racialization, in that it insisted upon the accountability of external and histor-ical factors—prior enslavement—rather than individual inadequacy or innate inferiority for an impoverished condition.[15]

The behavior of workers and middling people of color, on the other hand, offered a different kind of categorical resistance to racial characterization. Simply inserting themselves successfully into an economy and, sometimes, a polity in which they were assumed to be unable to function constituted a form of resistance to racial production. By the 1790s, people of color had begun to assume diverse roles in the economy. In probates, ledgers, and other records, they appear among the creditors listed in the estate inventories of whites, as owners of estates themselves, as holders of securities, and (rarely) as bond-holders of laborers of color. The visible participation of such hard-working people of color on a day-to-day basis in the ongoing economic lives of their communities offered potent resistance to assumptions about the inherent de-pendency and disorderliness of free people of color. On the other hand, as James Brewer Stewart points out in his essay in this volume, the success of some blacks sparked deep resentment on the part of whites who saw it as a dangerous pretension to social equality and responded with behavior ranging from ridicule to riots. Also, such industry for the majority of working people of color was rewarded still by low pay, uncertainty and irregularity of em-ployment, and relegation to poor quality housing, their living conditions of-ten seemed to whites to confirm, rather than refute, claims of the "degraded condition" of people of color.[16]

Black leaders and intellectuals participated in the discourse of race most di-rectly in their engagement with the "condition" issue. The condition argument can best be understood as an attempt by people of color to account for the racial stratification of republican America—a stratification they interpreted as the failure of republican ideology to deliver on its revolutionary promises. This stratification left most free people of color suffering under circum-stances of systematic "prejudice," if not outright poverty, unemployment, and overall marginalization in postrevolutionary American society. Black intel-lectuals endlessly debated the problems of locating responsibility for the "de-graded condition" of most people of color, understanding its relation to the pervasive "prejudice" of whites, and determining a course of action that could ameliorate both condition and prejudice. They looked for a strategy that would enable them to become full and equal inheritors of the republican promises of opportunity for self-making and for citizenship.[17]

The discourse of condition was the discourse of identity and of race; "con-dition" provided the context in which people of color interrogated the meaning and permanence of physical difference, the precise terminology that they should use to identify themselves as a group, and the sources of the persistent "prejudice" of whites against them. These issues in turn informed an ongoing debate over what it was exactly that defined them as a group separate and distinct from other Americans, that could constitute a common identity. Did such an identity lie in a shared descent from African peoples? A shared experience of oppression? A common range of skin color and other physical characteristics?

As early as 1780, northern free people of color recognized in their condition the legacy of failed revolutionary promises. In that year in Dartmouth, Massachusetts, a small group of free people of color petitioned the revolutionary legislature to relieve them of poll and estate taxes on the grounds that "we are not allowed the Privilege of freemen of the State having no vote or Influence in the Election of those that Tax us." They also saw their situation as a direct consequence of former enslavement—New England enslavement. "(B)y Reason of Long Bondag and hard Slavery we have been deprived of Injoying the Profits of our Labouer or the advantage of Inheriting Estates from our Parents as our Neighbouers the white peopel do."[18]

By the turn of the nineteenth century, the condition of the growing number of free people of color had not improved. Nonetheless, black leaders of the revolutionary generation still expected that the republican promise would be fulfilled for them, and they still retained a vivid memory of the experience of slavery. Their leaders, linking these two factors, sought to explain their persistent suffering as the failure of republicanism to overcome the legacy of the form of despotism that slavery represented. An exemplar of this kind of thinking was Lemuel Haynes, black minister and revolutionary veteran. In an 1801 Fourth of July address entitled "The Nature and Importance of True Republicanism," Haynes set out several of the themes that would become elements of intense argument in the ensuing years against a backdrop of the recent, historical experience of local enslavement. Asking a Vermont audience of whites to consider "the poor Africans, among us," he inquired,

> What has reduced them to their present pitiful, abject state? Is it any distinction that the God of nature hath made in their formation? Nay—but being subjected to slavery, by the cruel hands of the oppressors, they have been taught to view themselves as a rank of beings far below others, which has suppressed, in a degree, every principle of manhood, and so they become despised, ignorant, and licentious. This shews the effects of despotism.[19]

Here, Haynes rejected biological explanations of difference and forcefully indicted slavery as the original cause of the "pitiful, abject state" of free people of color; at the same time, he found the behavior of people of color themselves to be the proximate cause of their "abject" condition, invoking environmental theories of difference to argue that their behavior had been corrupted by the "effects of despotism." Drawing upon republican ideas of benevolence and affection as the ties that would bind together a republic, Haynes saw clearly that it was the responsibility of whites to undo the effects of despotism by extending benevolence to people of color, "to meliorate the troubles of life, and to cement mankind in the strictest bonds of friendship and society." Haynes, black minister to a white parish, was convinced that whites both had the power to unite their interests with those of people of color and could be persuaded to do so by the compelling argument that the virtue and well-being of the republic depended upon this union. Bound in a reciprocal exchange of benevolence with whites, free people of color could shake off their "ignorance and licentiousness," legacies of despotism, and regain their "principles of manhood" (that is, the pride, dignity, and strength of character common to all free human beings).[20]

By the 1820s and 1830s, however, the context for discussing the condition of free people of color, and the frame of reference of leaders of color themselves, both had changed dramatically. New black leaders who confronted the "degraded" condition of free people of color in New England were a generation distant from the personal experience of enslavement—their own or that of family and friends. Fundamental attitudes in the white community toward the effects of enslavement on "character" had changed as well. Most northern whites had allowed the middle member in the progression "'negro' > slave > servile" to wither along with the institution of slavery itself, fixing permanent inferiority upon people of color as a group and undermining prospects for Haynes's hoped-for extension of benevolence. The new racial antipathy could be demonstrated by the fate of Haynes himself, who had been dismissed from his parish after twenty years of service because, as an acquaintance reported that Haynes had told him wryly, "the congregation had just then discovered that he was a colored man."[21]

While the memory of local slavery had receded and a conviction that blacks were racially inferior had become widespread among whites, the problem of condition itself remained largely unchanged for the vast majority of free people of color: But how could their condition be improved, and their American citizenship be claimed, as long as whites insisted upon treating them almost universally as an inferior people? As Abraham Shadd put it in his address to the Third Annual Convention of the Negro People in 1833, "a deep and solemn gloom has settled on that once bright anticipation, and that monster prejudice, is stalking over the land, spreading in its course its pestilential breath." Hosea Easton, in his *Treatise on the Intellectual Character, and Civil and Political Condition of the Colored People of the United States*, offered a devastating and painful condemnation of white racist language and its effects:

Negro or nigger, is an approbrious [*sic*] term, employed to impose contempt upon them as an inferior race, and also to express their deformity of person. Nigger lips, nigger shins, and nigger heels . . . are intended to apply to colored people, . . . as being expressive or descriptive of the odious qualities of their mind and body. . . . See nigger's thick lips—see his flat nose—nigger eye shine—nigger, where you get so much coat?"[22]

While people of color clearly recognized "prejudice" as an important factor in their oppression, there was considerable disagreement on how exactly it related to physical difference, and what in fact the meaning of physical difference was.

People of color were as keenly interested as whites in explaining human variety. Some leaders of color continued to insist upon environmental explanations of physical difference, attributing variety in skin color to diet, culture, and climate, long after most authorities had succumbed to biological theories. James McCune Smith, a physician, even elaborated a theory linking human character traits with culturally distinct modes of intake of food and use of air. Nonetheless, the increasing popularity of an essentialist vocabulary of nature and "blood" to explain human behavior frequently led people of color to confront essentialist constructions of their own difference in equally essentialist terms.[23]

Although nearly everyone vigorously rejected interpretations of their own oppressed status as evidence of innate inferiority, they often adopted the language of "biology" and "character" to describe what they continued to regard as a mutable condition. For example, Martin Delany quite self-consciously explored the connection between experience and biology.

The degradation of the slave parent has been entailed upon the child . . . in regular succession handed down from father to son—a system of regular submission and servitude, menialism and dependence, until it has become almost a physiological function of our system, an actual condition of our nature. Let this no longer be so.[24]

Such adoption by leaders of color of the essentialist language of whites as a goad to induce change in their own constituency was a common tactic and one which may have been intended at least partly to subvert the essentialist construction itself; but in a discourse of black inferiority so pervasive, this strategy undoubtedly had an unintentionally reinforcing effect.

By the 1820s and 1830s, the dominant discourse of variety or difference had become one of hierarchy, supported by the emerging "science" of race along with the longstanding Biblical arguments concerning the curse of Canaan, son of Ham. Many black intellectuals challenged these frameworks. *Freedom's Journal* insisted editorially that "there are no facts . . . which authorise the conclusion that any one of the several varieties of our race is either intellectually or morally superior to the rest." Hosea Easton thought it "a settled point with the wisest of the age, that no constitutional difference exists in the children of men, which can be said to be established by hereditary laws . . . whatever differences exist, are casual or accidental." But a great and growing number of whites held otherwise; and, by the late 1820s, intellectuals of color had begun countering widespread assumptions of "natural" black inferiority in their own terms—with claims of innate black superiority.[25]

Some of these arguments were based on physical comparisons. As early as 1827, *Freedom's Journal* was quoting Herodotus on the physical superiority of Africans to whites. By 1859, John Rock of Boston, a dentist who was also an attorney, was lecturing regularly on the greater physical beauty and strength of constitution of people of color, contrasting their "beautiful, rich color" with whites' "wan color," their "gracefully frizzled hair" with whites' "lank hair," and so forth." More subtly, Henry Highland Garnet sometimes referred to whites as "our colorless brethren."[26]

But, more than a defense against accusations of inferiority, people of color longed for a unifying identity powerful enough to allow them to contest whites' exclusive claim to that all-powerful identity, "American citizen," to which people of color were entitled but which they were unable to enact successfully. They sought this identity in the languages of descent ("African") and physiognomy ("black" and "of color").

For the first two centuries, people of African descent in New England called themselves variously "Blacks," "Negroes," and "Africans." They most frequently used the term "African" for the independent institutions they began forming in the last two decades of the eighteenth century and the first decade of the nineteenth, following the lead of Absalom Jones and Richard Allen in their establishment of the Free African Society in 1787 in Philadelphia. The use of "African" by people of color probably reflected several factors: African cultural influence, the common usage of the surrounding community, and a desire among a largely enslaved people to define themselves by a point of origin at which they or their ancestors all had been free persons.[27]

After 1820 free people of color increasingly substituted the term "coloured" and sometimes "black" for the term "African." One factor in this change undoubtedly was the perception that it had become dangerous for people of color to suggest an origin or allegiance outside the United States in the face of the American Colonization Society's determination to send them "back" to their African "homeland." But the growing use of terms such as "black" and "colored" in preference to "African" (in public discussion, at least) may reflect the increasingly pervasive discourse of physical difference and "essence" as well.[28]

A few people of color vehemently opposed the use of physical language, although it is difficult to pin down the precise meaning of their opposition. William Whipper, a lumberman from Pennsylvania, led the charge against language that supported what he called "complexional distinctions" of any kind. Whipper's denunciation of "color-phobia" on the part of people of color themselves, and his injunction to blacks to "throw off the distinctive features in the charters of our churches and other institutions," often are read as evidence of shame about African ancestry. Yet another reading is possible, especially in light of Whipper's 1849 call for a "national existence as a people" for people of color. His earlier denunciations of "complexional" terms and even institutions may simply reflect a rejection of physical difference as the basis of social organization and of physical language as the expression of identity.[29]

Some people of color continued to use the term "African" in the early antebellum years in preference to "of color" without any apparent objection to the latter term but with a different agenda. Maria Stewart, a Hartford-born woman of color who became a Boston lecturer, writer, and celebrity, commonly referred to her people as "daughters of Africa" and "sons of Africa" in contradistinction to "the Americans" (whites). A profound admirer of the Boston black nationalist, David Walker, Stewart insisted, as he did, upon a distinct identity for people of color and a leadership role for them in ending slavery and ameliorating their condition in the North as well. By continuing to use the term "African," Stewart seems to have been addressing African men and women as sojourners, marooned in a country in which they had earned, by their labor, a property right, but in which they had been unable to claim a right of citizenship. Her lack of concern that the term "African" might weaken the claims of free people of color to an enfranchised American citizenship may rest partly on the fact that, as a woman who frequently shaped her remarks to women, Stewart may have found the issue of literal enfranchisement somewhat irrelevant. Stewart was the exception, however, in a swelling chorus of voices identifying themselves as "coloured citizens."[30]

Establishing a collective name for people of color was not only, or even primarily, a strategic choice between an integrationist approach (employing no distinctive name at all) and a nationalist one (using "African" or "colored"). It also involved, quite importantly, another kind of strategic choice—a Hobson's choice, in fact—between locating the source of a distinctive collective identity in the body, with all the assumptions about innate mental and moral incapacity that had become fused with it in the course of gradual emancipation; and fashioning a coherent national identity out of African origin, which could encourage expatriation efforts and which heightened the identification of American blacks with peoples thought by whites to be sunk in darkness and depravity.

Many leaders of color of the 1830s and after resolved this dilemma by adopting elements of both strategies and employing the strengths of one to counter the damning aspects of the other. They chose the language of physical difference as their primary form of identification as a present, living group in order to avoid weakening their claim to American citizenship; at the same time, they renewed their historical identification with the Africa of antiquity—emphasizing the glories of ancient Egypt and Ethiopia, whose achievements stood as a powerful rebuttal to accusations of innate inferiority associated with that physical identity.[31]

Of course, it was not a distant, glorious past in Africa but a devastating experience of slavery in America that produced the current condition of poverty of northern free people of color and the climate of persistent prejudice against them. As Hosea Easton said,

> Color . . . cannot be an efficient cause of the malignant prejudice of the whites against the blacks; it is only an imaginary cause at the most. It serves only as a trait by which a principle is identified. . . . The true cause of this prejudice is slavery. . . . Its effect [is] in the character of prejudice.[32]

But which slavery accounted for the condition of free people of color—the slavery of their own northern ancestors in the past, or the ongoing bondage of the majority of American people of color in the South?

Northern whites, friend and foe alike for the most part, were busily effacing the historical experience of maintaining enslaved Africans on New England soil. For example, Silas M'Keen of Vermont asked, "What part of our country is freer from the guilt of slavery than New England?" acknowledging, however, that the region had been "most active of all our citizens in the slave trade." Leonard Bacon, Connecticut colonizationist, insisted in 1825, "slavery never existed here to any considerable extent, and for years it has been a thing unknown." Even Jeremy Belknap (founder of the Massachusetts Historical Society), though conceding the existence of northern slavery, insisted that "[t]he condition of our slaves . . . was far from rigorous. No greater labor was exacted of them than of white people. . . . Such of them as were prudent and industrious purchased their freedom" and "the former condition of most of them [slavery] was preferable to the present."[33]

The point here, of course, was to disavow slavery—for abolitionists, in order to magnify the distinction between a virtuous free North and a slaveholding South; for colonizationists, to focus attention on the distressing anomaly of "degraded" people of color in a free white society. But absent an explanation rooted in their historical experience of an oppressive institution of slavery in the North, the debased condition of free people of color could be understood as the logical consequence of their own innate inferiority, as many colonizationist sermons and burlesquing broadsides claimed.

Only rarely, however, did voices of color fix the blame for the oppressed condition of northern people of color squarely on the shoulders of those who had enslaved them in the North. One instance was an 1837 article in *The Weekly Advocate*, which described "prejudice which was always felt against [our people of color] because they were slaves," which had "descended like a curse upon their free children." Downing and others occasionally referred obliquely to northern slavery, but few people of color were willing to resurrect the memory of it as bluntly as had *The Weekly Advocate*. Why alienate the few white abolitionist friends they had? By and large, abolitionists were no more eager than colonizationists to remember northern slavery.[34]

The fading away of a legitimizing historical context for the oppressed condition of northern free people of color lent a special urgency to the program of self-improvement or "uplift" that constituted the dominant strategy of a majority of northern leaders of color of the 1820s and 1830s. The self-improvement agenda engaged the condition argument head-on. It challenged charges that people of color were innately mentally incapable by demonstrating their potential for achievement; it countered claims that they were naturally immoral by demonstrating their capacity for moral rectitude. *Freedom's Journal* editorialized in 1827, "It is for us to convince the world by uniform propriety of conduct, industry and economy, that we are worthy of esteem and patronage."[35]

But the uplift agenda struck some leaders as an abandonment of their southern brethren to the terrors of bondage. In 1838 the *Colored American* railed at free people of color to "Witness our criminal apathy and idiot coldness in the antislavery cause!" To stimulate support for abolition, many leaders insisted that it was southern slavery that debased northern people of color. Along with "W," they insisted, "Slavery must be abolished before the colored man can rise." In his address to the 1848 national convention, Douglass insisted, "We ask you to devote yourselves to this cause as one of the first and most successful means of self-improvement."[36]

Yet, claiming that southern slavery was the real source of northern "prejudice" further effaced the history of northern slavery. Such a disconnection from their history, again, left free people of color, demonstrably poorer and less literate than whites, prey to charges of innate inferiority.

There was no way out of the circularity of these arguments. The antebellum struggles of free people of color to define and assert an identity that would empower them, and their efforts to explain and transform their condition, were enmeshed in the postrevolutionary discourse of race; their struggles shaped, as well as were shaped by, that discourse. There was no place to stand, so to speak, outside the pervasive discourse of race.

The identity that people of color struggled to define in the years before the Civil War was a racial identity—an identity in which difference was embodied—because, Whipper's early longings to the contrary, by 1800 a nonracial identity had become an oxymoron. And even when the Civil War abolished southern slavery, northern free people of color were not liberated thereby from racial thinking and practices whose origins were lost in a largely suppressed history of northern slavery and emancipation and whose evolution had provided the context for their long struggle to empower and define themselves as a people.

NOTES

1. "Minutes of the New England Colored Citizens Convention," in Philip S. Foner and George E. Walker, eds., *Proceedings of the Black State Conventions, 1840–1865* (Philadelphia, 1979), 211.

2. David Waldstreicher discusses the emergence of "nationalist regionalisms" in the antebellum period and New England's claim to embody the nation in *In the Midst of Perpetual Fetes: The Making of American Nationalism, 1776–1820* (Chapel Hill, 1997), 251–69. Harlow Elizabeth Walker Sheidley shows how Massachusetts conservative elites in particular worked to stabilize American identity around a set of cultural, moral, and political values forged in the revolutionary struggle of New England patriots. See Walker, "Sectional Nationalism: The Culture and Politics of the Massachusetts Conservative Elite, 1715–1836" (Ph.D. diss., University of Connecticut, 1990). In *Mind and the American Civil War: A Meditation on Lost Causes* (Baton Rouge, 1989), 35, 51–53, Louis Simpson describes the intensification of New England nationalism in a sort of dialectical relationship with escalating southern nationalism.

3. The ideas in this paper are fleshed out much more fully in Joanne Pope Melish, *Disowning Slavery: Gradual Emancipation and "Race" in New England, 1780–1860* (Ithaca, 1998), esp. chap. 7. In this paper I have reluctantly abandoned placing the word "race" in quotation marks to resist its reification, as I did in my book, having been persuaded by Matthew Jacobson and others that it is inconsistent to place "race" in quotes without similarly marking "white," "black," etc., which would bury my work in an impenetrable thicket of quotation marks. This should not suggest that I am in any way moving away from a baseline assumption that race is an ideological construction, as Barbara Fields and many others have argued. A second assumption is that, as Alexander Saxton suggests, racism is a theory of history in that it imputes historical causation to racial difference. See Barbara J. Fields, "Ideology and Race in American History," in J. Morgan Kousser and James N. McPherson, eds., *Region, Race and Reconstruction: Essays in Honor of C. Vann Woodward* (New York, 1982); and Alexander Saxton, *The Rise and Fall of the White Republic: Class Politics and Mass Culture in Nineteenth-Century America* (London, UK, 1990), 14–15. For a compelling argument against the "inconspicuous racial logic" of placing some designations of difference in quotation marks and not others, see Matthew Frye Jacobson, *Whiteness of a Different Color: European Immigrants and the Alchemy of Race* (Cambridge, MA, 1998), ix.

4. A New England boosterism that touted the historical absence or insignificance of slavery in the region and contrasted its proud heritage of free white labor with the "negroization" of the South emanated from a wide range of sources—colonizationists, especially, but also abolitionists, travelers, journalists, and others. See, for example, Jeremy

Belknap, *Liberator*, Feb. 26, 1831; and Silas M'Keen, *Sermon delivered before the Vermont Colonization Society at Montpelier, Vermont, October 5, 1828* . . . (Montpelier, 1828). See also Melish, *Disowning Slavery*, 210–37. For references to the distinctiveness of northern racism, see, for example, Harriet Beecher Stowe, *Uncle Tom's Cabin* (1852; rep., New York, 1966), 195; James Weldon Johnson, *Autobiography of an Ex-Coloured Man*, in *Three Negro Classics* (1912; rep., New York, 1965), 488; and Zora Neale Hurston, quoted in Robert Hemenway's introduction to Hurston, *Dust Tracks on a Road: An Autobiography* (1942; 2d ed., Urbana, 1984), xxix-xxx.

5. See Melish, *Disowning Slavery*, chap. 2, *passim*; and Arthur Zilversmit, *The First Emancipation: The Abolition of Slavery in the North* (Chicago, 1967), *passim*.

6. See, for example, Levi Hart, "Some Thoughts on the Subject of Freeing the Negro Slaves in the Colony of Connecticut . . . ," (c.1775), 7, Miscellaneous Manuscripts (Connecticut Historical Society), typeset by Doris E. Cook. On prospective management of free blacks, see, for example, The Convention of Delegates from the Abolition Societies in the United States [Joseph Bloomfield, President], "To the Free Africans and other free People of color in the United States," May 1797 (Broadside Collection, Boston Public Library).

7. For an extensive range of examples of these activities, see Melish, *Disowning Slavery*, chap. 3.

8. The most detailed monograph on New England slavery remains Lorenzo J. Greene, *The Negro in Colonial New England* (New York, 1942). In *Black Bondage in the North* (Syracuse, 1973), Edgar J. McManus, describes the social history of slavery in the Mid-Atlantic as well as New England states. William D. Piersen focuses on the development of African-American culture in New England in *Black Yankees: The Development of an Afro-American Sub-culture in Eighteenth-Century New England* (Amherst, 1988). Arthur Zilversmit covers the legal history of emancipation in the New England and Mid-Atlantic states in *The First Emancipation*.

9. George Louis Leclerc, Comte de Buffon, *Histoire Naturelle,* trans. *In Barr's Buffon: Buffon's Natural History* . . . (3 vols., London, UK, 1797), III, 324–25, 334–40, 348–52; Samuel Stanhope Smith, *An Essay on the Causes of the Variety of Complexion and Figure in the Human Species* . . . (2d ed., New Brunswick, NJ, 1810), 152–55.

10. See, for example, James Bate, "An Account of a remarkable alteration of colour in a negro woman . . . ," *American Museum,* 4 (Dec. 1788), 501–02; Robert White, "A Curious Historical and Entertaining Narrative of the Captivity and almost unheard-of Sufferings and cruel Treatment of Mr. Robert White, Mariner," in *Bickerstaff's Boston Almanack, or Federal Calendar for 1791* (Boston, 1790).

11. For accounts in which both servile blackness and republican whiteness are essentialized, see, for example, "Account of a Negro Woman Who Became White," *American Magazine of Wonders,* 2 (1809), 312–13; John Vandike, *Narrative of the Captivity of John Vandike* . . . (Leominster, MA, 1801). For emerging scientific thinking on essentialized racial difference, see, for example, John Augustine Smith, "A Lecture introductory to the second Course of Anatomical Instruction . . . ," *New York Medical and Philosophical Journal and Review*, 1 (1809), 84–96; Samuel George Morton, *Crania Americana*; or, *A Comparative View of the Skulls of Various Aboriginal Nations of North and South America, to which Is Prefixed an Essay on the Varieties of the Human Species* (Philadelphia, 1839), 1–3. For an overview of the development of scientific racism, see William Stanton, *The Leopard's Spots: Scientific Attitudes toward Race in America 1815–59* (Chicago, 1960).

12. John Hough, *Sermon Delivered before the Vermont Colonization Society at Montpelier, October 18, 1826* (Montpelier, 1826), 8–10. Ventriloquistic broadsides that represented African Americans as pretenders to citizenship aping white middle-class culture have been discussed by several scholars. See, for example, Shane White, "'It Was a Proud Day': African Americans, Festivals, and Parades in the North, 1742–1834," *Journal of American History*, 81 (June 1994), 35–38; and Philip Lapsansky in "Graphic Discord: Abolitionist and Antiabolitionist Images," in Jean Fagan Yellin and John C. Van Horne, eds., *The Abolitionist Sisterhood: Women's Political Culture in Antebellum America* (Ithaca, 1994), 216–19. The most comprehensive treatment of the American Colonization Society and its antebellum movement to resettle free blacks in Africa is P. J. Staudenraus, *The American Colonization Society, 1817–1930* (New York, 1961).

13. See, for example, William Lloyd Garrison, *Thoughts on African Colonization* (Boston, 1832), 128–29.

14. Hopkinton Justice Court Records, Oct. 8, 1793 (Hopkinton, RI, Town Hall). Ruth Wallis Herndon and Ella Wilcox Sekatau discuss the redesignation of persons with Narragansett ancestry successively as "Indians," "Mustees," and finally, "blacks" or "negroes" in "The Right to a Name: The Narragansett People and Rhode Island Officials in the Revolutionary Era," *Ethnohistory*, 44 (Summer 1997), 445–47.

15. See William Piersen, *Black Yankees: The Development of an Afro-American Subculture in Eighteenth-Century New England* (Amherst, 1988), 33–34, for some expressions of former slaves' attitudes.

16. James O. Horton and Lois E. Horton have explored the communities and culture of northern free people of color in *In Hope of Liberty: Culture, Community and Protest Among Northern Free Blacks, 1700–1860* (New York, 1997). Harry A. Reed, *Platform for Change: The Foundations of the Northern Free Black Community, 1775–1865* (East Lansing, MI, 1994), compares the development of infrastructure in the black communities of Boston, New York, and Philadelphia. A clear, detailed analysis of the concerns, goals, and strategies of northern free people of color from 1830 to the eve of the Civil War is provided by Jane H. Pease and William H. Pease, *They Who Would Be Free: Blacks' Search for Freedom, 1830–1861* (New York, 1974). Leon F. Litwack, *North of Slavery: The Negro in the Free States, 1790–1860* (Chicago, 1961), remains the classic exposition of the social and political context of free blacks' struggles. Hard evidence of the emergence of a small black middle class in the North must be culled from many different sources: for occupational data, see, for example, *The African Repository*, 13 (Mar. 1837), 90; and the "Report of the Committee upon the Condition of the Colored People," in *Minutes of the National Convention of Colored Citizens* (Buffalo, Aug. 1843), in Howard H. Bell, ed., *Minutes of the Proceedings of the National Negro Conventions, 1830–1864* (New York, 1969), 38–39; statewide estimates of business assets of free black citizens were presented to the Colored National Convention of 1855 (Philadelphia, 1855), in Bell, *Minutes of the Proceedings of the National Negro Conventions*.

17. The contemporary arguments themselves are found throughout the black newspapers in the 1820s, 1830s, and 1840s, especially *Freedom's Journal, The Rights of All, The Weekly Anglo-African,* and *The Coloured American*, as well as in the minutes of the state and national Negro conventions between 1830 and 1859. See Bell, ed., *Minutes of the Proceedings of the National Negro Conventions*; and Foner and Walker, eds., *Proceedings of the Black State Conventions*.

18. Petition "Negroes Protest Against Taxation," in Herbert A. Aptheker, ed., *Documentary History of the Negro People in the United States* (New York, 1969), 14–16.

19. *Black Preacher to White America: The Collected Writings of Lemuel Haynes, 1774–1833*, ed. Richard Newman (Brooklyn, 1990), 82.

20. Newman, ed., *Black Preacher to White America*, 80–84. I owe my interpretation of Haynes's position on the relationship between American postrevolutionary "racial" problems and republicanism to John Saillant's very illuminating discussion, "Lemuel Haynes's Black Republicanism and the American Republican Tradition, 1775–1820," *Journal of the Early Republic*, 14 (Fall 1994), 293–324.

21. Ebenezer Baldwin, *Observations on the Physical, Intellectual, and Moral Qualities of our Colored Population: With remarks on the subject of Emancipation and Colonization* (New Haven, 1834), 46.

22. *Minutes and Proceedings of the Third Annual Convention, for the Improvement of the Free People of Colour* (New York, 1833), 32, in Bell, ed., *Minutes of the Proceedings of the National Negro Conventions;* Hosea Easton, *A Treatise on the Intellectual Character, and Civil and Political Condition of the Colored People of the U. States, and the Prejudice Exercised Towards Them. By Rev. H. Easton, A Colored Man.* (Boston, 1837), 41.

23. *Anglo African Magazine* (Jan. 1859), 5–9. Earlier examples are *Freedom's Journal*, May 18, 1827, 37, May 2, 1828, 51, and Sept. 19, 1828, 201–03.

24. Martin Robison Delany, *The Condition, Elevation, Emigration, and Destiny of the Colored People of the United States. Politically Considered* (Philadelphia, 1852), 47–48.

25. See *Freedom's Journal*, July 13, 1827, 69; Easton, *A Treatise*. See Melish, *Disowning Slavery*, chap. 4, for a discussion of developing racial essentialism.

26. *Freedom's Journal*, Mar. 20, 1827, Feb. 14, 1829; *The Liberator*, Mar. 12, 1858; Henry Highland Garnet, *The Past and Present Condition and the Destiny of the Colored Race* (1848; rep., Miami, FL, 1969), 11.

27. See Carol V. R. George, *Segregated Sabbaths: Richard Allen and the Emergence of Independent Black Curches, 1760–1840* (New York, 1973), for a detailed description of the establishment of African-American denominations.

28. The most comprehensive discussion of what has been called "the names controversy" among antebellum people of color is Sterling Stuckey's chapter, "Identity and Ideology: The Names Controversy," in *Slave Culture: Nationalist Theory and the Foundations of Black America* (New York, 1987), 193–244.

29. Stuckey describes the efforts of William Whipper and others to discard the words "colored" and "African" and to dissolve organizations based in "complexional distinctions" as part of an integrationist position that dominated the leadership of free people of color in the mid-1830s; a countervailing nationalist position, represented by Henry Highland Garnet and others, began to become dominant after 1840. For a taste of Whipper's argument, see *The Colored American*, Jan. 12, 1841; for Stuckey's conclusions, see *Slave Culture*, 210–11. The deteriorating position of free people of color is usually cited as the basis for the transformation in strategy, outlook, and language of Whipper and others who underwent a significant transformation in thinking and embraced nationalism in the late 1840s and especially after 1850. See, for example, Pease and Pease, *They Who Would Be Free*, 251–76. I do not disagree with this interpretation; I would argue, however, that some seemingly antinationalist or integrationist thinking of the 1830s may reflect a more complex awareness of the political implications of the embodiment of "race" and its expression in language by people of color themselves.

30. Marilyn Richardson, ed., *Maria Stewart, America's First Black Woman Political Writer* (Bloomington, IN, 1987), 34, 37, 38.

31. See, for example, *Freedom's Journal*, Apr. 6, July 6 and 13, Aug. 31, 1818, Feb. 7, 1829; Garnet, *The Past and Present Condition*, 11–12.

32. Easton, *A Treatise*, 38.

33. M'Keen, *Sermon* . . . October 5, 1828, 11; Leonard Bacon, *A Plea for Africa, delivered in New-Haven, July 4, 1825* (New Haven, 1825), 12; Jeremy Belknap, "History of Slavery in Massachusetts. Judge Tucker's queries respecting slavery, with Dr. Belknap's Answers," in installments in *The Liberator*, Vol. 1, Feb. and Mar. 1831, nos. 8–12.

34. *The Weekly Advocate*, Feb. 11, 1837.

35. *Freedom's Journal*, Mar. 30, 1827.

36. *The Colored American*, May 3, 1838; *ibid.*, June 24, 1837; "Report of the Proceedings of the Colored National Convention, held at Cleveland, Ohio, . . . 1848," in Bell, ed., *Convention Minutes*, 18.

BIBLIOGRAPHY

Aptheker, Herbert, ed. *A Dictionary History of the Negro People in the United States.* New York: Citadel Press, 1951.

Bell, Howard Holman, ed. *Proceedings of the National Negro Conventions, 1830–1864.* New York: Arno Press, 1969.

Foner, Philip, and George E. Walker. *Proceedings of the Black State Conventions, 1840–1865.* 2 vols. Philadelphia: Temple University Press, 1979.

Goodman, Paul. *Of One Blood: Abolitionism and the Origins of Racial Equality.* Berkeley: University of California Press, 1998.

Horton, James Oliver. *Free People of Color: Inside the African American Community.* Washington, DC: Smithsonian Institution Press, 1993.

Horton, James Oliver, and Lois E. Horton. *In Hope of Liberty: Culture, Community, and Protest among Northern Free Blacks, 1700–1860.* New York: Oxford University Press, 1997.

Melish, Joanne Pope. *Disowning Slavery: Gradual Emancipation and "Race" in New England, 1780–1860.* Ithaca: Cornell University Press, 1998.

Miller, Floyd J. *The Search for a Black Nationality: Black Emigration and Colonization, 1787–1863.* Urbana: University of Illinois Press, 1975.

Pease, Jane H., and William H. Pease. *They Who Would Be Free: Blacks' Search for Freedom, 1830–1861.* Urbana: University of Illinois Press, 1974.

Stewart, James Brewer. "The Emergence of Racial Modernity and the Rise of the White North, 1790–1840." *Journal of the Early Republic* 18 (Summer 1998): 181–217.

Stuckey, Sterling. *Slave Culture: Nationalist Theory and the Foundations of Black America.* New York: Oxford University Press, 1987.

White, Shane. "'It Was a Proud Day': African Americans, Festivals, and Parades in the North, 1742–1834." *Journal of American History* 81 (June 1994): 13–50.

5

"Here in America There Is Neither King Nor Tyrant": European Encounters with Race, "Freedom," and Their European Pasts

Jon Gjerde

Historians have been especially attentive to a series of dualities set in tension that serve to define crucial issues in the early republic. The subject of this issue is an examination of one duality that has occupied historians of the early national period (and elsewhere) in recent years: the juxtaposition of a whiteness and nonwhiteness. By being "white" or by becoming "white," historians have noted the privileges of naturalization and citizenship accorded to some and denied to others. If one was considered white, he or she was consequently free to celebrate the freedoms of the United States. In contrast, those who were not defined as white were subject to legal and extralegal inequities of nonmembership and, for many, unfreedom.

A second and related duality is the countervailing, yet inextricably connected, facts of slavery and freedom. Historians can cite countless Americans who prized life in the United States because, unlike conditions in most of the world at the time, it promised an unmistakable freedom. They can in turn enumerate millions of others who lived as chattel slaves. Moreover, because liberty was so prized and slavery so close at hand, Americans who enjoyed their perceived freedom were obsessed with maintaining it. They wrote of the slavery of alcohol;[1] of the bondage of the family; of the servitude of labor.[2] Those who were not free were haunted by a freedom so close at hand that it surely sharpened their need to escape slavery. Frederick Douglass's *Autobiography*, for example, resonates with the dualisms of slavery and freedom. "The wretchedness of slavery, and blessedness of freedom," he remembered, "were perpetually before me." Likewise, whereas slavery was "a stern reality" with "robes already crimsoned with the blood of millions," in the distance there "stood a doubtful freedom . . . beckoning us to come and share its hospitality."[3]

The referents of freedom and slavery, and of whiteness and nonwhiteness, were polar opposites, inextricably linked and starkly juxtaposed.[4]

It is tempting to stress the parallels inherent in these dualities. Because slavery-freedom and nonwhite-white are such compelling juxtapositions, the modalities are often portrayed by historians in stark—one might say, black-and-white—terms. Yet there are shadings of freedom and unfreedom, white and nonwhite that clearly complicate the story. The place of white women, for example, provides no easy formulation of relative freedoms and slavery. The fact that some American Indians became slaveholders as they became "civilized," only to be forced westward as their claims of citizenship, civilization, and land entitlement were denied by the United States government, likewise confounds parallels between nonwhiteness and freedom.

European immigrants are another curious example because their position in early national American society was so unclear and so contested. Scholarship of late has opened up the field—masterfully articulated in this book and elsewhere by David Roediger—in its exploration of the relationship between immigrants and race and, put simply, of how the Irish became white.[5] In this narrative, immigrants from Europe in the early nineteenth century were able to utilize legal precedents already established in the preceding century to become citizens and develop a base of political power. By becoming white, they were able to etch out a niche amid the uncertainties of the early national era. In an effort to make certain that the larger society differentiated them from the nonwhite, the unfree, and disempowered, these immigrants became among the most vociferous advocates of a *herrenvolk* republic.

Yet this is only one facet—although a very important one—in the way that European immigrants forced themselves into the American polity and society and into the American imagination. This essay is an attempt to suggest that a broadened scope be used to explore the issues of race and freedom embedded in American society. Because immigrants arrived from Europe with different frames of reference from those American-born and because Europe itself played an important role in the nation's imagination, we profit from enlarging the purview of liberty and servitude, of freedom and slavery beyond the United States as we explore American myths in the era. By viewing the objective fact and subjective experience of immigration, I will suggest in this essay that the modulating dualities of freedom-unfreedom and whiteness-nonwhiteness were connected inextricably to the meaning of the immigrant as European in the United States and the meaning of the United States as free to the antebellum European immigrant. Only after some time in the United States did immigrants come to understand the linkages within the United States between race and levels of freeness. And it was in their political education that vague notions of freedom held by immigrants slowly were politicized by concrete issues of slavery and race as the antebellum era progressed.

First, let us consider how the European presence informed the American imagination. In such a consideration, yet another juxtaposition—the duality of Europe and America—is brought into play. One might argue that a crucial project among Americans was to maintain the United States as a society distinct from Europe. Many of the foundation myths of the United States were both teleological in their definition of a new providential movement of history and dichotomous in their differentiation of the societies and polities of America and Europe as illustrations of that movement. As John Adams would write in 1765, "I always consider the settlement of America with Reverence and Wonder—as the Opening of a grand scene and Design in Providence for the Illumination of the Ignorant and Emancipation of the slavish Part of Mankind all over the Earth."[6] In spite of a flourishing slave system in the South, Americans in the North not only stressed the ostensible freedom that the United States offered its citizens, but the many threats that the Republic faced in defending it. If thousands later joined the movement to abolish slavery in part because of these inherent contradictions between freedom and slavery, others focused on the unfreedom that characterized Europe. In so doing, Americans were able to juxtapose their world from that which continued to exist in Europe. Not a few coupled their hatred of chattel slavery with their fears of European encroachment onto American shores.

Perhaps the best example of these fears of Europe is found in the common portrayal of Roman Catholicism in the United States.[7] Anti-Catholicism stemmed from a well-developed, hoary tradition in Anglo-American culture in the early nineteenth century, and influential anti-Catholic tracts were penned in the 1830s when Lyman Beecher, Samuel F. B. Morse, and ghost-writers for Maria Monk associated Catholicism with unfreedom and captivity.[8] It was no accident that these concerns were expressed amid the stirring of a Roman Catholic migration to the United States when fears of an undermined republic were expressed. Benighted Catholic immigrants, under the thumb of a powerful priesthood, were perceived as individuals both unfit for republican citizenship and lacking the "respectability" described by James Brewer Stewart in his article in this collection. Significantly, moreover, the peculiarities of Catholicism were likened to the peculiar institution of the South. Northern antislavery observers were quick to condemn the southern slaveowners who held their slaves and their region in bondage. Yet the specters of the despotic European monarch and the authoritarian Catholic priest were threats that at least prior to 1854 were much closer at hand in the North, threats that might also undermine and ultimately destroy the American experiment.[9] The iconography of the Roman Catholic Church in this critique in many ways paralleled that of the slaveholder. The church was characterized as a hierarchical force that inhibited individual freedoms; it was "irrational"; it kept its victims in "slavery"; and it had vast implications for the development of the West and ultimately of the Republic.[10]

Thomas R. Whitney, founder of the Order of United Americans who served in Congress in the 1850s, was among the more explicit in his correlations of liberty and slavery in republicanism and Romanism—"two isms . . . for all time." "Romanism," Whitney began simply, "is diametrically opposed to Republicanism." The opposition was due politically to the hostility of the Roman Catholic Church to "our free institutions." "The simple fact," Whitney argued, "that one is an *absolute* government, and the other a *popular* government, establishes the antipodal." The consequences of this "simple fact" were profound and wide-ranging. "American Republicanism" cultivated intelligence among the people and ensured the freedom of the press whereas "Romanism" suppressed intelligence and silenced the press. "American Republicanism" secured "the full liberty of conscience to all its people" as Romanism pronounced "liberty of conscience to be a wicked heresy." "In a word," Whitney concluded ominously, "American Republicanism is FREEDOM; Romanism is *slavery*."[11]

What was more, Catholicism—like the system of slavery—was flourishing as it undermined "temperate liberty." Immigrants, who were allegedly thralls of a Catholic power, were condemned by Americans for their inability to discern the difference between liberty and license. A reproach that was not entirely consistent with one that denounced their adherence to authoritarian Roman Catholic forms, it was nonetheless linked to immigrants' political participation and ultimately to their political power. This was not a new concern: Thomas Jefferson, as early as 1784 in *Notes on Virginia*, predicted the ill effects of diversity. The United States, he held, could expect "the greatest number of emigrants" who had come of age under the aegis of monarchy. Such immigrants would "bring with them the principles of the governments they have imbibed in early youth; or if able to throw them off, it will be in exchange for an unbounded licentiousness." Vacillating from one extreme to the other, "it would be a miracle were they to stop precisely at the point of temperate liberty." They would share these principles with their children and together they would play a role in the creation of law. In that enterprise, they would "infuse into [legislation] their spirit, warp and bias its direction, and render it a heterogeneous, incoherent, distracted mass."[12] From this perspective, incoherent heterogeneity needed to be replaced by harmonious homogeneity.

The most obvious indication of the dangers of heterogeneity was interethnic violence. As some American-born set these ideas to pen, others acted them out on the street. Recurrent urban riots and violence in antebellum America often combined anti-Catholic and anti-European themes. A few examples must suffice. Following the 1844 Philadelphia riots, for example, Representative Lewis C. Levin spoke on the floor of Congress of the "drilled bands of armed foreigners" that was "an imported element—a European weapon—one peculiar only to the feudal institutions of the Old World."[13] Perhaps more curious—and more revealing—was the Astor Place riot in New York City in 1849 that pitted the American-born against English sentiments and in so doing exposed a series of perspectives of the urban mob. A seemingly bizarre debate over whether an American or Englishman ought to play Macbeth at the Astor Place Opera ended in riots and a police action that fired upon a crowd, killing some thirty and wounding scores of people. Handbills posted prior to the riot merged a disparate number of sentiments in their call to action. There existed a nationalism, a sense of yet another American Revolution, when one poster answered the question "shall Americans or English rule in this city?" with the observation that a "crew of the English steamer have threatened all Americans who [dared] to express their opinions." Importantly for our purposes, moreover, is the powerful rhetoric of American freedom versus English authoritarianism. The preriot handbill that conflated the opera house with "Englishness" and "aristocracy" gave way to even more forceful expressions after the police action. One New York City politician speaking the day after the riot considered the military that fired on the crowd to be "the slaves of her Majesty of England." Another compared the militia unfavorably to that of the czar of Russia. Even though the czar held "the lives of people in little better estimation than that of dogs," he required that his military discharge blanks before firing a round of lead into a citizenry. Here was expression of a fear that the authoritarian forms of Europe were in the process of retrenchment in America's cities.[14] Significantly, disorder spread westward as European settlement swelled and as national issues—such as slavery and temperance—became increasingly politicized in the years prior to and during the Civil War.

There was reason, of course, for these fears among the American-born. A transforming economy in this era caused many urban workers to see an emergence of Europe on American streets.[15] Would a new aristocracy arise from economic centralization? Yet there was more for many observers. America was not only in danger of becoming like Europe; Europe—and one of the most regressive institutions that characterized European society—was moving to the United States. Here was a source of an anti-Catholicism that was expressed by many native-born evangelical Protestants: immigrants and especially Catholic immigrants in the antebellum era symbolized actors in a process in which "un-American," "foreign," and "unfree" elements were infiltrating republican

America, planting "foreign" and "unfree" institutions, and endangering the Republic. Their immigration and the concomitant migration of their institutions were threats to "freedom" and republican forms of government, not least because they were accorded rights of citizenship by virtue of their "whiteness." From this perspective, white immigrants, rather than initially serving as defenders of a *herrenvolk* republic, were an ominous internal threat. The key ambition was to convert them—perhaps to Protestantism, certainly to an allegiance to the United States. The great irony is that many were converted by the Democratic Party, which itself posed a political threat to the nativists who swelled the ranks of the Whig and Republican parties and who gave voice to different expressions regarding slavery and freedom.

If many Americans attached a fear of European despotism to the appearance of the European immigrant, how did immigrants view their own arrival? How did they grapple with the freedoms they associated with the United States and the oppression of Europe? How did they couple questions of freeness with questions of race? Whereas every immigrant was forced in one way or another to address these questions, the sum total of their answers resulted in complex and occasionally contradictory answers. A key factor in the spectrum of these reactions, moreover, was the context in which European immigrants found themselves. The famine Irish, for example, who dwelt in the burgeoning cities of the eastern seaboard—a ground zero of violent racial antagonism in the antebellum North—differed radically from the swarms of immigrants living in enclaves in the western states, enclaves that so concerned American-born observers but which were nonetheless isolated from other racial groups.

In these differing contexts, European immigrants and ethnics pieced together narratives to explain their encounters with the American Republic and with others about them. The duality of freedom-unfreedom for nineteenth-century European immigrants thus was informed not only by chattel slavery, but also by frames of reference that separated the United States from Europe, and which encompassed a history of servitude and unfreedom that immigrants had escaped. As David Brion Davis suggests in his essay, the immigrants' peasant forebears had been viewed as unfree, even black. Thus, European immigrants tended to equate both freedom with the United States and slavery—or unfreedom and despotism—with Europe, as they learned to differentiate themselves both from their European past and from Americans in the present who were enslaved or whose forebears had been enslaved. Over time, they learned to celebrate the freedom—particularly in the antebellum era—that seemed to exist for them in the United States that enabled them to develop their own sense of a race for "respectability" as described by Jim Stewart. Over time, they also learned to differentiate those who, unlike them, were unfree.[16]

Immigrants utilized these frames of reference to write their own foundation myths even before the United States was a nation-state. In 1764, Christopher Saur, a Philadelphia German cleric, would write "whether you are Englishmen, Germans, Low-Germans or Swedes, whether you are of the High Church, Presbyterians, Quakers, or of another denomination, by your living here and by the law of the land you are *free men, not slaves*."[17] And Henry Miller, in a patriotic litany penned shortly before the Declaration of Independence was signed, reminded his readers, "Remember—and remind your families—you came to America, suffering many hardships, in order to escape servitude and enjoy liberty; Remember, in Germany serfs [*leibeigene*] may not marry without the consent of their master. . . . They are regarded as little better than black slaves on West Indian Islands."[18] A pliant use of the abstraction of freedom, set in a context of the unfreedom of the European world, thus was a useful rhetorical device for understanding life in the American Republic.

The rhetoric of freedom, a freedom that ostensibly was offered to "white" European immigrants, became an increasingly powerful ideological force in the nineteenth century in integrating immigrants of a variety of stripes into American society, in encouraging what Herbert Marcuse called "repressive tolerance," and in exacerbating racial fault lines. A significant phase in the creation of an ethnic identity in the antebellum United States was the affirmation of Europe as a negative reference to the freedoms of the United States. Already in the 1830s French visitor Michel Chevalier remarked that democracy so pervaded all "national habits" in the United States that "it besets and startles at every step the foreigner [presumably immigrant or visitor alike] who, before landing in the country, had no suspicion to what a degree [his] every nerve and fibre had been steeped in aristocracy by a European education."[19] This pervasive democracy was expressed particularly by those immigrants who had been touched by the flames of republicanism in Europe or were influenced by the pronouncements of American liberty and opportunity. "In America," trumpeted *Nordlyset*, a Norwegian-language paper that would support the Free Soil party in the 1840s, "liberty advances as proudly and deliberately as its gigantic rivers. [In Europe], absolute despots or kings are everywhere in power. . . . Just let them sit on their thrones, wearing their robes of sable, and oppressing mankind! Here in America at any rate, there is neither king nor tyrant."[20]

Johan R. Reiersen, learning from his journey through the United States in 1843, agreed. Since the American government was unhampered by monarchical and aristocratic interests, he argued, there was created a "spirit of progress, improvements in all directions, and a feeling for popular liberty and of the rights of the great masses exceeding that of any land in Europe." As a result, republican government would not fail, in large part because "the masses" would never be "reduced—through the power of individuals or of capital—to the same slavish dependence that supports the thrones of Europe." "Personal freedom," he asserted, "is something the people suck in with their mother's milk." "It seems to have become as essential to every citizen of the United States as the air he breathes," Reiersen concluded. "It is part of his being, and will continue to be until his whole nature is cowed and transformed in the bondage of need and oppression."[21]

These sentiments were also maintained privately. A German immigrant, writing to his kin in Europe in 1838, compared his former home to his new one. In Germany, "alas, common sense and free speech lie in shackles," he observed. If his relatives wished "to obtain a clear notion of *genuine* public life, freedom of the people and sense of being a nation," he contended, they should emigrate. "I have never regretted that I came here, and never! never! again shall I bow my head under the yoke of despotism and folly."[22] Other immigrants writing one decade later and speaking a different tongue used nearly identical imagery: Norwegians, they wrote, enjoyed tasting "the satisfaction of being liberated from the effect of all yoke and despotism."[23]

If European immigrants continued to develop a tradition that invoked the rhetoric and institutions of an American exceptionalism, the ways in which they deployed this rhetoric correlated both with their past experience and with the level of satisfaction they felt with the purported freedoms of the United States. Some immigrants, such as German Forty-eighters who left Europe with republican visions, seized on the liberal republican possibilities of the United States. Others, and especially those from Roman Catholic traditions, at once celebrated the possibilities of American freedom—and especially religious freedom—while they powerfully assailed instances of hypocrisy when the purported freedoms of America were abused, although not usually with regard to chattel slavery. When public schools utilized the King James Version in scriptural study, for example, Roman Catholic immigrants and their religious leadership pointed out that despite professions to the contrary, public institutions did enable a freedom in the practice of religion.[24] Thus Forty-eighters and Catholics of German descent used expressions of freedom to advance beliefs that were anathema to the other group.

As American nativism grew more riotous in the antebellum period, tensions between immigrants and native-born and between Protestant and Catholic immigrants increased. In 1846, Father Joseph Cretin wrote that the American government "was decidedly Protestant; above all, since the war with Mexico which it regards as a war of religion." "There are already rumors of sending 5 or 6 thousand yankees to Mexico to civilize that country, that is to say, to Protestantize it," he continued. "They are people whom one must handle very delicated [*sic*] like puffed up persons." Years later, Andre Trevis agreed. "The agitation," he wrote, "caused here by the question of slavery. . . . may be followed in a few years by open war against Catholicism. . . . Under the pretext of assuring liberty, [Republican leaders] will try to drive out of the Northern States Catholicism, the pretended enemy of the independence of the U.S. and the patron of slavery." "It may not be impossible," Trevis concluded ominously, "that the palm of martyrdom may one day be reaped in America on the borders of the Great Lakes and the Mississippi."[25]

Significantly, then, as "white" immigrants warred over the outcomes of the American Republic, they accepted its premises. And whether or not they were disillusioned with pretenses of American opportunity and freedom, the steady rhetoric about salutary encounters with American conditions tended to mute the criticism of their new nation, if not that of other cultural groups in their midst. Gilbert Osofsky has argued as well that immigrants (and especially poor Irish Catholics) were driven to express superpatriotic affirmations toward the United States to temper the barrage of criticism they themselves faced.[26] The predisposition to glorify the possibilities of American citizenship, oftentimes uncritically, likely worked both to hasten the integration of the immigrants into American society and to differentiate themselves from others not so fortunate.

That integration was facilitated by the opportunity to refashion aspects of the immigrants' cultural pasts. We are well aware that immigrants seized on common national, linguistic, and religious traditions as cornerstones to create ethnic collectivities. These ethnic groups maintained boundaries, oftentimes reconfiguring common pasts, that were instrumental for ethnic leaders in a pluralist society.[27] Ethnic institutions, based on common intellectual, geographical, or linguistic pasts originating in Europe, were created in the United States to support interest group associations in the polity and society. Yet this process of "ethnicization" did not necessarily nullify the development of loyalties to the United States. Rather than competing, the dual loyalties to nation and subgroup, invented under the auspices of an American creed that stressed freedoms of religion and speech, could be complementary. This "complementary identity," which I have described in greater detail elsewhere, enabled immigrants to nurture simultaneously their bond to nation and to ethnic or religious subgroups. Tropes of "freedom" and "liberty," because their meaning was so pliant, proved to be malleable concepts that fostered an opportunity to remodel systems of belief and an appreciation among immigrants of the responsibilities and rights of American citizenship.[28] Thus although European immigrants began to recognize an "other" in terms of nonwhiteness and unfreedom, they did not necessarily identify themselves as white. Rather, they saw themselves — and this was especially the case in secluded enclaves — as

Pomeranians, Vossings, or from County Cork. Unlike W. E. B. Du Bois's sense of "two-ness" as an African American, European immigrants and their children could merge multilayered ethnic and national identities. Pluralism for them was embedded into loyalty to nation.

The ways in which this rhetoric had an impact on issues of race were expressed both privately and in the public discourse regarding slavery and freedom, and race. If immigrants were familiar with the dissimilarities between the United States and Europe that they often used to justify their emigration, they were forced to learn about race and slavery in America. Indeed, early images of slavery often were connected to the Islamic world rather than to African Americans.[29] Nonetheless, an American education was fostered through the spoken and written word in which slavery became racialized. Some immigrants, before they had stepped off the boat, might have read immigrant guidebooks such as the following by Ole Rynning in 1838: "An ugly contrast to this freedom and equality [of the United States] which justly constitute the pride of the Americans is the infamous slave traffic, which is tolerated and still flourishes in the southern states. In these states is found a race of black people, with wooly hair on their heads, who are called negroes, and who are brought here from Africa, which is their native country."[30]

Yet private discussions of the issues of race and slavery reveal greater confusion, especially among those immigrants sequestered in communities that had little contact with slavery or with African Americans, than Rynning's depiction that predicted that the slavery question would culminate in a civil war. Consider the thoughts of Gottfried Duden writing from the slave state of Missouri in 1827. As he remarked to his friend while traveling through the state, "people in Europe will not and cannot believe how easy and how pleasant it can be to live in this country." It resembled a "fairy-tale world," a place that at once was "too strange, too fabulous." Yet when he noted the blemishes of American life in the presence of slavery, he focused less on African-American slaves than on German redemptioners, or "white slaves" as he called them, whose "fate is far worse than that of the Negro slaves." As late as 1856, Martin Weitz, while saluting the freedom of America, rued its slavery that held both whites and blacks in chains. "There are already 15 states in the South with slavery," he wrote, "and the slaveholders own 3 million slaves, of which there are many white ones."[31] Despite these condemnations of white slavery in this fairy-tale land, Duden in the same breath considered how black slaves were a means of immigrant mobility. With a sum of money to start a farm, a German in Missouri could "buy two adult slaves (one male and one female) . . . and establish himself in such a manner that he can live more happily and, especially in regard to the future lot of numerous descendants, with many less worries than if he possessed six times that amount in Germany."[32]

Implicitly, white freedom and black servitude were deemed normal, and, despite ruing the abnormality of white slaves, slavery was a means of mobility and greater freedom.

Immigrant women were also well aware of the significance of race. In her letter written home in 1856, a Swedish-American maid living in Chicago praised the United States "for here *white* people are free." These white people, she continued, enjoyed freedoms nonexistent in Sweden. The servant because she was white and free was able to quit her work if she so desired. And women servants were not made "to toil in the fields and not even feed the animals or milk the cows." Whereas she did not argue that her freedom was built on the slavery of others, she was aware of the freedoms that did not exist in Sweden or for nonwhite people in the United States.[33] Yet her views were perhaps more perceptive than most: only a few years later in New York City, a German immigrant woman wrote that neither black nor white Americans would harm members of her group "since the blacks are very happy when you don't do anything to them, the only thing is the problem with language."[34]

In places where slaves and free people of color were uncommon, nonwhites as a group were effaced. As Gjert Hovland would write without irony in a letter back to Norway in 1838, "*everybody* has the liberty to travel about in the country, wherever he wishes, without any passports or paper. Everyone is permitted to engage in whatever business he finds most desirable, in trade or commerce, by land or by water."[35] American Indians, like African Americans depicted by Lois Horton and Joanne Pope Melish in their essays in this book, tended to be erased in the mind of the European immigrant.

If private attitudes are difficult to discover, sentiments regarding race and slavery were expressed more powerfully in public debate that was part and parcel of the political education that immigrants were receiving in the United States. And as abolitionism grew as a movement, as slavery became a national political issue in the 1840s, the coupling of race and unfreedom became even more closely entwined. Differentiation of immigrants as "white," especially in places of racial contestation, became increasingly common, and Europeans also participated in Jim Stewart's "modernization of racial difference" as political identities were articulated.

I cannot explore this complex process of the development of political allegiance among members of immigrant groups in depth in this short essay. Nonetheless, it is important to consider three factors. First, ethnic and religious groups brought predispositions to the political debate that served to channel them into specific political entities. Kathleen Neils Conzen, for example, has illustrated how German Catholics carried a communal localism from Europe that accorded well with the precepts of the Democratic Party.[36] Likewise, immigrants maintained varying senses of the propriety of slavery.

Pietist sects, to use another example, were more likely to condemn slavery and to comment on race. For example, the "Old Constitution" of the Eielsen Synod, a pietistic Norwegian Lutheran sect, cited Matthew 7:12 (the "Golden Rule") when it condemned "the fearful sin of . . . the slave traffic." Other Scandinavian Lutheran bodies regarded those who defended the sin of slavery by appealing to scripture to be guilty of blasphemy against God as a prostitution of the Word.[37] In contrast, other church organizations—specifically Roman Catholics and more liturgically oriented Protestants—were softer on the issue, so much so that the Norwegian Synod, to take one example, became embroiled in a heated debate about the absolute sinfulness of slavery during the Civil War.[38]

Second, as they brought these inclinations to the political arena, immigrants were schooled by their political parties. It is difficult to discover the degree to which or the speed with which these people, who were only decades removed from Europe and often living in local societies defined by religious belief and non-English language traditions, identified with the American debate. Specifically, we do not know how many immigrant men joined the chants of "white men, white men" in the Lincoln-Douglas debates that David Roediger mentions in his essay.[39] Yet we do know that these expressions were learned in the United States, and that the schooling came in part from the political party apparatus. If a German immigrant espoused the Democracy because it accorded well with his beliefs in localism, he was encouraged as well to accept the party's views on race and become a white man. On the other hand, others rapidly learned from their political organizations about antislavery as exemplified in the christening of one John Brown Olson, born in an isolated southeastern Minnesota rural settlement to recent Norwegian immigrants in 1859.[40] Third, the parties brought together local ethnic, religious, and (in places) racial groups into national coalitions. If Democrats in Illinois were chanting "white men" in the late 1850s, others in Minnesota were "civilized" Indians who forged a singular alliance with German Catholics and upland southerners.[41]

Members of immigrant groups arrayed with cultural baggage carried from Europe and mindful of the purported freedoms in the United States thus began their American political education, an education that was sporadic and imperfect. Simply put, for many the negative reference to the freedoms allegedly inherent in the United States pivoted from a despotic and unfree Europe to an enslaved and unfree nonwhite. If ethnic and religious predilections were powerful forces in informing partisan allegiance, the political education in turn hardened their ideological positions. Principally through the print media and political gatherings, immigrant voters were instructed about race, slavery, and freedom. And those who hewed to the Democratic Party, we have been told, were more likely to view their whiteness as a basis for freedom and as a mark of status denied those defined as nonwhite. Ralph Ellison is thus correct when he suggests that immigrants in the countryside but more pointedly in the city came to learn to differentiate themselves from nonwhites and came to understand the power of whiteness. Attempting to distance themselves both literally and figuratively from unfree Europe, the European born in the United States nonetheless arrived at varying conclusions regarding their nonfree and nonwhite neighbors.

It might be too much to ask, borrowing from Ellison, what America would be like without European immigrants. But this essay has touched on two aspects of that question. It has illustrated first how the European immigrant for many American-born represented a threat of unfreeness to the unfolding of the American Republic. As a minion and as a dupe of a Roman Catholic conspiracy, the European immigrant potentially could lead the nation to ruin. This concern ebbed and flowed in correlation with the volume of the immigration, but it is a significant—and largely untold—story of how the "white" foreigner, in part *because* he was white, could undermine the nation. Scholars need to connect the story of how the immigrant became white with that of how the immigrant ceased to be a threat to the Republic.

The second aspect concerns the European immigrants themselves who perceived the United States as a place that simultaneously promised them a freedom to replant ethnic and religious institutions and fostered a condition that helped them transform themselves from the "foreign" to the "naturalized." Because they were "white," immigrants were able both to attain citizenship and practice forms of belief often denied them in their former homes. And in celebrating the freedoms of the United States they were aware of the many meanings of freedom and the escape from a sense of European bondage. Yet they also saw a positive type of freedom: the freedom to build ethnic and religious communities based not so much on "whiteness" as on a constructed, and ostensibly common, past. In these ethnic groups, white immigrants and their children maintained specific sensibilities regarding their faith, family, society, and polity that had been nurtured in Europe. They were nudged toward celebrating membership in the United States because it permitted them the opportunity to practice transplanted beliefs, beliefs ironically that many native-born Americans felt might undermine the nation. This American education was related to the creation and the definition of the ethnic group, each with its own distinctive qualities that in turn were connected to learning to differentiate one group from another. As they began to label themselves in relation to others, European immigrants transposed the despotism of Europe to the unfreedom of the nonwhite as a vehicle to juxtapose their freedom in the United States. As historians have illustrated time and time again, this transformation from the unfree European to the free American tragically was connected to the denial of freedom to others.

NOTES

1. In 1828, Heman Humphrey, in *A Parallel Between Intemperance and the Slave Trade*, argued that "where the slave trade opens *one* grave, hard drinking opens *three*." That same year, Lyman Beecher compared the middle passage with the slavery of alcohol in his *Six Sermons on the Nature, Occasions, Signs, Evils, and Remedy of Intemperance*. "In this nation," he wrote, "there is a middle passage of slavery, and darkness, and chains, and disease, and death. But it is a middle passage, not from Africa to America, but from time to eternity, and not of slaves whom death will release from suffering, but of those whose sufferings at death do but just begin." Cited in Robert H. Abzug, *Cosmos Crumbling: American Reform and the Religious Imagination* (New York, 1994), 89, 95.

2. The charge of "wage slavery," for example, was common.

3. *Narrative of the Life of Frederick Douglass: An American Slave. Written by Himself*, ed. David W. Blight (Boston, 1993), 86, 98.

4. The coupled relationships of slavery-freedom and white-nonwhite were not the only dualities that preoccupied antebellum Americans. A third relationship that complicates the discussion was the contestation between liberty and order. Americans steadfastly prizing freedom, nonetheless frequently expressed concern that that liberty could lead to license, and that freedom had to be constrained or it could lead to excesses that would undermine the Republic. Already in the *Federalist Papers*, Madison argued that "liberty is to faction what air is to fire." These concerns would occupy the thoughts of Americans and notable visitors to the United States, most notably de Tocqueville, some forty years later. And this riddle would be forcefully put in context of the European immigrant, as we shall see below. "Publius" [Madison], "Number 10: The Same Subject Continued," in Isaac Kramnick, ed., *The Federalist Papers* (1788; rep., New York, 1988), 123.

5. The most influential work on this issue is David Roediger, *Wages of Whiteness: Race and the Making of the American Working Class* (New York, 1991). The turn of phrase comes from Noel Ignatiev, *How the Irish Became White* (New York, 1995).

6. Cited in Arthur Mann, *The One and the Many: Reflections on the American Identity* (Chicago, 1979), 59.

7. See, for example, Ray Allen Billington, *The Protestant Crusade 1800–1860: A Study of the Origins of American Nativism* (New York, 1938); and David Brion Davis, "Some Themes of Counter-Subversion: An Analysis of the Anti-Masonic, Anti-Catholic, and Anti-Mormon Literature," *Mississippi Valley Historical Review*, 47 (Sept. 1960), 205–24.

8. Anti-Catholicism was connected in many ways to the portrayal of Spain as the despotic other to England.

9. Stephen E. Maizlish, "The Meaning of Nativism and the Crisis of the Union: The Know-Nothing Movement in the Antebellum North," in Stephen E. Maizlish and John J. Kushma, eds., *Essays on Antebellum Politics, 1840–1860* (College Station, TX, 1982), 166–98; Tyler Anbinder, *Nativism and Slavery: The Northern Know Nothings and the Politics of the 1850s* (New York, 1992), 44–47.

10. Significantly, however, this correlation was not advanced universally. A critical exception was William Lloyd Garrison who saw Know-Nothingism as a movement with a thinly masked proslavery stance. See Gilbert Osofsky, "Abolitionists, Irish Immigrants, and the Dilemmas of Romantic Nationalism," *American Historical Review*, 80 (Oct. 1975), 889–912.

11. Thomas R. Whitney, *A Defence of the American Policy* (New York, 1856), 94–96. Italics in original. If Whitney's analysis of the implications of slavery among the "Romanists" and freedom among the "American Republicans" was among the more explicitly defined, he was not alone in perceiving the presence of slavery and freedom in the respective systems. C. B. Boynton, in fact, was even more explicit in connecting the slaveholder to the priest. The central belief of the nation, he argued, was that the government "was designed for the overthrow of slavery." Protestantism, moreover, was central to liberty and it was "not Protestantism led in chains by a priesthood, nor betrayed by a jesuit [*sic*], not liberty cherishing and endeavoring to perpetuate a system of chattelism for millions of Americans." Rather it was Protestantism "with the right will, and power to defend itself, and Liberty seeking deliverance for all." Boynton concluded that "there are two dangers which threaten our noble Republic": "the Papacy and Slavery." With God's help, however, "the American eagle [would] never dwell in peace with [the] coiling serpent of slavery." With God's help, America would be "Protestant and Free!" C. B. Boynton, *Address Before the Citizens of Cincinnati, July 4, 1855*, cited in Maizlish, "Meaning of Nativism," 177–78.

12. Thomas Jefferson, *Notes on Virginia* (Paris, 1784), in Adrienne Koch and William Peden, eds., *The Life and Selected Writings of Thomas Jefferson* (New York, 1944), 217–18. Jefferson thus suggested that a slower natural growth of American-born citizens was preferable to immigration. In this way, the government would be "more homogeneous, more peaceable, more durable."

13. Cited in Billington, *The Protestant Crusade 1800–1860*, 233.

14. Joel Tyler Headley, *The Great Riots of New York, 1712 to 1873; Including a Full and Complete Account of the Four Days' Draft Riot of 1863* (New York, 1873), 120; Richard Moody, *The Astor Place Riot* (Bloomington, IN, 1958), 130, 189–94.

15. Michael F. Holt outlines the influence of economic change on mid-century nativist organization in "The Politics of Impatience: The Origins of Know Nothingism," *Journal of American History*, 60 (Sept. 1973), 309–31.

16. This tendency by European immigrants to equate freedom with the United States seemingly diminished later in the nineteenth century. See, for example, the essays in Marianne Debouzy, ed., *In the Shadow of the Statue of Liberty: Immigrants, Workers, and Citizens in the American Republic, 1880–1920* (Urbana, 1992).

17. Christopher Saur, *Eine zu dieser Zeit höchstnöthige Warnung und Erinnerung an die freye Einwohner der Provintz Pennsylvanien*, cited in Willi Paul Adams, "The Colonial German-language Press and the American Revolution," in Bernard Bailyn and John B. Hench, eds., *The Press and the American Revolution* (Boston, 1981), 180 (my emphasis).

18. Henry Miller, *Staatsbote*, Mar. 9, 1776, cited in Adams, "The Colonial German-language Press and the American Revolution," in Bailyn and Hench, eds., *The Press and the American Revolution* (Boston, 1981), 209–10.

19. Michel Chevalier, *Society, Manners and Politics in the United States* (Boston, 1839), 187.

20. *Nordlyset* cited in Ole Munch Raeder, *America in the Forties: The Letters of Ole Munch Raeder,* trans. and ed. Gunnar J. Malmin (Minneapolis, 1983), 180.

21. Johan Reinart Reiersen, *Pathfinder for Norwegian Emigrants by Johan Reinert Reiersen*, trans. and ed. Frank G. Nelson (Northfield, MN, 1981), 176, 183.

22. August Blümner to his relatives, Apr. 3, 1838, in Walter D. Kamphoefner, Wolfgang Helbich, and Ulrike Sommer, eds., *News from the Land of Freedom: German Immigrants Write Home* (Ithaca, 1991), 103. The exact text: "Denn dort liegt leider Gottes der gesunde Menschenverstand und die freie Sprache in Fesseln . . . . Indessen lade ich Euch ein, wenn Ihr Euch einen klaren Begriff vom *eigentlichen* Volksleben, Volksfreiheit u. Volksnationalität verschaffen wollt, hier mal rüber zu kommen." See also similar letters, *ibid.*, 164, 307, 393, 427, 478, 481–82, 494, 585, 602.

23. Lars Fletre, "The Vossing Correspondence Society of 1848 and the Report of Adam Lövenskjold," *Norwegian-American Studies*, 28 (1979), 267.

24. See, for example, John T. McGreevy, "The Eliot School Rebellion, Boston, 1859: Freedom and Catholicism on the Eve of the Civil War," unpublished manuscript in possession of author.

25. Joseph Cretin to Mathias Loras, Aug. 17, 1846, cited in M. M. Hoffman, ed., "From Early Iowa to Boston," *The Iowa Catholic Historical Review*, 1 (1930), 9. Father Andre Trevis to friends in France, cited in M. M. Hoffman, "'Clement Smith' Second Bishop in Iowa," *Iowa Catholic Historical Review*, 9 (1936), 13. By 1864, a Minnesota soldier remarked on his uneasiness when traveling through a Roman Catholic rural settlement: "One would imagine," he wrote, "while passing along the road that he was traveling in Mexico. Every four or five miles there are great crosses erected with Latin inscriptions on the bar." His conclusion, like the earlier Roman Catholic, was not far-fetched that "the next internal struggle will be a war upon the Catholics." Letter in the Hastings (MN) *Conserver*, Mar. 17, 1864, cited in Kathleen Neils Conzen, *Making Their Own America: Assimilation Theory and the German Peasant Pioneer* (New York, 1990), 18. Eleven years later, President Ulysses S. Grant would opine that in the next great national contest, the "dividing line will not be the Mason and Dixons [*sic*] but between patriotism and intelligence on the one side and superstitions, ambition, and ignorance on the other." Jon Gjerde, *The Minds of the West: Ethnocultural Evolution in the Rural Middle West, 1830–1917* (Chapel Hill, 1997), 290–91.

26. See Osofsky, "Abolitionists, Irish Immigrants, and the Dilemmas of Romantic Nationalism," 900.

27. Jonathan Sarna notes that larger collectivities were configured out of previously divisive groups. Jonathan D. Sarna, "From Immigrants to Ethnics: Towards a New Theory of 'Ethnicization,'" *Ethnicity*, 5 (1978), 370–78. On "boundaries," see Fredrik Barth, *Ethnic Groups and Boundaries: The Social Organization of Cultural Difference* (Boston, 1969), 9–38. See also William L. Yancey *et al.,* "Emergent Ethnicity: A Review and Reformulation," *American Sociological Review*, 41 (June 1976), 391–403; and Nathan Glazer and Daniel P. Moynihan, *Beyond the Melting Pot* (Cambridge, MA, 1963).

28. As always, the devil is in the details. Although varying groups could agree on broad—one might say platitudinous—ideals of "freedom" and "liberty," they came into conflict over how those rights might be used or what they meant. On the concept of "complementary identity," see Gjerde, *The Minds of the West*, 59–66; Peter A. Munch, "In Search of Identity: Ethnic Awareness and Ethnic Attitudes Among Scandinavian Immigrants, 1840–1860," in J. R. Christianson, ed., *Scandinavians in America: Literary Life*,

(Decorah, IA, 1985), 1–24; David M. Potter, "The Historian's Use of Nationalism and Vice Versa," in Potter, *History and American Society*, (New York, 1973), 74–75; and Morton Grodzins, *The Loyal and the Disloyal: Social Boundaries of Patriotism and Treason*, (Chicago, 1956).

29. "The strangest stories were told about America," wrote Svein Nilsson in 1868. "Some of the mountain people [of Norway] had heard that skippers often sold emigrants as slaves to the Turks." *A Chronicler of Immigrant Life: Svein Nilsson's Articles in Billed Magazin, 1868–1870*, trans. C. A. Clausen (Northfield, 1982).

30. Ole Rynning, *True Account of America*, trans. and ed. Theodore C. Blegen (Freeport, NY, 1971), 87.

31. Walter D. Kamphoefner *et al., News from the Land of Freedom: German Immigrants Write Home*, trans. Susan Carter Vogel (Ithaca, 1988), 356. The exact text: *die Sklavenhalten besitzen 3 Million Sklaven wovon vile weissen.*

32. Gottfried Duden, *Bericht über eine Reise nach den westlichen Staaten Nordamerikas* (1827), in *Report on a Journey to the Western States of North America and a Stay of Several Years Along the Missouri*, trans. James W. Goodrich *et al.* (Columbia, MO, 1980), 182–85. Elsewhere in his writings, Duden is more condemnatory of slavery. *Ibid.*, 105–17.

33. Letter written by Catharina Jonsdatter Rÿd, Mar. 15, 1856, cited in Werner Sollors, "How Americans Became White: Three Examples," in Ishmael Reed, ed., *MultiAmerica: Essays on Cultural Wars and Cultural Peace* (New York, 1998), 4. Exact quote: "*Ty här är hwit menniska fri.*"

34. Anna Maria Schano, in Kamphoefner *et al., News from the Lord of Freedom*, 539. Exact quote: *u. Was die Amerikaner anbelangt Weise u. Schwarze die thun ein auch nichts denn die Schwarzen sind [sehr] froh wenn mann ihn nichts thut, nur das einzige ist das bösse mit der Sprache.*

35. Gjert Gregorioussen Hovland, Apr. 22, 1835, in Theodore C. Blegen, "A Typical 'America' Letter," *Mississippi Valley Historical Review*, 9 (June 1922), 68–74 (my emphasis).

36. Kathleen Neils Conzen, "German-Catholic Communalism and the American Civil War: Exploring the Dilemmas of Transatlantic Political Integration," in Elisabeth Glaser-Schmidt and Hermann Wellenreuther, eds., *Bridging the Atlantic: Europe and the United States in Modern Times* (Cambridge, UK, forthcoming).

37. See E. Clifford Nelson and Eugene L. Fevold, *The Lutheran Church Among Norwegian-Americans* (2 vols., Minneapolis, 1960), I, 169–71; and Theodore C. Blegen, *Norwegian Migration to America: The American Transition* (Northfield, MN, 1940), 149.

38. The slavery controversy in the Norwegian Synod is ably described Blegen, *Norwegian Migration to America*, 418–53.

39. David Roediger, "The Pursuit of Whiteness: Property, Terror and Expansion, 1790–1860," in this book.

40. The child's baptism is noted in the Arendahl Lutheran Church records. See Jon Gjerde, *From Peasants to Farmers: The Migration from Balestrand, Norway to the Upper Middle West* (New York, 1985), 292.

41. See Kathleen Neils Conzen, "Pi-ing the Type: Jane Grey Swisshelm and the Contest of Midwestern Regionality," in Andrew Cayton and Susan Gray, eds., *The American Midwest: Essays on Regional History* (Bloomington, 2001) 91–110.

BIBLIOGRAPHY

Anbinder, Tyler. *Nativism and Slavery: The Northern Know-Nothings and the Politics of the 1850s.* New York: Oxford University Press, 1992.

Bennett, David H. *The Party of Fear: From Nativist Movements to the New Right in American History.* Chapel Hill: University of North Carolina Press, 1988.

Billington, Ray Allan. *The Protestant Crusade 1880–1860: A Study in the Origins of American Nativism.* New York: Macmillan, 1938.

Conzen, Kathleen. *Making Their Own America: Assimilation Theory and the German Peasant Pioneer.* New York: Berg, 1990.

Davis, David Brion. "Some Themes of Counter-Subversion: An Analysis of Anti-Masonic, Anti-Catholic, and Anti-Mormon Literature." *Mississippi Valley Historical Review,* 47 (1960): 205–24.

Franchot, Jenny. *Roads to Rome: The Antebellum Protestant Encounter with Catholicism.* Berkeley: University of California Press, 1994.

Gjerde, Jon. *The Minds of the West: Ethnocultural Evolution in the Rural Middle West, 1830–1917.* Chapel Hill: University of North Carolina Press, 1997.

Holt, Michael F. *The Political Crisis of the 1850s.* New York: Norton, 1978.

Ignatiev, Noel. *How the Irish Became White.* New York: Routledge, 1995.

Jacobson, Matthew Frye. *Whiteness of a Different Color: European Immigrants and the Alchemy of Race.* Cambridge: Harvard University Press, 1998.

Knobel, Dale T. *Paddy and the Republic: Ethnicity and Nationality in Antebellum America.* Middletown, Conn.: Wesleyan University Press, 1986.

Roediger, David. *The Wages of Whiteness: Race and the Making of the American Working Class.* New York: Routledge, 1991.

MONROVIA, LIBERIA.

This will Certify

that by a contribution of

dollars by is a member for *Life* of

the COLONIZATION SOCIETY

Secretary President

Early opponents of slavery thought to solve the "Negro problem" by colonizing freed slaves in West Africa. It was a program widely opposed by the free black community. *"Liberian Colonization Certificate" (Courtesy of Boston Athenaeum)*

Published by the American Anti-Slavery Society, the Liberty Bell challenged an
emerging racial essentialism by calling for a moral revolution. *"The Liberty Bell"*
(Courtesy of Library Company of Philadelphia)

James Forten, a prominent Philadelphia businessman, abolitionist, and black community leader, used his resources to educate "Young Black Artisans." *"James Forten" Leon Gardiner Collection (Courtesy of Library Company of Philadelphia)*

David Claypool Johnston's lithograph reflects whites' hostility to, and fear of, black Philadelphians who refused to remain in menial occupations. *"A Meeting of the Free & Independent Wood Sawyers, Boot Cleaners, Chimney Sweepers, Porters of Phila." David Claypool Johnston. (Courtesy of American Antiquarian Society)*

Edward Clay's satire neatly captures whites' contempt for black "respectability." *"Life in Philadelphia" Edward W. Clay. (Courtesy of Library Company of Philadelphia)*

Though supporters of white supremacy lampooned the potential personal consequences of racial equality, they feared that it might bring whites and blacks together sexually. *"Practical Amalgamation" Edward W. Clay. (Courtesy of Library Company of Philadelphia)*

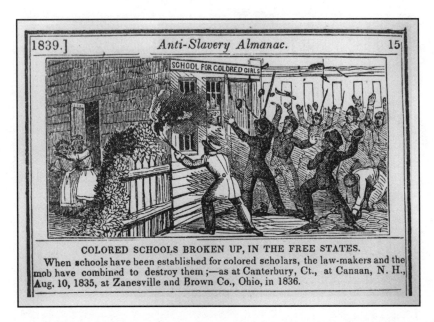

SCHOOL FOR COLORED GIRLS

COLORED SCHOOLS BROKEN UP, IN THE FREE STATES.

When schools have been established for colored scholars, the law-makers and the mob have combined to destroy them;—as at Canterbury, Ct., at Canaan, N. H., Aug. 10, 1835, at Zanesville and Brown Co., Ohio, in 1836.

African Americans desire for self-improvement and "uplift" were routinely met with white mob violence. *"Colored Schools Broken Up in the Free States" (Courtesy of Library Company of Philadelphia)*

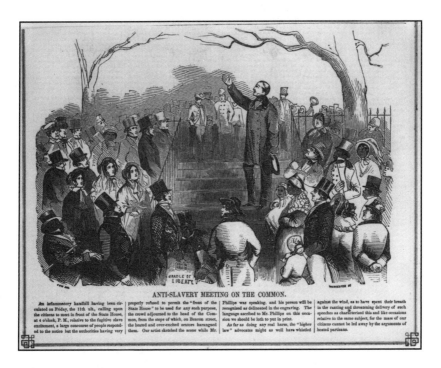

ANTI-SLAVERY MEETING ON THE COMMON.

An inflammatory handbill having been circulated on Friday, the 11th ult., calling upon the citizens to meet in front of the State House, at 4 o'clock, P. M., relative to the fugitive slave excitement, a large concourse of people responded to the notice but the authorities having very properly refused to permit the "front of the State House" to be used for any such purpose, the crowd adjourned to the head of the Common, from the steps of which, on Beacon street, the heated and over-excited orators harangued them. Our artist sketched the scene while Mr. Phillips was speaking, and his person will be recognised as delineated in the engraving. The language ascribed to Mr. Phillips on this occasion we should be loth to put in print. As far as doing any real harm, the "higher law" advocates might as well have whistled against the wind, as to have spent their breath in the ranting and threatening delivery of such speeches as characterized this and like occasions relative to the same subject, for the mass of our citizens cannot be led away by the arguments of heated partisans.

Wendell Phillips, like William Lloyd Garrison, devoted his life to abolition by challenging the mass-participation party politics that bolstered racism and the institution of slavery. *"Abolitionist Meeting on Boston Common." (Courtesy of Boston Athenaeum)*

Frederick Douglass's antislavery activism stands in stark counterpoint to Stephen Douglas's appeals for white supremacy. *"Frederick Douglass" (Courtesy of American Antiquarian Society)*

6

Modernizing "Difference": The Political Meanings of Color in the Free States, 1776–1840

James Brewer Stewart

As the decade of the 1830s opened, people living in the states "north of slavery" found themselves facing unprecedented dangers and opportunities that resulted from rapidly accumulating racial tensions. As crises multiplied, headlines of that time (even in generic form) conveyed their enormity and potential for violence—Nullification Spirit Sweeps South Carolina—Jackson Demands Cherokee Removal—Slaves Revolt and Murder in Southampton County Virginia—Walker's *Appeal* Found Among Southern Negroes—Garrison Demands Race Amalgamation—Abolitionists Gather Women and Negroes in Promiscuous Assemblies—Mobs Attack Negro Neighborhoods. At no previous time in the history of the "free states" did so many racially charged events overtake one another in such rapid succession. Never before were assumptions about the proper dynamics of "race relations" so suddenly and so heavily questioned, revisioned, and defended. Only during Reconstruction, or later still, during the post-World War II Civil Rights Movement, would people experience trauma more drastic than that which swept the free states in the late 1820s and early 1830s. And only in these much more recent struggles would the trajectory of history so suddenly open similar possibilities for democratic change, for brutal repression, and for new political understandings of what skin color differences ought to mean.

This essay seeks to explain what deeper historical developments led the North to this sudden conjuncture in the late 1820s and early 1830s, what its specific dynamics were, and how its long-term influence reshaped and reinforced the power of "race" to define the modernizing political culture of the free states before the Civil War. Before this watershed moment, from 1790 until around 1830, society in the North, though suffused with prejudice, nevertheless fostered a surprisingly open premodern struggle over claims of "respectability" and citizenship put forward by many social groups, and particularly by free African Americans. This effort to achieve respectability, in turn, stimulated deepening internal and external divisions among people of differing skin colors, and finally promoted the unprecedented interracialism of a nascent immediate abolitionist movement. By the opening of the 1830s, the compounding effect of these volatile contests had frayed the social fabric of free states to the point of disintegration. Then came Walker's *Appeal*, Turner's insurrection, South Carolina's nullification crisis, and, above all, Garrison's *Liberator*. When this publication announced that abolitionists—black and white, male and female—were embarking on a crusade for racial equality, the impact of this extraordinary venture transmuted the North's accumulating racial tensions into a general crisis that exploded into mob violence across the free states.[1]

By the late 1830s, as the mobs dispersed African-American neighborhoods and the beleaguered victims began to rebuild their lives, views of racial order had changed dramatically for practically everyone in the North. The abolitionists' first struggles to secure racial equality had instead spawned an unprecedented upheaval among the vast majority of whites in the free states that solidified into an unmovable political consensus of highly ordered white supremacy. "Color lines" that had hitherto been so sharply contested around conflicting claims of "respectability" now had become indelibly drawn. Nearly impossible to revise, they were buttressed by a system of democratic white politics premised on the modern assumption that "nature" had always divided "black" and "white" as inferior and superior, and always must. By the mid-1830s, just as the nation's system of mass participation two-party politics began to take hold, this harsh new spirit of modern racial essentialism was becoming all-pervasive. It obliterated in turn earlier relationships based on deference and "respectability" while profoundly reshaping the fundamental outlooks of even those who would continue to struggle for racial equality. In all these respects, the white North had emerged into an age of racial modernity, an era much more closely resembling the white supremacist tyranny of the late nineteenth century than the interracial contestation and alliance-building of the decades between 1776 and 1830. Moreover, protest movements contesting this new state of affairs much more resembled the racial activism of the twentieth century than they did those of the postrevolutionary era. How this crisis developed, why it concluded as it did, and what its implications were for the North's sectionalizing political system are the questions this essay seeks to answer.

The premodern racial landscapes of the early republican North gave few suggestions of the monumental upheavals that lay ahead. To be clear, deep-rooted racial prejudice was much in evidence as the dismantling of northern slavery ran its tortuous course after 1776. Far too many of those emancipated remained ensnared in restrictive apprenticeships, and too many more continued their enslavement until reaching ages required by manumission laws. All found themselves being pushed into a rapidly segregating and unequal social order by strengthening customs and newly enacted statutes. Churches that had once included African Americans now isolated or expelled them. Parades and festivals that had once been purposefully multiracial affairs now proceeded for the benefit of whites only. Court dockets and jail registers listed disproportionately high percentages of people of color.[2]

But from African Americans' perspectives, such trends fired ambitious visions even as they blighted immediate hopes. To the first generation of free African-American leaders, racial boundaries in the early republican North were detestably unfair, but it remained unproven that they could not be contested and redrawn. As a result, initiatives multiplied as the new century opened—Paul Cuffee launched an extraordinary quest to create an Africa-based, transatlantic, commercial empire. His kinsman, James Easton, developed an ambitious manual labor school for African-American youth at his foundry outside Boston. James Forten also reached outward to Africa while using his remunerative sail loft in Philadelphia to educate young black artisans. Forten's collaborator, Bishop Richard Allen, turned his single congregation into the nursery of an entire denomination, the African Methodist Episcopal Zion Church. New York City's John Teasman successfully promoted tax-supported schools to serve African Americans. Boston's Prince Hall dreamed of returning to Africa, but witnessed instead the spread of his idea of uniting free people of color under the banner of Freemasonry.[3]

For all the variety of their plans and visions, these early leaders drew common inspiration from the prospect of free people of color "uplifting" themselves to conditions of "respectability," an approach to securing equality that stressed patient incrementalism, strenuous self-improvement, deference from ordinary community members, and the guidance of patriarchal leaders. Such aspirations permitted free African Americans to build autonomous institutions that nurtured their sense of themselves as both "African" and "American," and which acted as "uplifting" agencies by which they could interject their egalitarian voices into the nation's political discussions. Persuasive historical analysis, such as that presented in this book by Joanne Pope Melish, has pinpointed the strengths and weaknesses of this approach: it was vital to giving free blacks a sense of cultural solidarity and achievement when facing a hostile white world, but it also deflected primary responsibility for improving "race relations" away from bigoted whites while conveying the fatal impression that African Americans, in their "non-uplifted" state, were, indeed, a "degraded people." But whatever the costs and gains, Cuffe, Easton, Allen, and the others had every incentive to embrace the goals of "uplift" and "respectability" as the 1800s opened.[4]

The strongest of these imperatives, to build solid communities where none had existed, compelled these early leaders to place stern demands on their neighbors and on themselves. Progress against discrimination, they insisted, required unflagging efforts by each to "uplift" all by living lives of "respectability" by striving to embrace piety, practice thrift and temperance, comport one's self with well-mannered dignity, and seek all advantage that education offered. Far from registering "white middle class" values, the distinguished "men of color" who set forth these daunting expectations registered a distinctly premodern African-American style of Federalist-era deference politics when giving direction to their own "lesser orders." Their didactic pronouncements responded to the consequences of slave emancipation that made community-building so difficult after 1776, namely, the streams of former slaves from the North, the South, and the Caribbean that flowed into northern cities, and the hostile critiques of whites who increasingly defined these congregating free people of color as an innately "turbulent, degraded race" that merited segregation and surveillance.

In the face of these obstacles, proponents of "uplift" and "respectability" succeeded magnificently in shaping ethnically diverse groups of urban transients into enduring communities. In so doing, they automatically rebutted imputations that blacks constituted a "degraded race" by empowering those very African Americans to demonstrate cultural parity with whites of the highest attainment, to scorn "degraded" slaveholders and racial bigots as inferiors, and to give the lie to those who judged all dark-skinned people by the behavior of a "degenerate" few. To live "respectably" also constituted an assertion of free African-American "manhood" and citizenship. It was a demonstration of personal independence embraced by males when protecting and directing their families, which was exactly what enslaved men throughout the South were presumably prevented from doing. Above all, "respectability" connoted the possession of the intellectual and literary skills necessary to allow African Americans to contribute their own authoritative political voices as equals to the nation's ongoing civic discussions. In sum, "respectability" initially expressed the free black elites' deepest abolitionist values.[5]

Judged by the impressive number of churches, schools, and benevolent associations they established by the 1820s, the accomplishments of these "uplifting" leaders were by any measure extraordinary, and the painstaking work of ordinary people all the more so. Yet the price that these successes exacted from many free African Americans was heavy, often requiring drastic alterations of identity and allegiance. Numerous members of "multiracial" families with bloodlines that had mixed African, Indian, and Euro-American ancestors

(Eastons and Cuffes prominent among them) now chose in the name of "respectability" to identify themselves as African Americans and, as a result, to allow themselves to be identified as members of the "Negro race," a rapidly compounding aggregate of ostracized dark-skinned peoples of differing origins and genealogies. Left behind in their quests for "respectability" were indigenous traditions that had stressed communal sharing and the suppression of individualism, qualities inimical to the progressive assumptions of "uplift." The embrace of "uplift" also exacted a second, related loss, the disintegration of traditional definitions of the "turbulent rabble" that had regulated social relations throughout the eighteenth century. In this earlier setting, as Lois Horton explains in her contribution to this collection, the inclusion of dark-skinned people in the ethnically diverse "lower orders" had served to inhibit naked repression exclusively against black people and fostered multicultural alliances among the poor of a variety of skin colors. But by the opening of the new century, these plebeian connections were beginning to unravel across the North as people of many backgrounds became increasingly caught up in a harsher regime of "race relations" in which the values of "respectability" began exerting greater influence over the minds of Anglo-Americans.[6]

For black New England's elite leaders, the implications of these developments were inescapable. Perforce, they must now undertake their own struggles for "uplift" in order to secure the future "respectability" of their (ever more stringently defined) "race." Though interracial alliances still remained, by the 1800s they involved only the haphazard patronage of individual philanthropists at the apex of the social order—elite Quakers, British reformers, and Federalist scions. Never again would support be found among a mass of poor Euro-Americans. Black Yankees, in short, had no choice but to begin pouring the resources of their "race" into programs that secured their claims to equality by "uplifting" themselves and their neighbors. Little wonder, given these circumstances, that while the Eastons, Fortens, and Allens despised this racial order, they also maintained that they could challenge and reshape it by promoting "respectability." Their impressive personal histories of accomplishment and recognition certainly suggested just how mutable "race relations" actually were and gave them little choice but to believe that a pious, energetic people could, with God's help, incrementally change those relations for the better.[7]

By choosing this course of action, free African Americans joined an intense and highly divisive race for "respectability" that set them against a formidable variety of Euro-American competitors. For white northerners from many walks of life in the early nineteenth century the claim of "respectability" came to serve similar functions as it did for African Americans. It valued and gave value to the achievements of piety, refinement, learning, and political engagement far above one's measurable economic position in a time of deepening inequality. As manufacturing, commerce, personal consumption, and class distinctions reshaped urban life in the North, so did rapid immigration from the British Isles and Western Europe. As a result, divisions grew between hard-pressed wage earners and an increasingly affluent middle class, as did ethnic tensions between long-settled Yankees and immigrants and even between newly arrived ethnic groups themselves. To assert one's "respectability" in the face of such deepening rifts meant insisting that workers and immigrants, rural no less than urban, could overcome foreign and plebean origins and claim parity with all other citizens. It also offered "ordinary" people the hope of upward mobility and republican equality, thanks to the strength of their moral character. From the wealthy, it required philanthropic effort to "uplift" the less fortunate who needed education and the benefits of sound morals in order to contribute to the nation's political life.

The race to attain "respectability," in short, seemed to promise cultural and political remedies for multiplying class divisions, ethnic conflicts, stresses of acculturation, and feelings of personal alienation. Equality was presumably attainable to all the "uplifted," whatever their occupation, income, ethnic group, or, as a Forten or an Easton would add emphatically, skin color. But as this contest unfolded it only intensified the very conflicts that it was presumed to mitigate. As a result, by the opening of the 1820s, people throughout the North found themselves engaged in ever more violent disagreements over how racial boundaries ought to be drawn to accord with conflicting claims of "respectability," citizenship, and heightening color consciousness. As Jon Gjerde explains in his contribution to this collection, this compulsion to embrace "whiteness" and "respectability" was strongly felt even among new immigrants in the rural North, people well removed from African-American population centers, but well-aware of "Indian Country" when formulating their initial claims to republican citizenship.[8]

These heightening senses of racial identity among whites and mounting inclinations among free blacks to push across racial boundaries increasingly influenced day-to-day urban life in the North in the early nineteenth century. For example, lower-class men, blacks and whites alike, now formulated understandings of the meaning of "respectability" that were very much in conflict with those of their social "betters." Plebeian blacks and whites quickly developed the habit of mixing in grog houses, cellar bistros, oyster houses, and lottery stalls, all elements of street culture that ran deeply counter to elites' "uplifting" values. Yet this was hardly a return to the interracial fraternization among the "lower orders" of prerevolutionary days. Instead, the situation fostered hostility between working men of differing skin colors over the preservation of "manly self-respect." Working-class whites now exhibited a volatile ambivalence toward African-American culture when they burlesqued it in black-faced minstrel shows, even as they also patronized black prostitutes, applauded black musicians, and drank their fill in black speakeasies. Now encountering the traumas of industrial labor, these white male wage earners, many of them immigrants, feared the "blackness" of those with whom they mingled as symbolic of their own personal "degradation." Such feelings in turn spurred their desires for emotional catharsis, and became an excuse for aggressive assertions of "manly self-respect." Street corner tensions deepened as black men responded with assertive behavior of their own, which fused assertions of gendered identity with those of color.[9]

Meanwhile, on the opposite end of the social spectrum, genteel white philanthropists and public officials who espoused colonizationism also blurred racial boundaries and fostered contention over claims of male "respectability" by inviting African-American elites to join them as "gentlemen" in "uplifting" the nation's free blacks. Through their American Colonization Society they proposed to "elevate" free African Americans from oppressive white bigotry by subsidizing their voluntary emigration to the West Africa colony of Liberia. But rather than cementing biracial cooperation among gentlemanly "respectables," this proposition prompted the black elites, including those truly interested in African resettlement, to mobilize their communities against the colonizationists. They denounced colonizationists in an unprecedented outpouring of pamphlets, speeches, sermons, and "indignation meetings" as "degraded" white conspirators who aimed to drive "upstanding" free people of color into exile. Here, in fact, were the first stirrings of both a formally organized elite black abolitionist movement and of a clearly identified "respectable" white opposition to it.[10]

On every social level, then, from barrooms to church meeting halls, the continuing efforts of African Americans to put themselves forward as equals provoked deepening racial resistance from whites preoccupied with their own pursuits of "manliness" and "respectability." When, for example, African-American men began staging marches commemorating their two most meaningful political events—northern emancipation and Haitian Independence—whites lampooned them in handbills and showered them with epithets and rocks, scorning their assertion that a citizen's right to the streets belonged as much to African Americans as to anyone. Even the very landmarks that bespoke the elites' successes in promoting "uplift" now served as catalysts for compounding white resentment. Whites rightly regarded the handsome new churches, meeting halls, and school buildings as both symbols of African-American communities' high aspirations and as agencies for amplifying the voices of its "uplifted" preachers, pamphleteers, and social activists. Consequently, white harassment increasingly marred Sabbath observances and school-day activities, and the buildings themselves became the targets of the earliest race riots that first erupted in the early and mid-1820s in Boston, New Haven, Providence, Pittsburgh, and Philadelphia.[11]

These violent episodes, unsettling in their own right, were actually skirmishes in a sustained assault against free blacks that gathered strength throughout the North in the 1820s. In the political sphere, state legislatures took the lead, and by late in the decade every one of them had either seriously debated or passed legislation that placed new restrictions on African Americans' voting rights, legal standing, and freedom of migration. To complete this sweeping confirmation of free blacks' ever more uniform "degradation," every legislature also enacted universal male suffrage for whites—the ultimate recognition of masculine social acceptability. The popular mandate supporting this legislation expressed fully in the North's newly emerging mass print culture, where cartoonists and editors found limitless audiences for woodcuts and sketches that demeaned African Americans in nearly every manner conceivable. By ridiculing blacks' physiognomy as simian, their speech as pidgin dialect, and all their attempts at "respectability" as outlandishly grotesque, these cartoons confirmed just how forceful free African-American activists had been in pursuing their goals, how much their successes at pushing through racial barriers had unsettled public culture, and how determined whites now were to suppress all such "uplifting" endeavors. What had begun in the 1790s as a quest for equality by "uplifted" African Americans was evolving by the late 1820s into a white crusade against free blacks in general. That such a crusade licensed terrorism became obvious when whites in Cincinnati launched vicious attacks on their black neighbors in 1829, leaving several hundred homeless and driving an undetermined number into exile in Canada.[12]

Among free blacks, such horrifying events evoked an understandable mixture of fear, anger, and alienation. Some elite leaders explored emigrating to Haiti or Upper Canada. Others speculated that violence-prone white Americans must have sprung from corrupted European origins and compared them to patiently struggling blacks who surely carried the legacy of culturally superior African beginnings. Nearly all responded warmly to the passionate writings of David Walker, whose extraordinary *Appeal* was published in 1829. In it he scorned the efficacy of African-American "uplift" without militant self-transformation, condemned colonization in unusually sweeping terms, and called for black people to defend their rights by force when necessary. The angry African Americans in several cities who protested the recapture of fugitives by hurling paving stones at whites obviously saw matters much as Walker did. Torn between the questionable alternatives of armed resistance, quiet submission, or self-exile, free blacks in the North faced a terrible impasse as the 1830s opened.[13]

Given these circumstances, the sudden appearance in 1831 of a militant white abolitionist movement must have seemed a godsend to free black leaders for, as crises deepened for free African Americans, racial tension erupted nationally as well. In South Carolina, militant planters courted civil war when they demanded the right to "nullify" on behalf of slavery. A massive slave insurrection in Jamaica, Nat Turner's rebellion in Virginia, and the discovery of Walker's *Appeal* in the possession of southern blacks stimulated premonitions among whites of an impending race war. As James Ronda reminds us in his contribution to this book, President Andrew Jackson's crusade to remove the Cherokee Nation linked racialized state coercion with mass expulsion in an unprecedented fashion. To African-American activists and white abolitionists, this only cast the American Colonization movement in a still more ominous light. Little wonder, therefore, that when Garrison and his associates, encouraged by activist African Americans, pledged to unmask that society, to promote equality for the North's free blacks, and to demand slavery's immediate abolition, the black elite responded enthusiastically. Yet in light of the increasingly volatile, gender-focused racial contentiousness of the late 1820s, compounded now by nullifiers and insurrectionists, it is impossible to imagine any event more disruptive than the sudden appearance of a biracial abolitionist movement that included women as well as men. Never before had struggles over racial boundaries and the masculine attributes of "respectability" carried such potential for violence as they did in 1831, when white Garrisonians invited people of all skin colors and both genders to crusade to "uplift" the free black community in the North and hasten the end of southern slavery.

Viewed from this perspective, the white men who mobbed abolitionists and terrorized black neighborhoods until the latter 1830s should be understood as having been absolutely correct when decrying their victims as racial "amalgamationists." For these new white abolitionists, "respectability" constituted a highly charged interracial imperative that black and white reformers, female as well as male, must collaborate to "uplift" northern African Americans into a racially inclusive middle class. This, they maintained, was essential to their overarching goal of obliterating caste oppression in all of its forms. To the men of the African-American elite, on the other hand, the prospect of an alliance with fellow "Christian gentlemen" such as Garrison, Lewis Tappan, and William Jay relieved their terrible impasse. Here, with unprecedented white assistance, was a unique opportunity once again to take action against white supremacism while recommitting their communities to the quest for "respectability."[14]

Whatever their motives, white and black abolitionists shared the revolutionary belief that African Americans had every right to speak the harshest truth to their "unregenerate" oppressors and to "rise" to social equality as rap-idly as possible. For this reason African-American authors were heavily fea-tured in white abolitionists' publications, an abrupt and unprecedentedly forceful intervention by African Americans into the nation's "marketplace of ideas." Meanwhile, white reformers also made unprecedented interventions by becoming deeply involved in renewed African-American campaigns of community "uplift" that blossomed in the early 1830s. They eagerly wel-comed African Americans into their rapidly multiplying antislavery societies and roundly denounced "colorphobia" among whites as supremely sinful and ignorant. But to the vast majority of northern white men in this already po-larized racial order, the very idea that blacks and whites of both genders would presume to "elevate" free African Americans to equal middle-class sta-tus and dictate morality to Euro-Americans "beneath" them meant unspeak-able "degradation." As prominent colonizationists, leading politicians, and ordinary day laborers prepared for mob action, it was clear to all but the abo-litionists themselves that their entrance into the highly contested race for "re-spectability" guaranteed the rapid suppression of the movement.

A survey of the antiabolitionist violence that tore through practically every major northern city and so many smaller towns amply confirms this truth. In nearly all of these thoroughly studied events, mob activity from 1831 to 1838 was triggered initially by a highly visible action that abolitionists regarded as part of their "respectable" promotion of African-American "uplift," but which whites of all classes abominated as degrading racial and sexual "amalgama-tionism": proposals for manual labor schools for black youths in New Haven, Connecticut, and in Canaan and Dover, New Hampshire; attempts to estab-lish academies for young African-American women in Canterbury, Connecti-cut, and in Cincinnati and Zanesville, Ohio; the "promiscuous" gatherings of abolitionists of both races and genders in public meeting halls in Boston, Utica, Pittsburgh, and New York City; and the "amalgamated" funding and leadership involved in building Philadelphia's Free Speech Hall. Equally pre-dictable were the specific targets of mob action—abolitionists of both races and genders whose pretenses to "respectability" had to be violently obliter-ated, and African-American neighborhoods, those magnets of "vice" and "debasement," where racial boundaries and white identities had been con-tested and compromised far too long.[15]

The complementary roles played throughout the rioting by white men on opposite ends of the social order were also consistent. As urban workers tore into black neighborhoods and shut down abolitionists' meetings, prominent businessmen, politicians, and editors, many of them colonizationists, con-demned the abolitionists as instigators of the riots, deploring only the mobs' "excesses." As abolitionists remarked at the time and as modern scholarship has since confirmed, the lower-class "tail" of urban white society worked easily with those at its "head" as both rich and poor whites drew from the cathartic violence an unprecedented sense of their brotherhood as *the* dominating "race." Theirs was a profoundly heightened activist identity that quickly expressed itself at the ballot box as well as in the streets.[16]

In retrospect, it seems all but inevitable that the abolitionists' drive for racially "respectable" inclusiveness would be overwhelmed by the growth of modern, white supremacist two-party politics. The spread of mob violence and the development of the second party system quickly linked rioters, their apologists, party spokesmen, and voters in common electoral purposes. Historians have long recognized the close relationship between the rise of universal white manhood suffrage and the systematic suppression of free African-Americans' rights. As part of this process, they have also stressed the northern Democratic Party's success in the 1830s in uniting its northern constituents through endorsements of bigotry and mob activity. Less understood, but equally important, was the northern Whigs' transformation of colonizationism from a poorly funded voluntary association into a major component in their party's ideology of "race." Throughout the early and mid-1830s, while many free state Democrats endorsed racial violence, northern Whig editors and party leaders generally mixed condemnations of abolitionist "amalgamationism" and working class "mob rule" with praise for the temperate statesmanship of Henry Clay, Edward Everett, and Daniel Webster, colonizationism's most prominent political spokesmen. In 1840 and 1844, when the national Whig party nominated presidential candidates, it was no accident that its choices were planter/colonizationists William Henry Harrison and Henry Clay.

By adopting this strategy, northern Whigs found an effective means of distinguishing their positions on issues of slavery and "race" from those of northern Democrats while satisfying fundamental rules that both parties obeyed—intersectional harmony and white supremacist solidarity. Though some Whigs like Clay believed deeply in voluntary emigration, most in the North who endorsed colonization were simply contrasting their party's new distinctive formulation of white supremacist politics to that of their Democratic opposition by stressing that free African Americans, ideally, should be "sent back to Africa." Their own allegiance to "whiteness" thus established, northern Whigs were free to attack their free-state Democratic opponents in sectional terms by condemning them as "tools" of southern planters because of their promotion of riots and their support for suppressing antislavery petitions in Congress. These tactics, however, did not undermine their party's unity, since southern Whigs appreciated the deeper support for slavery and white supremacy that underlay them, as well as the fact that they strengthened the party's overall performance against the Democrats in national elections.[17]

Despite this approach, the Whig party had to accommodate the supporters of maverick politicians such as John Quincy Adams and Joshua R. Giddings, who genuinely did hate slavery and its incursions on "northern rights" and who were truly disturbed by the plight of dark-skinned Americans. Soon too, strong criticisms also surfaced from a handful of antiabolitionist northern Democrats like Benjamin Tappan who nevertheless despised "aristocratic" slave holders and advocated the rights of their "chattel laborers" to freedom. In this respect, two-party racial politics ultimately stimulated authentic disagreements over the status of African Americans that wove themselves into conflicts over slavery's westward expansion. But in the meantime, the Democrats' blunt appeals to "white manhood" and the Whigs' more polished espousals of colonization conveyed identical conclusions regarding the newly modernized political meanings of color in the North. No matter how estimable their qualities or accomplishments, free African Americans had to be denied their claims of equal "respectability" and to be treated categorically as an "inferior race." Voters, in turn, had to express their party allegiances in terms of "white identity politics," rejecting all that was symbolized by both "abolitionism" and the possession of dark skin. Considering these precedents, it is little wonder that in later years northern free soil ideology and white racial bigotry were so often to become intertwined in the political crises leading to civil war.[18]

As their travails continued into the later 1830s, Garrison and his white associates also developed a quite new and unmistakably more modern understandings of racial identity and the political meaning of skin color. During the height of racial violence, all agreed that their crusade could no longer sustain its struggle for black "respectability." Especially in urban areas, abolitionists' efforts of racial "uplift" abruptly halted. The "moral bankruptcy" of their own white "race" caused these reversals, they now concluded; the sins of black enslavement in the South had now been shown to be powerfully reinforced by equally heinous crimes of politically mobilized whites throughout the free states. And as Garrison and his white coworkers reflected further, they also understood how deeply alienated they had become not only from the unrepentant slave holders in the South, but also from the vast majority of their fellow northern whites.[19]

The schisms that shattered white abolitionism in 1840 had many causes, but basic among them were deep disagreements over what these reformers believed was required of them now that they had become so self-consciously estranged from the white North. All concurred that their efforts must now be redirected to transforming the white majority's "corrupted" values, and as a result, for the first time in the nation's history, a white social movement put highest priority on wholesale ideological opposition to the northern racial prejudice of its own "race" rather than on attempting to lessen it by assisting free blacks to "rise." But almost immediately, white abolitionists also began articulating irreconcilable versions of their own "identity politics" as they disagreed over how best to challenge white supremacy in some fundamental way. As discord deepened, it became clear that their trials by violence had deeply altered their understandings of the political meanings of color in the North.[20]

To Garrison and his supporters, only a comprehensive espousal of women's rights, religious perfectionism, and nonresistance—the moral antipodes of mobs and mass parties—could inspire the transformation of "corrupted" majority values. To many of Garrison's opponents, however, it was the North's white voters, "enslaved" to the Whigs and Democrats, who must be morally liberated, and this could only be done by founding an emancipationist Liberty party. But beneath these controversies, serious as they were, lay the deeper acceptance by all parties that their overriding political challenges arose from bigoted constructions of "whiteness" that inspired mob rule and political repression within the free states. Both factions, in other words, now sought the liberation of the entire black population by overthrowing the North's newly organized white supremacist polity. No longer fixated on interracial "respectability," they were now eager to seek categorical equality for all northern blacks, "uplifted" or not, by challenging their own white "race."[21]

For Liberty Party members this objective required a concentrated effort in culturally homogenous rural areas such as Ohio's Western Reserve, western Massachusetts, and New York State's "Burned-Over District" where blacks and immigrants were few, where evangelical Yankees dominated, and where abolitionist sympathizers could be rallied to challenge the two major parties on egalitarian grounds. For Garrisonians it meant the wholesale condemnation of fellow whites of all institutions that nurtured "unregenerate" bigotry: religious denominations, electoral processes, courts of law, the constabulary, and the Federal Union itself. But whatever the particular strategy, behind it lay the white abolitionists' shared imperatives to pursue categorical equality for all black people by attacking white society for its uniform racial bigotry rather than by promoting the "uplifting" of individual African Americans.

Black activists, very predictably, adamantly embraced this agenda, and by 1840 were developing new political approaches that anticipated struggles for racial equality more familiar to our time. Utterly convinced by this time that equality could never be "respectability's" reward, African-American activists now embraced racial independence. As they did, these reformers helped to inaugurate a recognizable antecedent of the modern civil rights movement, for their stress was now on independent black leadership, mass participation, the development of distinctive black ideologies, and the importance of political coalition-building. Speaking no longer as individual exemplars of "uplift," they instead saw themselves as architects of a militant black movement that could ally with white reformers without compromising their own distinctive ends.

As a result, by the opening of the 1840s, broad-based interracial collaborations multiplied. In states where black men could vote, for example, African-American abolitionists worked with the white-led Liberty Party by campaigning and casting ballots for emancipationist candidates while simultaneously helping to build abolitionist constituencies. In certain states they also joined with sympathetic whites to agitate for color-blind male suffrage and the repeal of discriminatory "black codes," activities unthinkable in the 1820s and 1830s. Coalitions also developed between African-American activists and white Garrisonians that reflected an equally modern spirit. These alliances engaged in epochal battles against segregated schools and public facilities, which mobilized black communities for sustained periods while white reformers also played prominent roles. Henceforth until at least 1861, when black and white abolitionists worked together, it was invariably as a collaboration between members of distinct "races" united in the cause of unconditionally equal treatment for all African Americans, not as an alliance of "respectables," intent on incremental programs of melioration. Thus did abolitionists both black and white become egalitarian practitioners of modern racial politics, a fitting reversal of the essentialist white supremacist principles embraced in the 1830s by Whigs and Democrats when first inaugurating mass participation politics.[22]

Having moved in this fashion beyond the traumas of white supremacist politics, abolitionists also opened path-breaking ideological debates during the 1840s and 1850s that sustained the movement's vitality, deepened its radicalism, and documented its transformation into a recognizably modern enterprise. A simple listing of the topics that prompted their ideological disagreements goes far to suggest just how far these crusaders had evolved from their original commitments to "uplift," and just how closely their outlooks prefigured more recent struggles for racial equality: the conflicting values of racial integration and black separatism; the problems of racial bias and cultural antagonism between black and white egalitarians; the necessities and perils of pacifism and political violence; the contested positions of women, black and white, in a movement dominated by men; the multiple meanings of "Africa," emigrationism, and "pan-African" identity for African Americans; the debatable equation of the rights of citizenship with the imperatives of social justice. In the process, abolitionists clearly began recognizing some of the deeper complexities of color, gender, and cultural and class difference that David Roediger discusses in this collection when demonstrating the pertinence of critical race theory to the historiography of "whiteness."[23]

When Donald Yacovone, a talented historian of abolitionism, observed to this writer that "there is no controversy in today's struggle for racial justice that the abolitionists failed to address before the Civil War," he wisely identified why these now long-dead reformers continue to have so much to tell the generations of scholars who study them. Indeed, the abolitionists' presence has become inescapable in our historical vocabulary as we continue to struggle over the political meanings of color. On the most general level, representations of Frederick Douglass, Harriet Tubman, and Sojourner Truth join those of Martin Luther King and Malcolm X to dominate elementary and secondary curriculum. At the opposite end of the academic continuum, contemporary historiography, that extraordinary explosion of scholarship on abolitionism in all its varieties, now reverberates far beyond departments of history. It is a "supernova" of research and analysis radiating across the humanities that as often inspires professors of literary and cultural studies to excel in the historian's craft as it compels historians, as Roediger urges in his essay, to pioneer in interdisciplinary endeavor. In every academic setting abolitionism speaks at least as urgently to as many today as it did to the "neo-abolitionist" feelings of scholars and civil rights activists in the 1960s.[24]

In the last analysis, this contemporary sense of the abolitionists' immediacy best demonstrates just how modern their racial politics actually became after 1840. By the opening of that decade they had lived through the terrible process that had forged democratic white supremacy's "iron cages." While *herrenvolk* democracy was being built in the North on the wreckage of the abolitionists' hopes for immediate abolition and the "elevation" of "respectable" African Americans, their responses inaugurated an ever-compounding challenge to white supremacy even as civil war drew closer. Moreover, they mounted these challenges, as Lacy K. Ford Jr. makes clear in his essay, when facing a white South increasingly united by its own successful modernization of white supremacist political culture. From 1840 onward, therefore, abolitionists' immediate victories were rare and equivocal. Yet it is also difficult to deny that during this same period they did, indeed, strip white supremacism of its intellectual pretension, claims of moral sanction, and unchallenged power to shape social relations, thereby setting precedents and standards that continue to furnish some of our most compelling historical references. Had they chosen otherwise, the impoverishment of our efforts to convey the moral challenges of our history is easy to estimate. All we need do is imagine the duration of our silence.

NOTES

1. I wish to thank the following colleagues and friends for their critical contributions to the development of this essay: Dickson D. Bruce, Peter Hinks, James O. Horton, Lois

Horton, Carol Lasser, Joanne Pope Melish, Michael A. Morrison, Gary Nash, Rich Newman, George Price, Patrick Rael, Jean Soderlund, Clay Steinman, Dorothy C. Stewart,
Ronald Walters, and Donald Yacovone. It is also important to acknowledge the influence
of the burgeoning scholarship on racial "formation," with its emphasis that meanings of
skin color difference involve shifting ideological formulations and social relations. In this
regard, the title of this article, "Modernizing Difference," registers the idea that the role of
race in the political development of the early republic is best understood as a set of rapidly
evolving, conflicting ideological expressions by specific social groups over at least three
decades that heavily determined the development of the North's two-party system and of
the abolitionist movement as well. For discussions of this theme and methodology in current historiography, consult David R. Roediger, *The Wages of Whiteness: Race and the
Making of the American Working Class* (London, UK, 1991); Alexander Saxton, *The Rise
and Fall of the White Republic: Class, Politics and Mass Culture in Nineteenth Century
America* (New York, 1990); Joanne Pope Melish, *Disowning Slavery: Gradual Emancipation and the North, 1780–1860* (Ithaca, 1998); Stuart Hall, ed., *Representation: Cultural
Representations and Signifying Practices* (London, UK, 1997), 225–97; and Barbara J.
Fields, "Ideology and Race in American History," in J. Morton Kousser and James M.
McPherson, eds., *Region, Race and Reconstruction: Essays in Honor of C. Vann Wood-
ward* (New York, 1982), 143–78. As regards the present book, consult the introductory essay by Roediger that addresses the specific pertinence of cultural studies scholarship on
race to the history of the early republic: "The Pursuit of Whiteness: Property, Terror, and
Expansion, 1790–1860."

2. The literature describing the ending of northern slavery, the consolidation of free
black communities, and the development of white supremacist social practices includes,
James O. Horton and Lois Horton, *In Hope of Liberty: Culture, Community, and Protest
Among Northern Free Blacks, 1700–1860* (New York, 1997); Gary B. Nash, *Forging Free-
dom: The Formation of Philadelphia's Black Community, 1720–1840* (New York, 1991);
Graham Hodges, *Slavery and Freedom in the Rural North: African Americans in Mon-
mouth County, New Jersey, 1665–1865* (Madison, WI, 1997); Julie Winch, *Philadelphia's
Black Elite: Activism, Accommodation and the Struggle for Autonomy, 1787–1848*
(Philadelphia, 1988); Leonard P. Curry, *The Free Black in Urban America, 1800–1850:
The Shadow of a Dream* (Chicago, 1981); and Shane White, *Somewhat More Independent:
The End of Slavery in New York City 1770–1810* (Athens, GA, 1991).

3. See Carol V. R. George, *Segregated Sabbaths: Richard Allen and the Rise of Inde-
pendent Black Churches, 1760–1840* (1973, rep., Athens, GA, 1991); George R. Price and
James Brewer Stewart, *To Heal the Scourge of Prejudice: The Life and Writings of Hosea
Easton* (Amherst, 1999); Nash, *Forging Freedom*; Robert J. Swan, "John Teasman:
African-American Educator and the Emergence of Community in Early Black New York,"
Journal of the Early Republic, 12 (Fall 1992), 331–56; and Lamont D. Thomas, *Paul
Cuffe: Black Entrepreneur and Pan-Africanist* (Urbana, 1986).

4. See works cited in the previous note, and Gary Nash, *Race and Revolution* (Madison, WI, 1990), 57–87. For discussions of the strengths and weaknesses of "uplift" and
"respectability" in various formulations of free African-American ideology see in the present book Joanne Pope Melish, "The 'Condition' Debate and Racial Discourse in the Antebellum North"; Kevin Gaines, *Uplifting the Race: Black Leadership, Culture and Politics
in the Twentieth Century* (Chapel Hill, 1996), 17–91; and Horton and Horton, *In Hope of
Liberty*, 125–54.

5. This paragraph and that preceding it are based on James Oliver Horton and Lois E. Horton, "The Affirmation of Manhood: Black Garrisonians in Antebellum Boston," in Donald M. Jacobs, ed., *Courage and Conscience: Black & White Abolitionists in Boston* (Bloomington, IN, 1993), 128–53; Patrick Rael, "African American Elites and the Language of Respectability," paper presented at the Annual Meeting of the Organization of American Historians, San Francisco; and Price and Stewart, *Hosea Easton*, 3–57.

6. See James O. Horton's "Comment" in response to James Brewer Stewart, "The Emergence of Racial Modernity and the Rise of the White North, 1790–1840," *Journal of the Early Republic*, 18 (Summer 1998), 222–26; Horton and Horton, *In Hope of Liberty*, 30–54; Jeffrey Bolster, *Black Jacks: African American Seamen in the Age of Sail* (Cambridge, MA, 1997), 68–13; and particularly, in the present collection, Lois E. Horton, "From Class to Race in Early America: Northern Post-Emancipation Racial Reconstruction."

7. Linda Kerber, *Federalists in Dissent: Imagery and Ideology in Jeffersonian America* (Ithaca, 1970), chaps. 2–3; Robert Forbes, "Slavery and the Evangelical Enlightenment," in John R. McKivigan and Mitchell Snay, eds., *Religion and the Antebellum Debate Over Slavery* (Athens, GA, 1998), 68–106; Joanne Pope Melish, *Disowning Slavery: Gradual Emancipation and "Race" in New England, 1780–1860* (Ithaca, 1998), 84–118; Robert H. Abzug, *Cosmos Crumbling: American Reform and the Religious Imagination* (New York, 1994), 11–29; Horton and Horton, *In Hope of Liberty*, 55–76, 155–70.

8. The discussion of class formation and the ideology of "respectability" derives from Stuart Blumin, *The Emergence of the Middle Class: Social Experience in the American City, 1700–1900* (New York, 1989), 66–230; Richard Bushman, *The Refinement of America: Persons, Houses and Cities* (New York, 1992), 207–447; Karen Halttunen, *Confidence Men and Painted Women: A Study of Middle Class Culture in America* (New Haven, 1982); John Kasson, *Rudeness and Civility: Manners in Nineteenth Century Urban America* (New York, 1990); Tamara P. Thornton, *Cultivating Gentlemen: The Meaning of Country Life among the Boston Elite* (New Haven, 1989); Ronald Story, *The Forging of an Aristocracy: Harvard and the Boston Upper Class* (Boston, 1980); Roediger, *Wages of Whiteness*, 133–56; and in this collection Jon Gjerde, "'Here in America there is neither king nor tyrant': European Encounters with Race, 'Freedom,' and Their European Past"; and James P. Ronda, "'We Have a Country': Race, Geography, and the Invention of Indian Territory."

9. Eric Lott, *Love and Theft, Blackfaced Minstrelsy and the American Working Class* (New York, 1993); Michael Kaplan, "New York Tavern Violence and the Creation of a Male Working Class Identity," *Journal of the Early Republic*, 15 (Winter 1995), 592–617; Roediger, *Wages of Whiteness*, chaps. 3–5.

10. P. J. Staudenraus, *The African Colonization Movement, 1816–1865* (New York, 1967), 94–187; Hugh Davis, "Northern Colonizationism and Free Blacks, 1823–1837: A Case Study of Leonard Bacon," *Journal of the Early Republic*, 14 (Winter 1997), 553–75; George Fredrickson, *The Black Image in the White Mind: The Debate on Afro-American Character and Destiny* (New York, 1971), 1–27; Horton and Horton, *In Hope of Liberty*, 196–68; Paul Goodman, *Of One Blood: The Abolitionists and the Origins of Racial Equality* (Berkeley, 1998), 1–35.

11. Emma Jones Lapsansky, "'Since They Got Those Separate Churches': Afro-Americans and Racism in Jacksonian Philadelphia," *American Quarterly*, 32 (Spring 1980), 54–79; Shane White, "'It Was a Proud Day': African Americans, Festivals and Parades in the North, 1741–1834," *Journal of American History*, 81 (June 1994), 13–50; Paul J. Gilje, *The Road to Mobocracy: Popular Disorder in New York City, 1763–1834*

(Chapel Hill, 1987), 145–62; Patrick Rael, "'Besieged by Freedom's Army': Antislavery Celebrations, Black Leaders, and Black Society in the Antebellum North," unpublished paper in the author's possession.

12. The fullest overview of these developments remains Leon Litwack, *North of Slavery: The Negro in the Free States, 1790–1860* (New York, 1961). See also Richard C. Wade, "The Negro in Cincinnati, 1800–1830," *Journal of Negro History*, 35 (Jan. 1954), 39–51; John M. Werner, "Race Riots in the Age of Jackson, 1824–1849" (Ph.D. diss., University of Indiana, 1973). For a closely related analysis of these trends and their deeper meanings within the slave states, see, in the present collection, Lacy K. Ford Jr., "Making the 'White Man's Country' White: Race, Slavery, and State-Building in the Jacksonian South"; and respecting Cherokee removal, Ronda, "'We Have a Country.'"

13. Peter Hinks, *To Awake My Afflicted Brethren: David Walker and the Problem of Antebellum Slave Resistence* (University Park, PA, 1997); Bruce Dain, "Haiti, Egypt and Early Black Racial Discourse in the United States," *Slavery and Abolition*, 14 (Dec. 1983), 139–61.

14. Stewart, "Racial Modernity"; Bertram Wyatt-Brown, *Lewis Tappan and the Evangelical War Against Slavery* (Cleveland, 1969), 78–125; James Brewer Stewart, *William Lloyd Garrison and the Challenge of Emancipation* (Arlington Heights, IL, 1992), 40–74; Richard Newman, "The Transformation of American Abolitionism: People, Tactics and the Changing Meaning of Activism from the 1780s to the 1830s" (Ph.D. diss., State University of New York, Buffalo, 1997); James Huston, "The Experiential Basis of the Northern Antislavery Impulse," *Journal of Southern History*, 56 (Nov. 1990), 609–41; Mary Hershberger, "Mobilizing Women, Anticipating Abolition: The Struggle Against Indian Removal in the 1830s," *Journal of American History*, 86 (June 1999), 16–40.

15. The generalizations developed here regarding the importance of gender as well as racial antagonisms follow works that have carefully studied specific instances of anti-abolitionist and anti-free black rioting in New England, New York, and Pennsylvania. In addition to Leonard L. Richards, *"Gentlemen of Property and Standing": Antiabolitionist Mobs in Jacksonian America* (New York, 1971), 20–155; Roediger, *Wages of Whiteness*, 107–110; and Lott, *Love and Theft*, 28–29, 131–35; consult Susan Strane, *A Whole-Souled Women: Prudence Crandall and the Education of Black Women* (New York, 1990); Donald Yacovone, *Samuel Joseph May and the Dilemmas of the Liberal Persuasion, 1797–1871* (Philadelphia, 1991), 43–55; Margaret Hope Bacon, "By Moral Force Alone: Antislavery Women and Non-Resistence," in Jean Fagin Yellin and John Van Horn, eds., *The Abolitionist Sisterhood: Women's Political Culture in Antebellum America* (Ithaca, 1994), 285–90; John Runcie "'Hunting the Nigs' in Philadelphia: The Race Riot of August, 1834," *Pennsylvania History*, 39, (Apr. 1972), 187–218; John M. Werner, "Race Riots in the United States in the Age of Jackson," chaps. 3–4; Kerber, "Abolitionists and Amalgamators: The New York City Race Riots of 1834," *New York History*, 48 (Jan. 1967), 28–39; and Kaplan, "New York Tavern Violence and the Creation of a Male Working Class Identity."

16. For sources pertinent to this paragraph and the one preceding it, see Leonard L. Richards, *"Gentlemen of Property and Standing"*; Linda Kerber, "Abolitionists and Amalgamators," 28–39; Lott, *Love and Theft*, 63–88; Kaplan, "New York City Tavern Violence"; David Grimsted, "Rioting in its Jacksonian Setting," *American Historical Review*, 77 (Apr. 1972), 361–97; Dale Knobel, *Paddy and the Republic: Ethnicity and Nationality in Antebellum America* (Middletown, CT, 1986), 39–68; and Julie Roy Jeffrey, *The Great Silent Army of Abolitionism: Ordinary Women in the Antislavery Movement* (Chapel Hill, 1998), 14–95.

17. For analyses of the Whig and Democratic parties, slavery, colonization, white supremacy, and partisan loyalties that inform this paragraph and the one preceding it, see Leonard L. Richards, "The Jacksonians and Slavery," in Lewis Perry and Michael Fellman, eds., *Antislavery Reconsidered: New Perspectives on the Abolitionists* (Baton Rouge, 1979), 99–118; Richards, *"Gentlemen of Property and Standing,"* 8–10, 18, 29, 87, 114–22; Daniel Walker Howe, *The Political Culture of the American Whigs* (New York, 1980), 18–37, 165–80; John M. McFaul, "Expedience vs. Morality: Jacksonian Politics and Slavery," *Journal of American History*, 62 (June 1975), 24–39; John Ashworth, *Slavery, Capitalism and Politics in the Antebellum Republic,* Vol. I, *Commerce and Compromise, 1820–1850* (Cambridge, UK, 1995), 323–50; Michael F. Holt, *The Political Crisis of the 1850s* (New York, 1978), 17–33; James Brewer Stewart, "Abolitionists, Insurgents and Third Parties: Sectionalism and Partisan Politics in Northern Whiggery, 1836–1844," in Alan Kraut, ed., *Crusaders and Compromisers: Essays on the Relationship of the Antislavery Struggle to the Antebellum Party System* (Westport, 1983), 26–43.

18. A convenient, highly readable overview of Whig antislavery impulses is found in Leonard L. Richards, *The Life and Times of Congressman John Quincy Adams* (New York, 1986). See also, Ashworth, *Slavery, Capitalism and Politics,* 350–61; and James Brewer Stewart, *Joshua R. Giddings and the Tactics of Radical Politics* (Cleveland, 1970). For discussions of Democratic Party expressions of extreme antislavery sentiment (rare though they were in the 1830s and early 1840s), see esp. Daniel Feller, "A Brother in Arms: Benjamin Tappan and the Antislavery Democracy," paper delivered at the Annual Meeting of the Society for Historians of the Early American Republic, Lexington, KY, July 16, 1999; Sean Wilentz, "Slavery, Antislavery and Jacksonian Democracy," in Melvyn Stokes and Stephen Conway, eds., *The Market Revolution in America: Social, Political, and Religious Expressions* (Charlottesville, VA, 1996), 202–23; and Paul Goodman, *Of One Blood,* 161–75. The most discerning analysis of the relationships between white supremacy, racial egalitarianism, and northern opposition to slavery's westward expansion remains Eric Foner, *Free Soil, Free Labor, Free Men: The Ideology of the Republican Party before the Civil War* (New York, 1970), 261–317. Michael A. Morrison, *Slavery and the American West: The Eclipse of Manifest Destiny and the Coming of the Civil War* (Chapel Hill, 1997), contextualizes these racial themes in struggles between northern and southern politicians over conflicting understandings of the shared political traditions of republicanism. For Foner's most recent statement on issues of race, class, gender and contested definitions of freedom in antislavery ideology, see his trenchant and widely focused "Free Labor, Wage Labor and the Slave Power," in Stokes and Conway, eds., *The Market Revolution in America,* 128–46.

19. The most detailed and substantial analysis of the deeper issues involved in the schisms among white abolitionists and their relationship to issues of race and white supremacy remains Aileen Kraditor, *Means and Ends in American Abolitionism: Garrison and his Critics on Strategy and Tactics, 1834–1850* (New York, 1969). See also, James Brewer Stewart, "Peaceful Hopes and Violent Experiences: The Evolution of Conservative and Radical Abolitionism, 1831–1837," *Civil War History,* 17 (Dec. 1971), 293–309; Stewart, "Racial Modernity"; Alan Kraut, "'Vote as You Pray, Pray as You Vote': Church Oriented Abolitionism and Antislavery Politics," in Kraut, ed., *Crusaders and Compromisers,* 179–205; and Lawrence J. Friedman, *Gregarious Saints: Self and Community in American Abolitionism, 1830–1870* (New York, 1982), 43–67.

20. Stewart, "Racial Modernity," 210–13.

21. Vernon Volpe, *The Forlorn Hope of Freedom: The Liberty Party in the Old Northwest, 1838–1848* (Kent, OH, 1990); John W. Quist, "'The Great Majority of Our Subscribers are Farmers': The Michigan Abolitionist Conspiracy of the 1840's," *Journal of the Early Republic*, 14 (Fall 1994), 326–38; Alan Kraut, "Forgotten Reformers: A Profile of Third Party Abolitionists in Antebellum New York," in Perry and Fellman, eds., *Antislavery Reconsidered*, 119–45; James Brewer Stewart, *Liberty's Hero: Wendell Phillips* (1986; rep., Baton Rouge, 1997), 97–145; Stewart, "Boston, Abolitionism and the Atlantic World, 1820–1861," in Jacobs, ed., *Courage and Conscience*, 102–25; Friedman, *Gregarious Saints*, 43–126, 160–95; Jeffrey, *The Great Silent Army of Abolitionism*, 134–70.

22. Studies that document this crucial shift particularly well include Donald Yacovone, "The Transformation of the Black Temperance Movement, 1827–1854: An Interpretation," *Journal of the Early Republic*, 8 (Fall 1988), 282–97; Richard Newman, "Black Radical Politics in Jacksonian America," paper delivered at the Annual Meeting for the Society of Historians of the Early American Republic, Lexington, KY, July 16, 1999; and more generally C. Peter Ripley, Roy E. Finkenbine, Michael F. Hembree, and Donald Yacovone, eds., *Witness for Freedom: African American Voices on Race, Slavery and Emancipation* (Chapel Hill, 1993), 1–17. The most extensive study of black and white coalition-building in the name of racial integration and political equality remains Carleton Mabee, *Black Freedom: The Non-Violent Abolitionists* (New York, 1970). Other works that elucidate important aspects of this collaborative dynamic include Milton Sernett, *Abolition's Axe: Beriah Green, the Oneida Institute and the Black Freedom Struggle* (Syracuse, 1986); Horton and Horton, *In Hope of Liberty*, 64–65, 109, 126, 129, 152, 203–36; and James Brewer Stewart, *Holy Warriors: The Abolitionists and American Slavery* (1976; rev. ed., New York, 1997), 127–49.

23. For a most accessible primary source sampling of this range of discussion among African Americans, consult Howard Holman Bell, ed., *Minutes of the Proceedings of the National Negro Conventions, 1840–1864* (New York, 1969). See also Jane H. Pease and William H. Pease, "Black Power—The Debate of 1840," *Phylon*, 29 (Spring 1968), 19–26; Floyd J. Miller, *The Search For Black Nationality: Black Emigration and Colonization, 1787–1863* (Urbana, 1975), 90–249; and Howard Zinn, "Abolitionists, Freedom Riders and the Tactics of Agitation," in Martin Duberman, ed., *The Antislavery Vanguard: New Essays on the Abolitionists* (Princeton, 1965); Yacovone's comment is quoted with his permission from a longer discussion with the author of the subject of the "modernity" of abolitionism in the 1840s and 1850s at Legal Seafood Restaurant, Copley Plaza, Boston, March 18, 1997.

24. For instances of recent scholarship by members of departments of literature that eschew "poststructural" and cultural studies approaches in favor of almost "Rankean" efforts to reconstruct factual narrative, see Gary Collison, *Shadrach Minkins: From Fugitive Slave to Citizen* (Cambridge, MA, 1998); and Albert Von Frank, *The Trials of Anthony Burns: Freedom and Slavery in Emerson's Boston* (Cambridge, MA, 1997). For examples of historians of abolitionism whose work crosses over into interdisciplinary approaches, see David Blight, *Frederick Douglass's Civil War: Keeping Faith in Jubilee* (Baton Rouge, 1989); Nell Painter, *Sojourner Truth: A Life, A Symbol* (New York, 1997); and Horton and Horton, *In Hope of Liberty*. For a useful discussion of these interdisciplinary trends, consult Roediger, " The Pursuit of Whiteness: Property, Terror, and Expansion," in this book.

BIBLIOGRAPHY

Abzub, Robert W. *Cosmos Crumbling: American Reform and the Religious Imagination.* New York: Oxford University Press, 1994.

Ashworth, John. *Slavery Capitalism and Politics in the Antebellum Republic.* Vol. 1: *Commerce and Compromise, 1820–1850.* Cambridge: Cambridge University Press, 1995.

Horton, James Oliver, and Lois E. Horton. *In Hope of Liberty: Culture, Community and Protest among Northern Free Blacks, 1700–1860.* New York: Oxford University Press, 1997.

Jeffrey, Julie Roy. *The Great Silent Army of Abolitionists: Ordinary Women in the Antislavery Movement.* Chapel Hill: University of North Carolina Press, 1999.

Mayer, Henry. *All on Fire: William Lloyd Garrison and the Abolition of Slavery.* New York: St. Martin's Press, 1998.

Melish, Joanne Pope. *Disowning Slavery: Gradual Emancipation and "Race" in New England, 1780–1860.* Ithaca: Cornell University Press, 1998.

Price, George, and James Brewer Stewart, eds. *To Heal the Scourge of Prejudice: The Life and Writings of Hosea Easton.* Amherst: University of Massachusetts Press, 1999.

Richards, Leonard L. *Gentlemen of Property and Standing: Antiabolitionist Mobs in Jacksonian America.* New York: Oxford University Press, 1970.

Roediger, David. *The Wages of Whiteness: Race and the Making of the American Working Class.* New York: Routledge, 1997.

Stewart, James Brewer. *Holy Warriors: The Abolitionists and American Slavery.* New York: Hill & Wang, 1996.

Winch, Julie. *Philadelphia's Black Elite: Activism, Accommodation and the Struggle for Autonomy, 1787–1850.* Philadelphia: Temple University Press, 1988.

7

Making the "White Man's Country" White: Race, Slavery, and State-Building in the Jacksonian South

Lacy K. Ford Jr.

Any examination of race as a formative influence on the American South must first acknowledge the interpretation advanced decades ago by the putative founder of southern history as a field of study: Ulrich Bonnell Phillips. A Georgia-born Progressive and author of the first scholarly account of slavery to gain widespread acceptance in the national academy, Phillips surveyed the otherwise wrenching journey from Old South to New and found continuity in the timeless commitment of white southerners to the common cause of white supremacy. Phillips insisted that the "central theme" of southern history was "a single resolve indomitably maintained" that the South "was and shall remain a white man's country."[1] Long before the recent interpretive bent of cultural history refocused scholarly attention upon culturally and historically constructed definitions of race as critical factors shaping American society, Phillips posited a shared allegiance to white supremacy as the central theme of southern history and established an interpretation that would remain both influential and controversial for the remainder of the twentieth century.[2]

During the 1990s, practitioners of the new cultural history, influenced by anthropological research and the techniques of literary postmodernism, have maintained that most American historiography fails to account adequately for the social and cultural construction of race. Race, as postmodernists remind other scholars, emerges not as biologically determined from the genome, but as the product of distinct and identifiable social, cultural, and historical forces. Because it is culturally constructed rather than genetically determined, understandings of race and racism necessarily change over time, historically constructed and reconstructed by complex social negotiations within societies that also change.[3] From this valuable new understanding of race as a social and cultural construction emerged the current genre popularly known as "whiteness" studies. Roaming widely across chronological and disciplinary boundaries, "whiteness" scholarship has effectively returned race to the center of American historiography without diminishing related considerations of class and gender.[4]

In reminding American historians that race is a mutable historical construct, that ideas about race and racism change over time, "whiteness" scholars have also tied the Jacksonian reconsideration of race and racial ideology to other major trends of the era that have garnered recent historiographical attention. Certainly the Jacksonian reconsideration of race occurred within the context of a market revolution that touched almost every facet of American life. Driven by dramatic improvements in transportation and communication, the market revolution quickened the pace and broadened the scope of commerce in the new nation, both extending the boundaries of the market economy and intensifying the market orientation of many American households.[5] Second, the Jacksonian reconsideration of racial ideas emerged in response to the rapid spread of humanitarianism as a social ideal. Spawned and nurtured by widespread acceptance of evangelical Christianity during the Second Great Awakening, and spurred to extend its reach by the opportunities accompanying the market revolution, humanitarianism forced a dramatic rethinking of racial ideologies in both North and South during the Jacksonian era.[6] Finally, the potent egalitarian reform movement of the Jacksonian era, characterized by Robert Wiebe as an assault on gentry politics, not only drove most states toward more democratic political cultures and constitutions during the 1830s but also prompted a reevaluation of how racial differences defined American citizenship.[7] In a stimulating recent essay, James Brewer Stewart termed the product of this Jacksonian reconsideration of race the "emergence of racial modernity."[8] This new Jacksonian racial modernity denied the viability of a biracial republic, doubted the efficacy of efforts to promote respectability and social uplift among people of color, and conceded only a measure of white responsibility for the well-being of an allegedly "inferior" race.[9]

The coming of racial modernity in the South, which by the 1830s held more than ninety percent of the nation's African Americans and virtually all its slaves, looms as an especially inviting area of inquiry. Moreover, as scholars have explored "whiteness" as a national phenomena rather than as the source of southern exceptionalism, they have implicitly challenged southern historians to review and perhaps recast their understanding of precisely how the Old South became a white man's country. In response to these twin challenges, this essay will attempt to explain the triumph of racial modernity in the South of the 1830s by focusing on the political process through which race or "whiteness" became codified, formally and informally, as the defining characteristic of antebellum southern society. Put differently, it will describe how shapers of the Old South's Jacksonian political tradition ventured to make what U. B. Phillips later called "the white man's country" white.

A peculiar combination of economic circumstance and political ideology shaped the Jacksonian South's reconsideration of race and slavery. Contrasting subregional political economies, together with patterns of racial demography associated with these different political economies, ensured that questions relating to slavery and race were framed in different ways in different parts of the South. Central among these many internal variations in the Old South's political economy lay the growing contrast between the Upper South and the Lower South. Between 1800 and 1830, much of the Lower South swirled into the vortex of an economic transformation that Ira Berlin has aptly labeled the "cotton revolution."[10] The "cotton revolution" pulled slavery and plantation agriculture from its comparatively limited tidewater and alluvial strongholds and spread them across a vast plain of black and brown loam soils and through lush river valleys that became the Old South's rich Black Belt. It also promoted staple growing among the region's yeomen and helped spur the expansion of the cash economy in the red clay upland portions of the Old South. The process of cultivating cotton and complementary foodstuffs required steady attention for much of the growing season, making slave labor, with its high ratio of fixed to marginal costs, a highly profitable system. To a large extent, the cotton revolution transformed the Lower South into a true slaveholding region rather than a region characterized by important slaveholding enclaves known for their production of rice, sugar, and sea-island cotton. By doing so, it accelerated the movement of population, both slave and free, from long-settled regions to the frontier of the Old Southwest.[11]

In the Upper South, however, during the same three decades, the once dominant staple, tobacco, whose success had sustained first Chesapeake and later Piedmont demand for slave labor, fell into comparative decline. Alternative cash crops, including grains such as wheat and oats, emerged, but they required substantially less labor than tobacco, except during harvest. With sharp peaks and valleys in the demand for labor, grain cultivation rendered slavery, with its high fixed costs for labor, inefficient and financially unattractive. Thus, although some areas within the Upper South remained heavily dependent on slave labor, the future prospects for the region's slave-labor economy appeared problematic.[12]

By the early 1830s, an ominous antislavery challenge to the slaveholding social order of both the Upper and Lower South appeared from several different quarters. In 1827 the American Colonization Society first requested public funds from Congress; two years later, militant free black David Walker published an appeal for slaves to rebel against their masters; and in 1831,

William Lloyd Garrison ushered in a new era of abolition propaganda with *The Liberator*, a publication dedicated to "immediate" emancipation and effusive in its moral chastisement of slaveholders.[13] But no event focused southern attention on slavery and related issues as intensely as did the bloody if ultimately unsuccessful slave uprising led by Nat Turner in August 1831. Turner's rampage across a small swath of Virginia's lower Tidewater spread fear, rumor, and recrimination across the Old Dominion and sent waves of anxiety through the white population in other areas of the South.[14]

Virginia's Robert Pollard bluntly revealed the fears of Virginia's slaveholders in the wake of Turner's rebellion when he observed, "[E]very family that have slaves are in the power of those slaves, they sleep in our houses—they in this way have the power of cutting our throats or knocking our brains out while we sleep." News of the Southampton bloodbath also spawned fears in the deepest South. In the Natchez region, banker and planter Stephen Duncan confessed "a great apprehension that we will one day have our throats cut in this county."[15] The timing and particular conjunction of these events prompted not simply a short-term return of vigilance against slave rebellion, but also serious reconsideration of public policy toward slavery and the region's free black population precisely at the moment when mounting pressure from white egalitarians spurred most southern states to consider sweeping democratic revision of their existing state constitutions, thus giving southern constitution makers a chance to write a new racial order into fundamental law at their early convenience.

The Jacksonian South's political discussion of race and slavery revealed a variety of racial attitudes and ideologies ranging from exclusion and marginalization at one end of the spectrum to complete subordination of African Americans at the other end, with a bewildering array of selectively cobbled together variations on either the exclusion or the subordination themes, or both, lying in between. Full-voiced advocates of exclusion sought either to remove African Americans from southern society altogether, or, more realistically, minimize the role of blacks, slave and free, in the civic, social, and economic life of the South, much as had been done in northern society following the postrevolutionary emancipations. To implement their strategy, southern exclusionists advocated pushing free blacks further toward the margins of society and taking some cautious first steps toward putting slavery on the road to ultimate extinction. Thus they favored colonization because it reduced the free black population in the near term and established a working mechanism to facilitate gradual emancipation on a larger scale in the future. In essence, exclusionists wanted to "whiten" their society by reducing the size and diminishing the importance of the region's African-American population.

In contrast, champions of subordination recognized that the southern staple economy depended so heavily on slave labor that the region could not thrive without it. Subordinationists accepted racially justified slavery as a necessary labor system, and some argued affirmatively that the region's reliance on slaves for menial labor strengthened the virtues of independence and equality among whites. Viewing slavery as at least essential, arguably beneficial, and, in all likelihood perpetual, subordinationists sought to render white dominance of blacks as complete and thorough as possible.[16]

But if the ideological poles of the southern Jacksonian debate over race and slavery seemed well-defined, the actual terms and issues of the discussions varied widely across the region. In the Upper South, the debate occasionally focused on the future of slavery itself, and almost without exception, addressed the problematic role free blacks played in a slaveholding society. As a whole, the Upper South remained committed to a conception of slavery as a necessary (but possibly temporary) evil—an evil that could be at odds with the ideals of white independence and equality over the long term. Thus the arguments over race in the Upper South often centered on how the region might "whiten" itself, either through gradual emancipation and colonization of slaves, the colonization of free blacks, a gradual shift to free white labor facilitated by the sale of slaves to the cotton growing areas of the Deep South, or some combination of these approaches.[17] By contrast, in a heuristic "Middle South" of Tennessee and North Carolina, even though few saw slavery as a positive good, sentiment favoring emancipation on any terms nevertheless declined. In these states, the discussion of race centered on whether or not free people of color should have a political voice. In the Middle South, Whiggish paternalists defended the idea of promoting uplift and respectability among free blacks, while subordinationists championed disfranchisement.

In the Lower South, the case for slavery as a positive good remained in its infancy at the beginning of the Jacksonian era, and some of the peculiar institution's defenders still called it a necessary evil. But the "evils" of slavery were less and less often proclaimed openly, and public policy treated slavery as if it were a permanent institution, or one likely to thrive for as long as white southerners could imagine. Indeed, most Lower South political leaders considered slavery essential to the region's staple economy, which, despite fits and starts in the international market and vulnerability to unpredictable credit crunches, remained the bellwether of the region's prosperity. In the cotton South, the Jacksonian debate over race centered more on the prevention of insurrections, tighter regulation or removal of free blacks, and the desirability of regulating or even eliminating the interstate slave trade. Together, these three subregional debates constituted the larger Jacksonian South's attempt to define "racial modernity" and render it tangible in their political arrangements.

Upper South sentiment in favor of gradual emancipation, though always conditional, retained significant strength throughout the Jacksonian era. In the pensive months following Nat Turner's rebellion in the late summer of 1831, Virginia actively reconsidered its policy toward slavery and the free black population within its borders. Long time advocates of both gradual emancipation and colonization found full voice. Virginian John Marshall, the venerable Chief Justice of the United States Supreme Court, believed that the "removal of our free colored population" had emerged as a "common object" in postinsurrection Virginia and expressed a fervent hope that the legislature would seize upon "the excitement produced by the late insurrection" to pass sweeping legislation facilitating colonization. John Rutherford, a Richmond conservative, also denounced slavery as "the greatest curse that ever blighted the prospects of any people," and warned the legislature that the "evil" of "our colored population . . . increasing as it does so rapidly and so awfully, requires some prompt and energetic remedy." Thomas Ritchie urged Virginia lawmakers to do more than merely turn "their attention to preventing Insurrections" by considering a "more radical remedy," such as "an energetic system of manumission followed by a removal to Africa."[18]

Arguing an exclusionist position, Virginia's critics of slavery generally cited the harm the institution inflicted on white society, whether in retarding individual opportunity for ordinary whites, dragging the whole society down in comparison with the dynamic free labor society further north, or simply exposing whites to the horrors of insurrection and perhaps racial warfare. Virginia exclusionists believed that slavery bred personal arrogance and economic backwardness, and hindered the advancement of whites. During a heated debate over the issue in the Virginia House of Delegates 1831–32 session, Shenandoah Valley representative Samuel McDowell Moore blamed slavery for demoralizing the state's poorer whites, who, he insisted, viewed labor "as a mask of servitude."[19] Another Valley delegate, Charles J. Faulkner, echoed Moore's sentiments, explaining that the "independent yeomanry" west of the Blue Ridge feared losing its vitality to the "slothful and degraded African." Slaveholder and colonization advocate Thomas Marshall carried the curse of blackness argument even further, contending that both slavery and a large free black population "banishes the yeomanry of the country . . . until the whole country will be inundated by one black wave, covering its whole extent, with a few white faces here and there floating on the surface."[20]

As a rule, proslavery Virginians admitted the evils of the institution but argued that, for all its faults, slavery remained essential for maintaining racial control and ensuring the availability of an adequate agricultural labor supply. Only a small band of the Old Dominion's staunch subordinationists claimed that slavery enhanced white zeal for independence by daily presenting visible examples of the misery of abject dependency among black slaves. Summarizing the position of these diehard subordinationists, William Roane, son of distinguished Jeffersonian jurist Spencer Roane, claimed "that the torch of liberty has ever burnt brightest when surrounded by the dark and filthy, yet nutritious atmosphere of slavery." Like many proslavery conservatives, Roane rejected the "natural equality of man," and based his defense of slavery on the explicitly racist proposition "that the flat-nosed, wooly-headed black native of the deserts of Africa" was not the equal of "the straight haired white man of Europe."[21]

Not all Virginia opponents of emancipation shared Roane's assumptions about slavery's compatibility with white independence. Petersburg lawyer John Thompson Brown, a western Virginian by birth, understood his native region's desire for a "cordon sanitaire" protecting it from "the withering footsteps of slavery." Opposed to all legislative plans for emancipation, however, Brown preferred to keep the area west of the Blue Ridge free from slaves through the "fixed and unalterable laws of nature" rather than "legislative art." Thus Brown recommended reducing the influence of slavery in the Old Dominion by encouraging the "drain of slaves" from Virginia to the Lower South through the interstate slave trade, and he predicted that the cotton states would facilitate this process eventually by repealing all laws restricting the internal slave trade.[22] Some exclusionists who advocated colonization and gradual emancipation agreed with Brown about the probability of slavery's eventual decline in Virginia under the pressure of market forces but yearned to accelerate the process through government action.[23] Amid rumblings from Southside slaveholders about separation from the antislavery western portion of the state, the 1832 Virginia legislature rejected immediate emancipation as "inexpedient" by a vote of 73 to 58, but they endorsed the idea of emancipation at some undetermined future time by a vote of 67 to 60.[24]

After the legislative debate concluded, Thomas R. Dew, a young professor at William and Mary College, denounced "every plan of emancipation and deportation" that the legislature had considered as "utterly impracticable." Yet Dew predicted that slavery was headed toward "ultimate extinction" through the decline of tobacco as a staple and the steady flow of slaves to the newer cotton states of the Southwest. As slavery waned, Dew envisioned a new type of economic development for Virginia, driven by transportation improvements and the growth of towns, attracting "capitalists and free labourers of the north," and producing the consequent rise of manufacturing. Dew also believed that, despite their post-Southampton hesitancy, Alabama, Mississippi, and Louisiana would open their borders to additional slave labor and serve as an "absorbent" for Virginia's "excess" slave population.[25] Focusing on race as the basis of slavery in Virginia, Dew insisted that emancipation without removal was unthinkable since white society could neither absorb nor uplift a free colored population. "[T]he emancipated black carries a mark which no time can erase," Dew maintained; "he forever wears the indelible symbol of his inferior condition: the Ethiopian can not change his skin, nor the Leopard his spots."[26] The young Virginia ideologist nimbly advanced a market-driven exclusionist argument for noninterference with slavery, emphasizing racial differences as permanent and insurmountable obstacles to the successful uplift of blacks, whether slave or free.

Countering Dew, American Colonization Society supporter Jesse Burton Harrison, a native Virginian who moved to New Orleans to further his legal career, warned against the continued presence of "a distinct race of people within our bosom . . . soon to be more numerous than ourselves, exposed to every temptation . . . to become our deadliest foe." Also an exclusionist, Harrison admitted that his concerns about slavery were "founded but little on the miseries of the blacks" but instead "almost exclusively to the injuries slavery inflicts on the whites." Slavery degraded labor, Harrison contended, and created among whites "a disposition to look on all manual labor as menial and degrading." Slavery slowed the growth of manufacturing by retarding the "rearing of a large class of skillful mechanics." Slavery also discouraged immigration. With its slave-based staple economy stagnant, Virginia lagged behind much of the nation in wealth and population growth, and, Harrison insisted, as Virginia grew "blacker" such economic backwardness would only worsen. If slavery was gradually eliminated, Harrison contended, Virginia would hold "a thousand temptations" for "different sorts of immigrants, for capitalists, for free labourers, and for her own sons who meditate emigration." Thus he advocated colonization as a means both to stabilize the population ratio of the races in Virginia and to revive the state's languishing economy, an exclusionist prescription for steady movement toward "whiteness" and prosperity.[27]

Two years after the Virginia debate, memorials offered by antislavery societies sparked a brief consideration of emancipation at Tennessee's constitutional convention.[28] Rather than permit a lively public debate over the antislavery memorials, the convention appointed a special committee, chaired by East Tennessee delegate John McKinney, to respond. The McKinney committee's report rested its carefully qualified defense of slavery on racial grounds. Where the slave and master were of the "same race and wore the same complexion," the committee observed, slavery had "long ago been extinguished." But, in the American South, "the African slave stands in a different attitude— he bears upon his forehead a mark of separation which distinguishes him from the white man—as much after he is a free man as while he was a slave." Agreeing with the committee report, Terry Cahal, a nonslaveholder, professed regret "that domestic slavery ever found a home in our country," but he dismissed emancipation without colonization as absurd. Can the emancipator, Cahal asked, "change the African's skin, and elevate his feelings and his mental capacity to the dignity and honor of the white man's?"[29] On the key test vote, the Tennessee convention supported the McKinney committee report 42–12, and ultimately the new constitution barred the legislature from emancipating any slaves without the consent of their owners.[30]

In sum, the Jacksonian debate over slavery and race in the Upper South raged between, on the one hand, committed exclusionists who lacked the political muscle they needed to succeed, and on the other, apologetic but uncompromising subordinationists. Given the Upper South's large slave population, exclusion loomed a daunting task, and even its advocates recognized that it could be accomplished only gradually and with respect for the rights (including financial compensation) of slaveholders. But the putative defenders of slavery in the Upper South, tentative subordinationists if subordinationists at all, accepted many of the basic propositions advanced by the exclusionists. These opponents of legislative emancipation favored letting time and the market economy do the work of exclusion rather than using collective or state efforts to accelerate the process. The Upper South's defenders of slavery, however qualified their arguments, held the advantage of defending the existing social order. Proslavery ideology proved unconvincing to many in the Upper South, but slavery as a working institution remained firmly entrenched. In these Upper South debates, critics of slavery never found enough public support or legislative votes for emancipation, however gradual, and, advocates of colonization generally failed to find sufficient resources to accomplish anything more than a mere shadow of their ambition. Though heated at times, the Jacksonian-era debate over slavery and the status of free blacks yielded little more than a reluctant acceptance of the status quo in the Upper South.

By contrast, few in the Lower South doubted that slavery was anything but the single best passport to wealth and prosperity. Virtually no public figure in the Lower South seriously advocated or favored emancipation of any kind, including gradual and fully compensated emancipation. Even though many slaveholders and Jacksonian politicians in the Lower South still acknowledged that slavery was an evil, proposals for colonization of free blacks and small numbers of slaves voluntarily manumitted by their masters were crafted chiefly to strengthen the institution and better maintain public safety rather than as a modest first step toward a more sweeping emancipation. Ironically, exclusion as an ideology of racial control enjoyed currency in the Lower South during the Jacksonian era but as an approach to the "problem" of the region's substantial Native-American population. As James Ronda's essay demonstrates, a large majority of whites in the Lower South showed a singular determination to guarantee that their "white man's country" was not red, even when tribes like the Cherokees appeared to be strong supporters of slavery.[31]

In the Lower South, subordination prevailed as the preferred ideology of control for whites over blacks, but in pursuing their desired aims, subordinationists often disagreed sharply among themselves over strategy. Some Lower South subordinationists worried about the problems inherent in the presence of free blacks in a slaveholding society. Some favored removing as many free blacks (through colonization or expulsion) as possible, some preferred tight restriction on the activities of free blacks, especially concerning their interaction with slaves, while still others favored cultivation of a caste or cohort of socially respectable free blacks who might serve as a buffer between whites and black slaves. Subordinationists also fretted over both the absolute size and the proportion of the black population in the region even as faith in slavery as an economic benefit remained strong. Some subordinationists yearned to restrict the number of slaves allowed to enter their region as part of an effort to manage the region's racial demography; others thought slave labor so essential to the flourishing of the staple economy and upward social mobility among white southerners that no state should be legislatively or constitutionally deprived of the slaves it needed to prosper. Hence subordinationists often clashed among themselves over the regulation of the interstate slave trade. Thus, in the cotton South, where slavery seemed crucial to the continued economic prosperity of the region, the Jackson debate over slavery and race-related issues centered not on whether the region's peculiar institution should survive but over how best to manage its future.

Along the cotton frontier of the Old Southwest, dramatic increases in the slave population and concomitant fears of slave insurrection often prodded state legislatures into fits of action. In Jacksonian Louisiana, legislators viewed the rapid growth of their slave population with alarm. In 1826, the state approved a two-year moratorium on the interstate slave trade (excluding the importation of slaves by residents and immigrants) in an effort to control the growth of its slave population and slow the outflow of private capital. In 1829 Louisiana tried to insure itself against becoming a dumping ground for the troublesome slaves from older staple-growing states by establishing a "character" test for imported slaves. But the ongoing demand for slave labor on the cotton frontier rendered such restrictions unpopular and difficult to enforce.[32] As one Louisianan observed, the "situation of the Country" being "one in which we have to depend altogether on the labour of the Slaves for a support" led many to believe it "impracticable" to ban their introduction into the state.[33]

In the fall of 1831, news of the Turner insurrection and a bad crop year momentarily shifted planter opinion. A special session of the Louisiana legislature, eager to protect the state's white population against insurrection, again banned the activity of professional slave traders, allowing only citizens and immigrants who intended to settle permanently in Louisiana to bring slaves into the state and requiring even these to appear before parish judges to explain their intentions in detail.[34] Planter J. S. Johnston applauded the new restrictions not only because they provided safeguards against slave incendiaries, but also because they encouraged the retention of capital. Prior to the passage of such restrictions, Johnson complained, Louisiana was "every year drained of our Capital for the purchase of mere Negroes." Restrictions on the activity of slave traders, Johnston believed, ensured that slaves would "now be brought by actual settlers and our money returned to the country."[35]

In neighboring Mississippi, the perception that slavery, however profitable, remained a necessary evil rather than a positive good prevailed in the cotton-rich Natchez region. In 1831, Natchez attorney Sargent S. Prentiss summed up this view when he observed, "that slavery is a great evil, there can be no doubt—and it is an unfortunate circumstance that it was ever introduced into this, or any other country. At present, however, it is a necessary evil, and I do not think admits of a remedy."[36] Earlier in 1828, popular Governor Gerard Brandon complained that Mississippi had become a "receptacle for the surplus black population of the Middle States" and received a "vast number" every year, which "excited uneasiness in the minds of many of our fellow-citizens." To remedy the problem, Brandon advocated closing the interstate slave trade.[37]

In 1832, with slaves flooding into Mississippi and concerns about slave insurrections and an intensified abolitionist campaign running high, a state constitutional convention considered the regulation or prohibition of the slave trade. A coalition of Natchez area planters and piney woods' whites approved a clause prohibiting the introduction of slaves "as Merchandise" after March 1, 1833.[38] The new provision guaranteed Mississippi citizens and immigrants the right to import slaves for their own use until at least 1845. Grounded in the assumption that slaves who accompanied their owners and slaves purchased by Mississippi masters were of better character and less likely to incite rebellion, the constitutional ban on the activity of interstate slave traders emerged from a desire to prevent impecunious or alarmed planters in other states from "dumping" troublesome slaves on Mississippi. Yet by diminishing the supply of slaves, the constitutional provision also rendered the capital of Natchez area planters more valuable and gave these planters a protected market in which to sell their own surplus slaves.[39]

Popular opposition to the constitutional ban on the interstate slave trade surfaced immediately as demand for slave labor in the newly opened Choctaw and Chickasaw lands of northern and central Mississippi intensified.

Instead of supporting the constitutional prohibition on the slave trade with statutory penalties at its 1833 session, the Mississippi legislature proposed an amendment repealing the new constitution's prohibition on the interstate slave trade and submitted the amendment for popular approval at the fall elections. Though formerly an opponent of the trade, the conservative Natchez *Courier* endorsed the amendment because the ban on activity of professional slave traders ensured that "the rich may still import" while "the poorer class," who cannot afford to travel, "must either submit to the extortions of the wealthy or rest content with what they have."[40] When ballots were cast in November 1833, the amendment reopening the slave trade won a strong plurality of those voting on the question (4,531 in favor and 1,093 against), but it failed to receive the required majority of all votes cast in legislative elections. The unexpected failure of the amendment left Mississippi policy towards the interstate slave trade confused and uncertain. The next legislature failed to muster the votes needed to resubmit to the voters an amendment repealing the ban, renewing instead a 2.5 percent levy on the gross sale price of slaves, despite the constitutional prohibition on the trade. Thus while the supreme law of Mississippi prohibited the importation of slaves as merchandise after March 1, 1833, the legislature imposed no sanctions on violators and taxed the illicit trade.[41] Between 1833 and 1837, with no statutory penalties in place, slaves poured into Mississippi in record numbers. Finally, at the legislative session of 1837, a full four years after the constitutional prohibition was slated to take effect, the Mississippi legislature passed a bill imposing a system of fines and penalties for those who sold or purchased slaves imported solely for the purpose of sale or hire.[42]

This prolonged controversy over the slave trade revealed the fundamental contradictions and concerns of the cotton South during the Jacksonian era. Even as many Lower South whites yearned for enough slaves to bring cotton riches to themselves and their fellow citizens, they also fretted over the drain of capital to the Upper South and, more importantly, over the potential dangers of a large black population. As a result, they pondered ways to modulate their region's ever-volatile racial demographics. Within the emerging subordinationist consensus in the Lower South remained very substantial room for maneuver and internal disagreement; only external challenge inspired unified denunciation.

If the debate in the Upper South indicated that the momentum given the exclusion argument by the circumstances of the early 1830s could not overcome the power of entrenched proslavery interests, the experience of the Lower South suggested that even where subordination reigned, hegemonic issues related to slavery and race still held significant divisive potential, a potential that both Jacksonian-era parties in the region feared and manipulated over the

next two decades. But in the Middle South, exclusionists and subordinationists of varying stripes debated an issue central to defining the relationship of
race and citizenship: the question of free black suffrage.

A vigorous debate erupted over free black voting at the Tennessee constitutional convention of 1834. Tennessee's original 1796 constitution granted
the suffrage to all "freemen" who met minimal freehold or residency requirements, and thus permitted a rather small number of free blacks who were freeholders or long-time residents of a particular county to vote.[43] In 1834, however, egalitarian reformers who pushed hard for the extension of suffrage to
all whites also complained bitterly about the state's practice of allowing propertied free black men, otherwise considered "outside the social compact," to
vote. Contending that white Tennesseans "reprobate and abhor" black voting,
western delegate G. W. L. Marr declared that the "political fabric of Tennessee denied citizenship to all people of color, slave or free," and argued that
the "supposed claim" of free blacks "to exercise the great right of free suffrage" should be "prohibited." Marr insisted that the United States Constitution's phrase "We, the People" meant "we the free white people of the United
States and the free white people only."[44] Another western delegate, William
H. Loving, labeled it "an evil example to our slaves to allow free Negroes to
exercise the right of suffrage."[45] Egalitarian Terry Cahal worried that free
black suffrage threatened to transform Tennessee into "the asylum for free
Negroes and the harbour for runaway slaves."[46] Defending the 1796 provision, Robert Allen, a delegate from counties north of Nashville, opposed the
blanket disenfranchisement of free blacks, noting that many free blacks had
"exercised it [the suffrage] for thirty-eight years . . . without any evil growing out of it."[47] Ultimately, however, the convention disenfranchised all free
blacks, including freeholders, by a vote of 33 to 23.[48]

The question of voting rights for free blacks proved even more contentious
when debated at North Carolina's constitutional convention of 1835. The use
of the term "freeman" in the suffrage clause of North Carolina's constitution
of 1776 opened the door to voting rights for free blacks who met the constitution's freehold or taxpaying requirements.[49] Eligible free blacks voted regularly and with comparatively little controversy in most locales during the
first three decades of the nineteenth century.[50] When the convention met in
Raleigh in June 1835, however, James Bryan of Carteret County led a charge
for the disenfranchisement of free blacks, baldly declaring that the United
States was "a nation of white people—its offices, honors, dignities, and privileges, are alone open to, and to be enjoyed by, the white people."[51] Nathaniel
Macon, the venerable former speaker of the United States House, agreed, insisting that free blacks were "no part of the then political family" in 1776 and
that free black suffrage in North Carolina rested on a flawed interpretation of

the state's old constitution.[52] Treading carefully around the state's racial sensibilities, defenders of free black suffrage argued that respectable free blacks served as a valuable buffer between whites and slaves. Piedmont delegate John Giles urged retaining the suffrage for propertied free blacks as a "mode of raising them from their present degradation." Giles also believed that allowing free blacks to retain the suffrage "might attach them to the white population."[53] Presenting a consistent Whig ideology for protecting property and promoting uplift, jurist William Gaston, the most respected figure at the convention other than Macon, offered an eloquent defense of free black suffrage. "Let them know they are a part of the body politic," Gaston pleaded, "and they will feel an attachment to the form of government and have a fixed interest in the prosperity of the community, and will exercise an important influence over the slaves."[54] Judge Joseph Daniel of Halifax, an eastern district with the largest free black population in the state, proposed raising the property and taxpaying requirement for free-black voting to a freehold of $250. Such a substantial property requirement would allow "all colored men of good character and industrious habits" to vote and thus "conciliate the most respectable portion of the colored population" by giving them "a standing distinct from the slave population." Daniel contended that voting rights would "cultivate an inclination to protect the community against disorders" among propertied free blacks.[55] Gaston supported Daniel's proposal and warned the convention against leaving the respectable free black "politically excommunicated," with an "additional mark of degradation fixed upon him, solely on account of color." Prominent Whig planter John Morehead also warned that disenfranchising free blacks might "close the door entirely against this unfortunate class of our population," and hence encourage them to "light up the torch of commotion among our slaves."[56]

Leading a spirited attack on the "respectability" argument advanced by Daniel, Gaston, and Morehead, eastern delegate Jesse Wilson opposed any compromise based on property-holding or character in favor of a sweeping disenfranchisement of all free blacks. "Color is a barrier which ought not to be broken between the classes," Wilson argued. "If you make it your business to elevate the condition of the blacks," he contended, "in the same proportion . . . you degrade that of poorer whites."[57] Piedmont delegate Hugh McQueen concurred, arguing that "white portion of the population of this country constitutes the proper depository of political power" and complaining that "the exercise of the right of suffrage by free blacks was repugnant to public feeling in the State."[58]

After vigorous debate, the North Carolina convention approved a constitutional provision depriving all free persons of color by the relatively narrow margin of 67–62. A strong sectional component appeared in the voting. Seventeen of the twenty-five counties whose delegates voted against disenfranchisement lay in the Piedmont and Mountain regions, while nineteen of the twenty-six counties whose delegates voted entirely in favor of disenfranchisement lay in the heavily slaveholding East. There was also a crude relationship between party alignment and convention votes on the black disenfranchisement. The heavily Whig Piedmont and mountain regions tended to oppose disenfranchisement and the generally Democratic East tended to favor it.[59] With the constitutional decisions of Tennessee and North Carolina in 1834 and 1835, the last vestiges of political rights for people of color disappeared from all parts of the future Confederacy. The southern body politic had become an exclusively white preserve.

Out of the Old South's vigorous but varied debates over issues related to slavery and race during the Jacksonian era, complex patterns of racial thought emerged. In the Upper South, exclusionists seeking to lead the political economy of their region toward that of the free-labor North through gradual emancipation and colonization faced intractable, if sometimes apologetic, opposition from defenders of slavery who admitted "slavery in the abstract" an evil and who themselves often sought a whiter Upper South through the colonization of free blacks and the steady sale of slaves to the cotton South. In the Lower South, with its still burgeoning cotton economy and proportionately large black population, full-fledged exclusion was rejected long before the advent of Jacksonianism, and public opinion increasingly equated almost any interference with slavery, including colonization efforts, with abolition.

If subordination emerged as a hegemonic racial ideology in the Lower South, significant disagreement remained over which policies best promoted subordination, and concern over how "white" the cotton South should remain persisted. In the Middle South, open opposition to slavery proved decidedly weaker than in the more northern portions of the Upper South. Yet the status of free blacks in these slaveholding societies became a pressing issue during the Jacksonian era. Neither exclusionists nor subordinationists could fully agree on whether the removal of free blacks through expulsion or colonization was essential or even desirable, and even sharper disagreements emerged over the question of whether or not free blacks could serve as a valuable buffer between white citizens and black slaves. Self-styled conservatives and paternalists in the Middle South, though aware of the poverty and social ostracism experienced by many free blacks, tended to believe that social and moral uplift might raise a portion of the area's free black community into a respectable class whose service to society would prove valuable; white egalitarians tended to insist on drawing a strict racial line between freedom and slavery, between citizenship and bondage, between independence and dependence. Even though many in the Middle South remained unconvinced that subordination served whites best, arguments for subordination prevailed over Whiggish notions of paternalism and uplift in these lower reaches of the Upper South, although not without a struggle, and, in some instances, only by relatively narrow margins. Thus the Middle South stood as a middle ground; in North Carolina and Tennessee exclusion seemed impractical and garnered less support than in the more northern reaches of the Upper South, but subordination never gained the consensus support it eventually enjoyed in the cotton South.

In sum, racial modernism in the Jacksonian South wore several faces, all of them forbidding to blacks and supportive of white supremacy in some form. In nearly all of its southern guises, however, racial modernism viewed race as biologically determined and looked no further than skin color for the determination of racial categories. Except for paternalists increasingly on the defensive, character, reputation, and property made less difference than skin color in the public life of the Old South. Some diehard conservatives, like Virginia's William Colquohoun, openly scoffed at the supposed triumph of such *herrenvolk* egalitarianism, ridiculing the notion that the "mere animal man, because he happens to wear a white skin" was entitled to full and exclusive privileges of citizenship.[60] But across the Jacksonian South as a whole, such occasional conservative laments proved no match for the racial *esprit* and entitlement expressed and claimed in a young Mississippian's enthusiastic declaration upon coming of age that he was "*free, white, and twenty-one*."[61]

Thus in the Jacksonian South, as in the rest of Jacksonian America, the reconsideration of race produced an accomodation that enshrined whiteness as the standard measure of citizenship and racial entitlement. Proof of personal independence and public virtue deemed essential to republican citizenship no longer rested in the ownership of productive property, but instead hinged simply on "whiteness." To be sure, shared racism hardly united the Jacksonian South any more than it united the Jacksonian North. In the Upper South, belief in the permanent racial inferiority of nonwhites created a strong and continuing preference for racial exclusion, for a "whiter" society, one less dependent on slavery and characterized by a dwindling black population. Whites in the Lower South generally accepted slavery as an institution essential to the region's continued prosperity and agreed that the thorough subordination of blacks best served their society's interests. But even the cotton South's apparent consensus left considerable room for disagreement among whites over the status of free blacks, the regulation of the domestic slave trade, and the preferred racial balance of the population.

Yet despite these on-going disagreements, the Old South's contested decisions to emphasize whiteness at the expense of wealth, property, and character, choices most explicitly debated in the Middle South, revealed an important aspect of the great accommodation that held planter and plain folk in delicate political equipoise throughout the late antebellum era. However scornful of such claims in private, the slaveholding elite had to accept white equality, the spirit of *herrenvolk* democracy, in the public realm to ensure white solidarity in the coming stand against antislavery. Reluctant egalitarians to be sure, perhaps even hypocritical ones, the slaveholding elite of the Old South accepted the public creed of white equality as the price of broad support for slavery. At the same time, common whites found in the privileges of whiteness a social entitlement and a source of leverage they could employ with great effect in political debate. Lacking wealth but boasting numbers, white egalitarians used the ideological imperative of whiteness to wrest meaningful political concessions, if not outright control, from wealthy elites at key moments. Put another way, common whites in the Jacksonian South defined their whiteness as "property," as evidence of the requisite independence and virtue, and thus forged a southern *herrenvolk* republicanism, much in the same way that artisans and journeyman defined their skill as a sort of surrogate property and used it to forge artisanal republicanism in the urban North during the same era. In turn, by accepting, even tacitly, the legitimacy of slavery and the material inequalities it sustained, white egalitarians left the wealth and economic power of the planter elite secure.[62]

Thus the triumph of whiteness allocated valuable privileges, including voting and legal equality, solely on the basis of skin color, or at least on cultural perceptions and definitions of skin color, leaving race rather than class the key social divide in the public realm.[63] And that sense of white racial entitlement has proven tenacious indeed, surviving not only the collapse of slavery in the 1860s, but also (albeit in altered and sometimes disguised form) the dismantling of segregation a century later. By linking "whiteness" so closely to the prerogatives and rights of citizenship and political participation, the Jacksonian construction of racial modernity defined not merely the South but the entire American nation-state as a "white man's country." Thus racial modernity shaped a powerful national self-definition that would grudgingly sacrifice its gender dimension well before the Civil Rights Movement of the mid-twentieth century mounted a successful challenge to the claims for "whiteness" that lay at its very core.

NOTES

1. Ulrich B. Phillips, "The Central Theme of Southern History," *American Historical Review*, 34 (Oct. 1928), 30–43.

2. Daniel Joseph Singal, *The War Within: From Victorian To Modernist Thought in the South, 1919–1945* (Chapel Hill, 1982), 37–57.

3. Barbara J. Fields, "Ideology and Race in American History," in J. Morgan Kousser and James McPherson, eds., *Region, Race and Reconstruction: Essays in Honor of C. Vann Woodward* (New York, 1982), 143–78.

4. Among other things, these studies have found that racial ideology has not only served as a mechanism for elites to manipulate atavistic masses but also as leverage for white workers and immigrants to wedge their way into the American mainstream on the basis of skin color. For an introduction to "whiteness" historiography, see David R. Roediger, *The Wages of Whiteness: Race and the Making of the American Working Class* (London, UK, 1991); Alexander Saxton, *The Rise and Fall of the White Republic: Class Politics and Mass Culture in Nineteenth Century America* (New York, 1990); Noel Ignatiev, *How the Irish Became White* (New York, 1995); Michael Goldfield, *The Color of Politics: Race and the Mainsprings of American Politics* (New York, 1997); Cheryl Harris, "Whiteness as Property," *Harvard Law Review*, 106 (June 1993), 1709–91; David Stowe, "Uncolored People: The Rise of Whiteness Studies," *Lingua Franca*, 4 (Sept.-Oct. 1996), 68–77; and also the essay by David Roediger in this book. For recent applications of the "whiteness" approach to the study of the South, see Grace Elizabeth Hale, *Making Whiteness: The Culture of Segregation in the South, 1890–1940* (New York, 1998); and Bryant Simon, *A Fabric of Defeat: The Politics of South Carolina Millhands, 1910–1948* (Chapel Hill, 1998).

5. Charles Sellers, *The Market Revolution: Jacksonian America, 1815–1846* (New York, 1991), esp. 137; Melvin Stokes and Stephen Conway, eds., *The Market Revolution in America: Social, Political, and Religious Expressions, 1800–1880* (Charlottesville, 1996); Paul A. Gilje, *Wages of Independence: Capitalism in the Early Republic* (Madison, WI, 1997); James A. Henretta, "The 'Market' in the Early Republic," *Journal of the Early Republic*, 18 (Summer 1998), 289–304.

6. Thomas Haskell, "Capitalism and the Origins of the Humanitarian Sensibility," *American Historical Review*, 90 (Apr.-June, 1985), 339–61, 547–66; David Brion Davis, "Reflection on Abolitionism and Ideological Hegemony," *American Historical Review*, 92 (Oct. 1987), 797–812; John Ashworth, "The Relationship Between Capitalism and Humanitarianism," *American Historical Review*, 92 (Oct. 1987), 813–28; Robert Abzug, *Cosmos Crumbling: American Reform and the Religious Imagination* (New York, 1994).

7. Robert H. Wiebe, *Self-Rule: A Cultural History of American Democracy* (Chicago, 1995); Eric Foner, *The Story of American Freedom* (New York, 1998), esp. 47–94; Robert J. Stenfield, "Property and Suffrage in the Early American Republic," *Stanford Law Review*, 41 (Jan. 1989), 335–76; Lacy K. Ford Jr., "Popular Ideology of the Old South's Plain Folk: The Limits of Egalitarianism in a Slaveholding Society," in Samuel C. Hyde Jr., ed., *Plain Folk of the South Revisited* (Baton Rouge, 1997), 205–27; see also Fletcher M. Green, "Democracy in the Old South," *Journal of Southern History*, 12 (Feb. 1946), 2–23.

8. James Brewer Stewart, "The Emergence of Racial Modernity and the Rise of the White North," *Journal of the Early Republic*, 18 (Summer 1998), 181–217. See also the comments by Jean L. Soderlund, James Oliver Horton, and Ronald G. Walters along with Stewart's response in the same issue, 218–36. Though substantial quarrels over exactly how different racial modernity was from the systems of race relations and the racial ideologies that preceded it remain unresolved, it nevertheless appears that a new set of racial values emerged in the United States during the 1830s.

9. *Ibid.*, esp. 213–17. See also George M. Fredrickson, *The Black Image in the White Mind: The Debate on Afro-American Character and Destiny, 1817–1914* (New York, 1971), 1–164.

10. Ira Berlin, *Many Thousands Gone: The First Two Centuries of Slavery in North America* (Cambridge, MA, 1998), esp. 358–65. See also Joseph P. Reidy, *From Slavery to Agrarian Capitalism in the Cotton Plantation South: Central Georgia, 1800–1880* (Chapel Hill, 1992), 31–57.

11. Lacy K. Ford Jr., *Origins of Southern Radicalism: The South Carolina Upcountry, 1800–1860* (New York, 1988), 5–95; Bradley G. Bond, *Political Culture in the Nineteenth Century South: Mississippi, 1830–1900* (Baton Rouge, 1995), 43–80; Daniel S. Dupre, *Transforming the Cotton Frontier: Madison County, Alabama, 1800–1840* (Baton Rouge, 1997); John Hebron Moore, *The Emergence of the Cotton Kingdom in the Old Southwest: Mississippi, 1776–1860* (Baton Rouge, 1988); Ralph V. Anderson and Robert E. Gallman, "Slaves as Fixed Capital: Slave Labor and Southern Economic Development," *Journal of American History*, 64 (June 1978), 47–66; Gavin Wright, *The Political Economy of the Cotton South: Households, Markets, and Wealth in the Nineteenth Century South* (New York, 1978), 43–88. For purposes of this essay, I am defining the Lower South as those states heavily committed to the cotton economy. See the map in Wright, *The Political Economy of the Cotton South*, 16. Thus, in this essay, the terms Lower South and cotton South are essentially interchangeable.

12. Joseph C. Robert, *The Tobacco Kingdom: Plantation, Market, and Factory in Virginia and North Carolina, 1800–1860* (Durham, NC, 1938); Allan Kulikoff, *Tobacco and Slaves: The Development of Southern Cultures in the Chesapeake, 1680–1800* (Chapel Hill, 1986); John T. Schlotterbeck, "Plantation and Farm: Social and Economic Change in Orange and Greene Counties, Virginia, 1716–1860" (Ph.D. diss., The Johns Hopkins University, 1980); Paul G. E. Clemens, *The Atlantic Economy and Colonial Maryland's Eastern Shore: From Tobacco to Grain* (Ithaca, 1980). For purposes of this essay, I am defining the Upper South as all slaveholding states that were not heavily committed to the cotton economy. Thus the Upper South is essentially the noncotton South. Substantial cotton was grown in scattered locales across the Upper South, in Southside Virginia, in the southern Piedmont, and a few northeastern counties in North Carolina, and in parts of middle Tennessee; but neither Virginia, North Carolina, nor Tennessee could be accurately described as a cotton state during the Jacksonian era. As William Freehling has pointed out, given these differing subregional political economies, the so-called mind of the Old South was an often divided one, and one always shaped in part by the creative tensions among its various subregions; see Freehling, *The Road to Disunion: Secessionists at Bay, 1776–1854* (New York, 1990), esp. 13–38.

13. Robert H. Abzug, "The Influence of Garrisonian Abolitionists: Fears of Slave Violence on the Antislavery Argument, 1829–1840," *Journal of Negro History*, 55 (Jan. 1970), 15–28; James Brewer Stewart, "Peaceful Hopes and Violent Enterprises: The Evolution of Reforming and Radical Abolitionism, 1831–1837," *Civil War History*, 17 (Dec. 1971), 293–309; P. J. Staudenraus, *The African Colonization Movement, 1816–1865* (New York, 1961); William W. Freehling, *Prelude to Civil War: The Nullification Controversy in South Carolina, 1816–1836* (New York, 1966), 49–65.

14. Henry J. Tragle, *The Southampton Slave Revolt of 1831: A Compilation of Source Material* (Amherst, MA, 1971).

15. Robert Pollard to William C. Rives, Jan. 30, 1832, William C. Rives Papers (Library of Congress, Washington, DC); Stephen Duncan to Thomas Butler, Sept. 4, 1831,

Butler Family Papers, Louisiana and Lower Mississippi Valley Collection (Louisiana State University, Baton Rouge, LA).

16. My choice of terms requires some clarification. I have used the term "exclusion" to refer to the idea that African Americans, whether slave or free, should be either removed from American society or, failing that, pushed to its social, political, and economic margins. Thus it was an ideology of exclusion and/or marginalization. I have used the term "subordination" to refer to the idea that slaves were simply too numerous and their labor too valuable to the South to consider exclusion a viable option. Thus long-term southern dependence on slave labor must be accepted and measures taken to guarantee white domination and black subordination in a biracial, slaveholding society in which slavery was justified largely on racial grounds. Clearly exclusionists saw marginalization as a way of subordinating blacks who remained in their society, and just as clearly subordinationists wanted to exclude both slaves and free blacks from the realm of political and social equality. Although the terminology is my own, my thinking on these points has been influenced heavily by Freehling, *The Road to Disunion*, esp. 178–210.

17. The most thorough account of the Virginia slavery debate is Alison Goodyear Freehling, *Drift Toward Dissolution: The Virginia Slavery Debate of 1831–32* (Baton Rouge, 1982), esp. 122–95; for a more recent perspective, see Trenton E. Hizer, "'Virginia is Now Divided': Politics In the Old Dominion, 1820–1833" (Ph.D. diss., University of South Carolina, 1997), 269–379. Generally speaking, egalitarian constitutional reformers advocated exclusion, while conservatives tended to favor subordination.

18. Copy of letter from John Marshall to Reverend B. B. Gurley, Dec. 14, 1831, Faulkner Family Papers (Virginia Historical Society, Richmond); John Rutherford to William C. Rives, Nov. 6, 1831, Rives Papers; John Rutherford to William C. Rives, c. July 1832, John Rutherford Papers (William R. Perkins Library, Duke University, Durham); Thomas Ritchie to William C. Rives, Oct. 12, 1831, Rives Papers.

19. Richmond (VA) *Enquirer*, Jan. 19, 1832.

20. *The Speech of Charles J. Faulkner (of Berkeley) in the House of Delegates of Virginia on the Policy of the State with Respect to her Slave Population, January 20, 1832* (Richmond, 1832); *The Speech of Thomas Marshall (of Fauquier) in the House of Delegates of Virginia, on the Policy of the State in Relation to Her Colored Population: Delivered Saturday, January 14,1832* (Richmond, 1832).

21. Richmond *Enquirer*, Feb. 4, 1832.

22. *The Speech of John Thompson Brown, in the House of Delegates of Virginia, on the Abolition of Slavery. Delivered Wednesday, January 18, 1832* (Richmond, 1832).

23. Richmond *Constitutional Whig*, Mar. 28, 1832.

24. Alison Freehling, *Drift Toward Dissolution*, 159–69.

25. This gradual, market-driven revolution of the Virginia economy would accomplish the work of reform without legislative action by "increasing the prosperity of Virginia, and diminishing the evils of slavery without those impoverishing effects which all other schemes must necessarily have." Thomas Dew, "Abolition of Negro Slavery," *American Quarterly Review*, 12 (1832), 189–265. A few months later, the essay was reprinted in pamphlet form as *Review of the Debate in the Virginia Legislature of 1831 and 1832* (Richmond, 1832). A modern print of the original essay can be found in Drew Gilpin Faust, *The Ideology of Slavery: Proslavery Thought in the Antebellum South, 1830–1860* (Baton Rouge, 1981), 21–78.

26. Dew, "Abolition of Negro Slavery."

27. Jesse Burton Harrison, "Abolition Question," *American Quarterly Review* (Dec. 1832), 1–48. For biographical information on Harrison, see Michael O'Brien, *All Clever Men, Who Make Their Way: Critical Discourse in the Old South* (Fayetteville, AR, 1982), 55–57. Harrison confined his critique of slavery to its impact on the economy of Virginia. He conceded that the staple growing areas of the Lower South might prosper with slave labor and stopped well short of calling for general emancipation across the region. Harrison, "Abolition Question," 46–48.

28. Chase C. Mooney, *Slavery in Tennessee* (Bloomington, IN, 1957), 64–85; *Journal of the Convention of the State of Tennessee* (Nashville, 1834), esp. 70–71.

29. Nashville *Republican and State Gazette*, July 10, 1834; however, McKinney's committee also rejected the idea of a Virginia-style whitening of Tennessee through massive sales of slaves to the Lower South. Such action could hardly alleviate, and might actually increase, the plight and misery of slaves. "Let the slaves in the Unites States, by the operation of any cause whatever, be congregated together within the bounds of three or four states, so that they can ascertain by their own numbers and strength, concert plans among themselves, and co-operate with each other," the McKinney committee reasoned, "then what is to prevent a servile war?" As long as slavery existed in the United States, the committee believed, "the benefit of both the slave and the free man" hinged on the principle that "slaves should be distributed over as large a territory as possible, as thereby the slave receives better treatment and the free man is rendered more secure." Thus the Tennessee convention endorsed "diffusion" rather "exclusion" as the best policy for protecting whites from the dangers concomitant with slavery.

30. Chase C. Mooney, "The Question of Slavery and the Free Negro in Tennessee," *Journal of Southern History*, 12 (Nov. 1956), 487–509.

31. See James P. Ronda, "'We Have a Country': Race, Geography, and the Invention of Indian Territory," in this book.

32. The restriction on slave importation was repealed in 1828, a full year before its specified expiration. H. E. Sterkx, *The Free Negro in Antebellum Louisiana* (Rutherford, NJ, 1972), 285–315; Joe Gray Taylor, *Negro Slavery in Louisiana* (Baton Rouge, 1963), 21–58; Garry B. Mills, *The Forgotten People: Cane River's Creoles of Color* (Baton Rouge, 1977), 192–217; Ira Berlin, *Slaves Without Masters*, 108–32.

33. Thomas A. Scott to William S. Hamilton, Feb. 8, 1830, William S. Hamilton Papers (Louisiana State University); Alexander Barrow to William S. Hamilton, Jan. 25, 1830, *ibid*.

34. Taylor, *Negro Slavery in Louisiana*, 41–47.

35. J. S. Johnston to Thomas Butler, Mar. 12, 1832, Butler Family Papers.

36. George Lewis Prentiss, *A Memoir of S. S. Prentiss* (2 vols., New York, 1856), I, 107. That same year, spurred by news of Nat Turner's failed rebellion, the citizens of Natchez and Adams counties, where over one-third of all Mississippi's free people of color lived, petitioned the legislature for "the absolute and unconditional removal of free Negroes from the state." The legislature proved unwilling to enact such a draconian measure, but it agreed that the state needed better mechanisms for controlling its free black population and limiting its growth. Thus the legislature approved sweeping new legislation that required all free people of color to leave the state within ninety days on pain of being sold into slavery for five years. But Mississippi's lawmakers included a carefully conceived loophole in their otherwise bold measure. Free persons of color who could prove themselves of good character and not "a Class of undesirables" could receive a license to

remain in the state indefinitely. *Journal of the House of Representatives of the State of Mississippi* (1831), 7; Charles Sydnor, "The Free Negro in Mississippi," *American Historical Review*, 32 (July 1927), 769–88.

37. Brandon quoted in Charles Sydnor, *Slavery in Mississippi* (1933; rep., Gloucester, MA, 1965), 161–62. Mississippi's original state constitution, adopted in 1817, guaranteed immigrants the right to bring slaves into Mississippi but gave the state legislature "full power to prevent slaves from being brought into this State as merchandise." During its first fifteen years of statehood, however, Mississippi chose to regulate and tax the interstate trade rather than prohibit it. In 1822, the legislature approved a "character test" for imported slaves, requiring either the slave traders or prospective buyers to procure character references for the slaves in question from two freeholders in the slaves' previous state of residence. Designed to slow the work of slave traders, this regulation did not apply to either Mississippi residents or immigrants who intended to settle permanently in the state. In 1825, the legislature imposed a tax of 2.5 percent on all slaves purchases at auction. The following year, however, the legislature promptly lowered the tax to one percent in response to a vigorous public outcry, and, as new lands in central and northern Mississippi opened for settlement, the demand for slaves grew. See Winbourne Magruder Drake, "The Framing of Mississippi's First Constitution," *Journal of Mississippi History*, 29 (Apr. 1956), 79–110; Sydnor, *Slavery in Mississippi*, 162–65; Edwin A. Miles, *Jacksonian Democracy in Mississippi* (Chapel Hill, 1960), 41–42; and Oscar B. Chamberlain, "The Evolution of State Constitutions in the Antebellum United States: Michigan, Kentucky, and Mississippi" (Ph.D. diss., University of South Carolina, 1996), 89–123.

38. Natchez (MS) *Courier*, Nov. 9, 1832.

39. Largely isolated from staple agriculture, piney woods yeomen supported the ban to forestall the "blackening" of the state and preserve the value of their own labor. Winbourne Magruder Drake, "The Mississippi Constitution of 1832," *Journal of Southern History*, 23 (Aug. 1957), 354–70.

40. Natchez *Courier*, Aug. 23, 1833. The *Courier* also doubted that the legislature could draft an "effective" law that would be "respected" by citizens. A similar ban on the interstate slave trade in neighboring Louisiana, it noted, was "either evaded or openly violated."

41. Sydnor, *Slavery in Mississippi*, 164–71; Natchez *Courier*, Nov. 15, 1833.

42. One contemporary estimate placed the growth of the slave population between 1830 and 1837 at 74,000, a substantial portion of which entered Mississippi through the activity of slave traders, and the same observer claimed that the debts incurred by Mississippi slaveholders to slave traders between 1832 and 1837 totaled over three million dollars. *United States Reports*, 1841, 15 Peters (40), 449–517, esp. 481–89; Sydnor, *Slavery in Mississippi*, 164–70.

43. Mooney, "The Question of Slavery and the Free Negro," 487–509; Francis N. Thorpe, *Federal and State Constitutions*, Colonial Charters and Other Organic Laws of the State, Territories, and Colonies . . . (7 vols., Washington, DC, 1909), VI, 3426–44.

44. *Journal of the Convention of the State of Tennessee* (Nashville, 1834), 107.

45. Nashville *Republican and State Gazette*, July 5, 1834.

46. *Ibid.*, July 10, 1834.

47. *Ibid.*, July 1, 1834.

48. To further define blacks out of the body politic, the convention excluded them from militia service and excused them from paying the poll tax required of whites. See *Journal of the Convention of the State of Tennessee*, 209–14.

49. Harold J. Counihan, "The North Carolina Constitutional Convention of 1835: A Study in Jacksonian Democracy," *North Carolina Historical Review,* 46 (Oct. 1969), 335–64; John Hope Franklin, *The Free Negro in North Carolina, 1790–1860* (Chapel Hill, 1943), esp. 108–20; Thorpe, comp., *Federal and State Constitutions*, IV, 2787–94.

50. Franklin, *The Free Negro in North Carolina,* 107–08; Stephen B. Weeks, "The History of Negro Suffrage in the South," *Political Science Quarterly,* 9 (Dec. 1894), 676; John H. Bryan to Ebenezer Pettigrew, July 27, 1832, Pettigrew Family Papers (Southern Historical Collection, Wilson Library, University of North Carolina, Chapel Hill).

51. *Proceedings and Debates of the Convention of North Carolina Called to Amend The Constitution of the State* (Raleigh, NC, 1836), 62–69; *North Carolina Standard* (Raleigh), June 19, 1835.

52. *Proceedings and Debates of the Convention of North Carolina,* 69–70; *North Carolina Standard,* June 19, 1835. For an earlier but very similar statement of Macon's views, see Nathaniel Macon to John H. Bryan, Apr. 20, 1832, William S. Bryan Papers (Southern Historical Collection).

53. *Proceedings and Debates of the Convention of North Carolina,* 73–74.

54. *Ibid.,* 79; on Gaston's standing at the convention, see James W. Bryan to John H. Bryan, June 7, 1835, Bryan Family Papers (Perkins Library, Duke University).

55. Daniel praised the actual voting record of free blacks, noting that based on his observations of "their conduct for the thirty years" during which free blacks had "uniformly voted for men to represent them of the best character and talents." See *Proceedings and Debates of the Convention of North Carolina,* 60–62.

56. *North Carolina Standard,* June 19, 1835.

57. *Ibid.*

58. *Proceedings and Debates of the Convention of North Carolina,* 75–79.

59. Of the thirteen counties whose delegations split on the issue, seven lay in eastern North Carolina and six in the western portion of the state. Analysis based on information provided in Franklin, *The Free Negro in North Carolina,* 112–16. See also Thomas E. Jeffrey, *State Parties and National Politics in North Carolina, 1815–1861* (Athens, GA, 1989); and Marc W. Kruman, *Parties and Politics in North Carolina, 1836–1865* (Baton Rouge, 1983).

60. William S. Colquhoun to John Mason, May 10, 1851, Mason Family Papers (Virginia Historical Society).

61. Powhatan Ellis Jr. to Mrs. Charles Ellis, June 21, 1850, Mumford-Ellis Family Papers (Perkins Library, Duke University).

62. For comparative purposes, see Sean Wilentz, *Chants Democratic: New York City & the Rise of the American Working Class, 1788–1850* (New York, 1984), esp. 61–63.

63. An intriguing parallel, suggested in James Ronda's essay in this book, emerges from the efforts of the Cherokees to prevent whites and blacks from becoming citizens of the Cherokee nation. See also the essays by Lois Horton, James Brewer Stewart, and Joanne Pope Melish in this collection.

BIBLIOGRAPHY

Ashworth, John. *Slavery, Capitalism and Politics in the Antebellum Republic.* Cambridge: Cambridge University Press, 1995.

Berlin, Ira. *Many Thousands Gone: The First Two Centuries of Slavery in North America.* Cambridge: Harvard University Press, 1998.

Davis, David Brion. *The Problem of Slavery in the Age of Revolution, 1770–1833.* Ithaca: Cornell University Press, 1975.

Fields, Barbara J. "Ideology and Race in American History." In *Region, Race, and Reconstruction: Essays in Honor of C. Vann Woodward*, ed. J. Morgan Kousser and James McPherson. New York: Oxford University Press, 1982.

Ford, Lacy K., Jr. "Popular Ideology of the Old South's Plain Folk: The Limits of Egalitarianism in a Slaveholding Society." In *Plain Folk of the South Revisited*, ed. Samuel C. Hyde Jr. Baton Rouge: Louisiana State University Press, 1997.

Franklin, John Hope. *The Free Negro in North Carolina, 1790–1860.* Chapel Hill: University of North Carolina Press, 1943.

Fredrickson, George M. *The Black Image in the White Mind: The Debate on Afro-American Character and Destiny, 1817–1914.* New York: Irvington, 1971.

Freehling, William W. *The Road to Disunion: Secessionists at Bay, 1776–1854.* New York: Oxford University Press, 1990.

Genovese, Eugene D. *The Slaveholders' Dilemma: Freedom and Progress in Southern Conservative Thought, 1820–1860.* Columbia: University of South Carolina Press, 1992.

Mooney, Chase C. "The Question of Slavery and the Free Negro in Tennessee." *Journal of Southern History* 12 (November 1956): 487–509.

Oakes, James. *The Ruling Race: A History of American Slaveholders.* New York: Knopf, 1982.

Roediger, David. *The Wages of Whiteness: Race and the Making of the American Working Class.* New York: Verso, 1991.

Sellers, Charles. *The Market Revolution: Jacksonian America, 1815–1846.* New York: Oxford University Press, 1991.

Stewart, James Brewer. "The Emergence of Racial Modernity and the Rise of the White North, 1790–1840." *Journal of the Early Republic* 18 (Summer 1998): 181–217.

8

"We Have a Country": Race, Geography, and the Invention of Indian Territory

James P. Ronda

In 1859, some two decades after the Trail of Tears, Principal Chief John Ross surveyed the Cherokee Nation and confidently announced "we have a country." And this was, so he told his fellow citizens, no ordinary country. Drawing on a geographic vocabulary already centuries old, Ross described the Cherokee portion of Indian Territory as "salubrious in climate, rich in soil, and abounding in the resources of mineral wealth."[1] But Ross and other Indians had not always been so enthusiastic in their assessment of the trans-Mississippi West. Twenty years before, in the heat of the removal crisis, Ross labelled what became Indian Territory as "the wilderness of the West."[2] This was no isolated outburst of dismissive eastern prejudice. Like many speaking against removal, he repeatedly described the proposed western Indian country as "a barren and inhospitable region," a land where "water and timber are scarcely to be seen."[3]

Perhaps without fully recognizing it, Ross was part of the continuing invention of Indian Territory. In the first three decades of the nineteenth century, Indian Territory did not exist as a clearly defined geopolitical region, marked out by a widely recognized set of boundaries. Instead, the place that became Indian Territory first had to be imagined and then created. Space had to become place. Indian Territory was an idea—or a cluster of ideas—in search of a place. This act of geographic fashioning came through the efforts of an unlikely combination of politicians, bureaucrats, missionaries, and explorers. In this story of imagination, geography, and race, Cherokee politician John Ross marches in company with James Monroe, John C. Calhoun, and Andrew Jackson. Here missionary Isaac McCoy has much in common with the strident Georgia apologist Wilson Lumpkin. And the story reaches out to explorers like Zebulon Montgomery Pike, Stephen H. Long, and Thomas

159

Nuttall as well as the literary adventurer Washington Irving. What they shared was a set of assumptions about race and geography, national sovereignty and cultural identity. As fortune had it, the same attitudes about race and geographic boundaries played a central role both in removal as expulsion and in the Native American creation of Indian Territory as new homelands.

When it came to the trans-Mississippi West and Native Americans, Thomas Jefferson lived in, and sometimes between, two tightly comparmentalized worlds. Those worlds had unequal measures of fact and fantasy, information and illusion. In one part of his spacious imagination Jefferson constructed a place where Indians would willingly abandon traditional ways, take up the plough, and eventually melt into the larger white population. This was the romantic, utopian Jefferson, the American *philosophe* who saw native people as children of nature who might become adult participants in the new world of the American Republic. But that same imagination also had space for a profoundly different conception of the Republic. Writing to Indiana Territorial governor William Henry Harrison, the president revealed a space defined by the absence of native people as either a distinct polity or culture. "They will in time," Jefferson predicted, "either incorporate with us as citizens of the United States or remove beyond the Mississippi."[4] In the first months of 1803 Indian removal and resettlement outside of the United States was a geopolitical idea in search of a space. Beyond the Mississippi there were neither known places nor available spaces for natives unwilling to become Americans. The West might be the Garden of the World, but it seemed already occupied by Spanish or French gardeners. By the end of the summer all of that had changed.

More than any other event, the Louisiana Purchase provided the energy and the physical space for the white version of Indian Territory. Delaware Senator Samuel White, no friend to Jefferson's dreams of a western empire, caught that sense of new space when he described greater Louisiana as a "new, immense, unbounded world."[5] Jefferson soon grasped the geographic relationship between his earlier observation about Indian removal and the newly acquired territory. When Revolutionary War veteran General Horatio Gates wrote offering his congratulations on the purchase, the president's response was blunt and revealing. Western lands would be "a means of tempting all our Indians on the East side of the Mississippi to remove to the West." And the West was a good country, "not inferior" to the East in "soil, climate, productions, and important communications." The West was bait, a certain solution to the frontier troubles of the new republic.[6]

The Louisiana Purchase offered Jefferson and his successors a western space to think about race, place, removal, and resettlement. But it was the War of 1812 that provided fresh reasons to continue inventing Indian Territory. Historians eager to portray Jefferson as the father of an American empire in the West often overlook the powerful imperialist energies present in the administration of James Monroe. The president, Secretary of State John Quincy Adams, and Secretary of War John C. Calhoun were all fully committed to territorial expansion, the reestablishment of an American military presence on the frontier, and a systematic review of federal Indian policy.

In that atmosphere of renewed interest in the West, the Committee on Public Lands revisited the idea of an Indian territory beyond the Mississippi. Its January 1817 report offered a version of the present and a vision of the future that combined notions about geography, race, and national destiny. Thinking in terms of geographic relationships between peoples and races, the committee argued that "the present irregular form of the frontier, deeply indented by tracts of Indian territory, presents an extended boundary on which intercourse is maintained between the citizen and the savage, the effect of which on the moral habits of both is not unworthy of regard." Such personal encounters produced situations "by which the civilized man cannot be improved, and by which there is ground to believe the savage is depraved." The committee's answer to all this was Indian removal and resettlement west of the Mississippi. But now came an added twist. The new Indian frontier was to be a straight line, a European-style border, not an "irregular" or "deeply indented" zone of encounter. The line was a racial divide, an unmistakable signal that Indians must live separate from their white neighbors. What the committee report proposed was a geography of race, a geography that promised a sovereign solution to the Republic's "Indian problem."[7]

The Monroe administration agreed. Borders and boundaries needed to be fixed and enforced, whether they were lines separating nations or races. Calhoun was fully persuaded that the "Indian Civilization" policy championed by so many reformers and missionaries was unworkable and doomed to failure. In early 1820 he told the House of Representatives that "until there is a radical change in the system, any efforts which may be made must fall short of complete success." The radical change Calhoun envisioned demanded that independent Indian entities, whether political or cultural, cease to exist east of the Mississippi.[8] And it did not take Calhoun long to inform Indians about this reconfiguring of the nation and its living spaces. In 1824, when a Cherokee delegation protested on-going tensions with Georgia, Calhoun bluntly told the Indians, "It will be impossible for you to remain, for any length of time, in your present situation, as a distinct society or nation, within the limits of Georgia, or any other state." Like Jefferson, Calhoun offered native people a stark choice: either "cease to be a distinct community or remove beyond the limits of any state." What attracted Calhoun was the tidy geography of division. As for the nature of new Indian homelands, the secretary could only promise that a good country would be found "in a quarter most convenient."[9]

It was against the backdrop of Calhoun's advocacy of resettlement and the seemingly successful migration of some Cherokees to Arkansas in 1817 that Monroe drafted the first comprehensive presidential proposal for removal. What he called for was a fundamental reordering of the national landscape by means of large-scale migration and the imposition of racial borders. Convinced that Indian migration and separation was of "high importance" to the nation, Monroe also persuaded himself that the policy would "promote the interest and happiness" of the native nations. To move Indian Territory from rhetoric to reality, the administration advanced two legislative strategies. First, ownership of the new homelands would be vested in the tribes by means of a "good title." How much land and how it might be allocated remained uncertain. With only a hazy sense of western geography, Monroe's only comment was that the land be "adequate." The second element in the proposal was more complex—complex in possible execution and potential for controversy. When Monroe and Calhoun thought about an Indian "territory," they did not envision a territory in the constitutional sense as necessarily leading to a Native-American state. At the same time, Monroe recognized that whatever political place the federal government created required some form of "internal government" beyond, or perhaps in addition to, tribal government. But the president had not given up key aspects of the older civilization program. Indian territory might provide the best place for comprehensive social change. "By the regular progress of improvements and civilization"—a process best suited to the isolation of an Indian territory—native people would be saved from "the degeneracy which has generally marked the transition from the one to the other state."[10] Native people might become like their white neighbors but not alongside them. Civilization for Indians required separation from whites.

Monroe's invention of an Indian territory prompted a flurry of activity within the federal establishment. As management of Indian affairs moved from the Monroe administration to that of John Quincy Adams, new Secretary of War James Barbour prepared the first detailed plan for the creation of Indian Territory. Like Calhoun, Barbour was convinced that all civilization programs aimed at incorporating native people within existing states were doomed to failure. Turning to what he called "more modern plans," Barbour offered his scheme combining removal with resettlement, social engineering with sharply defined racial boundaries. A large, but geographically unspecified, portion of the country west of the Mississippi "is to be set apart" for the "exclusive abode" of native people. The removal process would involve individuals, not tribes. Once native people were settled in the West, federal authorities would establish and maintain a territorial government. Barbour was quite plain about his proposed western place as home not to tribes but to individuals. For Barbour, removal and civilization sought the same end—to weaken and finally eliminate native nations both as an expression of geography and a source of identity.[11]

Conventional wisdom notwithstanding, Andrew Jackson neither originated the policy contained in the 1830 Indian Removal Act nor created Indian Territory as an expression of race and geography. Instead, Jackson inherited from his predecessors an already fully formed geographic idea. Jefferson, Monroe, and a whole host of federal officials were the initiators of what historical geographer D. W. Meinig calls "this immense American project," the first "great geographic transformation in the West prompted by the Louisiana Purchase."[12] Others fashioned a vocabulary ready for Jackson to use in defining and describing Indian Territory. This language—with its images of expulsion, separation, and resettlement—suggested new ways to define both the existing states east of the Mississippi and those lands west of the river. The American states were now free of what one Georgia politician called "a race not admitted to be equal to the rest of the community," and others described as a peculiar people, a race set apart.[13] The western country was reshaped as well, both in terms of geographic boundaries and the presence of new peoples. What some had labeled as the "great American desert" was now transformed into a good country suitable for honest agricultural labor and civilized institutions.

In a series of important messages on removal and resettlement between 1829 and 1835, Jackson gave the weight of federal power to a sweeping imperial and racial geography. In 1829 the president's conception of an Indian territory was vague at best. He promised "an ample district west of the Mississippi" for each emigrant tribe. Rejecting notions of individual removals and resettlement as impractical, Jackson reluctantly accepted tribal governments as a permanent feature of the western political landscape. White Americans, with the exception of appropriate federal officials and missionaries, would be barred from permanent settlement in the native homelands. As Jackson imagined it, such an "interesting commonwealth" would serve to "perpetuate this race."[14] A year later Jackson revisited the removal and resettlement issue. He did so in an atmosphere still charged with controversy over the recently signed Indian Removal bill. Contending that "the removal of the Indians beyond the white settlements" was rapidly approaching "a happy consumation," the president centered his attention on the benefits offered by western homelands racially defined. With a demographic power vested only in American presidents, Jackson proclaimed the lands west of the Mississippi virtually empty except for "a few savage hunters." The empty West seemed the ideal place for Indian resettlement. Once native people lived lives separate from whites, Jackson was convinced that Indians would be free "to pursue happiness in their own way and under their own rude institutions."[15]

In his 1833 message to Congress Jackson moved even closer to using race and notions of racial incompatibility as the imperial rationale for both removal and the establishment of Indian Territory. Native people simply could not exist "surrounded by our settlements and in continued contact with our people." Abandoning any commitment to the civilization or moral uplift policy of earlier times, the president insisted that Indians possessed "neither the intelligence, the industry, the moral habits, nor the desire for improvement which are essential to any favorable change in their condition." Native Americans were not just ordinary human beings laboring under the burden of a deficient culture. They were a separate people living "in the midst of another and superior race and without appreciating the causes of their inferiority or seeking to control them." Jackson's ingenious argument condemned native people to permanent racial inferiority, and at the same time, charged them with failing to understand and therefore transcend the reasons for that inferiority.[16]

No official pronouncement more fully elaborated all the various geographic and racial themes in removal and resettlement than the 1836 Report of the Committee on Indian Affairs. In many ways the report is a compendium of official thinking on race and Indian Territory. The committee made no pretense that Indians were anything other than a "race under the peculiarities of constitution," a people intrinsically different from and inferior to their white neighbors. Those enduring differences were made plain, so the committee insisted, by four unchanging and unalterable patterns of behavior—an "irresistable thirst" for alcohol, an "unnatural predilection" for war and violence, an "inordinate fondness" for hunting as a way of life, and "an unconquerable aversion" to personal or societal betterment.[17] These racial differences made separation a national necessity. The very presence of Indians in American communities continued to inflame white prejudice and spark Indian revenge. Indian Territory was a place demanded by the very nature of race and racial differences.[18]

At least for committee members, race and geography worked as one to create a separate world where native people could "live to themselves." The report advanced the image of Indian Territory as "an immense body of fertile soil, elevated and healthy in appearance, well adapted to agriculture and grazing, and lying within the latitudes within which the tribes generally resided." And west beyond Indian Territory, so the committee believed, the land was barren and wholly uninhabitable. Never again would Indians and whites live in close proximity one to the other. Just how sharply these racial and geographic boundaries were to be drawn became clear when the committee closed its report, promising that Indians "are on the *outside* of us, and in a place which will ever remain an *outside*."[19]

By the end of the 1830s the official white invention of Indian Territory was nearly complete. What had begun nearly three decades earlier with Thomas Jefferson and the Louisiana Purchase was now a full-blown geographic and political reality. As D. W. Meinig explains: "In the 1830s the United States formalized a large sector of its western borderlands in unprecedented ways. A broad belt of country between the Platte and the Red River was set apart as the 'Indian Territory' or 'Western Territory' and subdivided into a set of territorial allotments to accommodate a great variety of Indian groups."[20] But presidents, politicians, and bureaucrats were not the only white Americans who busied themselves redefining national space in racial terms. Among those inventors of Indian Territory outside official Washington none was more outspoken and more influential than Isaac McCoy. Baptist preacher, government teacher, and explorer, McCoy was an indefatigable proponent of the Indian Territory idea.

McCoy's ideas first took written shape in 1827. Responding to Monroe's initiative, McCoy enthusiastically endorsed removal as the only way to preserve and elevate native people. "The colonizing plan," he explained, "proposes to place Aborigines on the same footing as ourselves." Believing in the redemptive power of private property and deeply distrustful of tribal and communal ways, McCoy envisioned each native family as a separate social and economic unit. Indian Territory would be much like any place east of the Mississippi except that "the colony would be *outside* of us."[21] Although the government creators of a separate Indian country used the word "outside" to mean both separate and inferior, McCoy meant something quite different— something that might remind twentieth-century readers of the phrase "separate but equal." When the influential *Missionary Herald* reprinted part of McCoy's *Remarks* in 1828, the editors chose that section directly addressing race and Indian "character." "Indians are not untameable," McCoy insisted. "Give them a country of their own, under circumstances which will enable them to feel their importance, where they can hope to enjoy, unmolested, the fruits of their labors, and their national recovery need not be doubted." Like many others, McCoy saw Indian Territory as the native promised land, the best place for civilized, Christianized Indians to thrive.[22]

Unlike the official inventors of Indian Territory, McCoy's geography was based on first-hand travel experience in the West. Between 1828 and 1831 he made four journeys into what is now Kansas and eastern Oklahoma. Those expeditions provided McCoy with the geographic detail contained in *Country for the Indians West of the Mississippi* (1832), his most important statement on Indian Territory. Evaluating what is now eastern Oklahoma, McCoy described the country as "fertile, and mostly so surrounded and interspersed with wood that most of it can be cultivated." Here was a vision of a green country with water enough for domestic use as well as the possible introduction of mills for grinding corn and grain. There were, so McCoy reported, extensive beds of coal, salt springs, and abundant stands of hardwood for buildings and fences. Working to counter those in the antiremoval movement who depicted Indian Territory as a wilderness wasteland, McCoy insisted that it could easily support "an immense population." And if "the spirit of uniting in one territory" could find acceptance in Indian country, McCoy was persuaded that "hopes unknown before would animate every tribe, and lead to virtue, industry, and enterprize."[23]

McCoy's Indian Territory was the result of personal experience in the West, a genuine if naive commitment to the welfare of native people, and a millennial faith that emigration would inaugurate a new day for Native Americans. In perhaps his most striking statement about the promise of Indian Territory, he compared the removal and resettlement era to the years of the American Revolution. The revolutionary generation had participated in a heady moment of liberation and nation-building. The creation of Indian Territory could signal a similar age for native people. Brimming with faith and optimism, McCoy confidently told readers: "We account ourselves happy in being the people to usher in this Halcyon era."[24]

The white inventors of Indian Territory did not fashion that new place out of thin air. Washington bureaucrats and committee room politicians enjoyed their fair share of pure fantasy when it came to the West, but they also grounded their conceptions in what seemed reliable information about lands beyond the Mississippi. Federal officials and congressional advocates on both sides of the removal issue repeatedly turned to published accounts by army explorers and frontier travelers. Because these adventurers moved through several geophysical environments—from the Ozark Plateau to the High Plains and the edge of the Rockies—their records contained diverse and often contradictory images of the western country. Policy makers could find geographic representations to fit nearly every view of Indian Territory, whether as garden or desert. Travelling through eastern Kansas in September 1806, Zebulon Montgomery Pike reported that "nature scarcely ever formed a more beautiful place to farm."[25] But when Pike's fellow explorer Lt. James B. Wilkinson made his way through the Arkansas River valley in late fall 1806, he found a very different country. Wilkinson described a "desolate" landscape dotted with only a few stunted cottonwoods growing in sterile soil.[26] Readers of Pike's 1810 *Account* might conclude that Native-American pioneers in Indian Territory would either grow prosperous in a rich country or starve in a barren one.

Expedition reports by Major Stephen H. Long and civilian botanist Thomas Nuttall presented eastern readers with an equally confusing set of geographies. Long's 1819–1820 reconnaissance of the Great Plains took his party across Nebraska, south through Colorado, and then, in two separate groups, to explore the Arkansas and Canadian rivers. It was Long's report, written by botanist Edwin James, that put the Great American Desert on the map and into the geographic lexicon. In what is probably the most often quoted description of the plains, Long and James characterized the lands beyond the Mississippi as "wholly unfit for cultivation" and "uninhabitable by a people depending upon agriculture for their subsistence."[27]

At the same time as Long's army explorers were traveling the central Great Plains, botanist Thomas Nuttall made two important forays into the southern plains. Setting out from Fort Smith in mid-May 1819, Nuttall joined a military detail evicting whites illegally squatting on Indian land in the Red River country. From early July to late September Nuttall made a far more extensive trip along the Arkansas River through present-day Oklahoma. As an experienced field botanist, Nuttall appreciated the many different environments that became Indian Territory. In what is now eastern Oklahoma he recorded a landscape of "forest, hill, and dale richly enamelled with a profusion of beautiful and curious flowers."[28] Near present-day Guthrie on the Cimarron River he found the soil poor and the barren countryside dotted with scrubby oak.[29] Passing through what later became Tulsa, Nuttall observed important terrain feature changes, writing that "the scenery was not without beauty; wooded hills of gentle slope everywhere bordered the river; and its islands and alluvions, still of considerable extent, are no way inferior to the lands of the Ohio."[30] And as his eastern readers were sure to know, "Ohio" was just another way to say fertile lands and abundant harvests.

Though readings of Pike, Wilkinson, Long, and Nuttall gave geographic comfort to both camps in the removal controversy, the most widely circulated travel account to report on what became Indian Territory painted a picture of unequivocal optimism. In the fall of 1832 Washington Irving joined a government expedition led by Indian Commissioner Henry L. Ellsworth on a fact-finding journey through eastern Oklahoma. Irving mined his own journals to write *A Tour on the Prairies*, published in 1835. Mixing romantic imagery with the daily details of frontier travel, Irving produced a very popular book. In *Tour on the Prairies*, Indian Territory emerged as "a vast and magnificent landscape."[31] Proponents of removal and resettlement could find encouragement in reading this passage, describing the country northwest of Fort Smith: "Beyond the river the eye wandered over a beautiful champaign country of flowery plains and sloping uplands, diversified by groves and clumps of trees, and long screens of woodlands; the whole wearing the aspect of complete and even ornamental cultivation, instead of native wildness."[32]

For Native-American politicians intent on defeating removal and reset-tlement plans, Indian Territory seemed at best a foolish fantasy and at worst a dangerous destination. No sooner had the Monroe administration begun to develop their removal plans than a Cherokee delegation presented what be-came the standard southern Indian view of the West. Tribal representatives insisted that there was "not a spot, outside of the limits of any of the states or territories thereof, and within the limits of the United States, that they would ever consent to inhabit." The Cherokee argument was based on both an attachment to traditional home places and a revealing acceptance of con-temporary cultural evolutionary theory about the relationship between place, economy, and culture. "Removal to the barren waste, bordering on the Rocky Mountains, where water and timber are scarcely to be seen, could be for no other object or inducement, than to pursue the buffalo, and to wage wars with the uncultivated Indians of that hemisphere." Sounding like good European social theorists, the Cherokees maintained that resettlement in Indian Territory would reverse their rising fortunes, reducing them to hunters and warriors. Like the earnest Quakers in Daniel K. Richter's essay, Ross and many Cherokees saw hunters as distinctly inferior to farmers. The land was a desert, and resettlement promised only social decay and national decline.[33]

Over the next two decades tribes threatened with removal expanded and re-fined that view of Indian Territory. The country set aside for them the great American desert. Resettlement meant poverty and the loss of identity in a des-olate place. John Ross, perhaps the most outspoken Cherokee critic of re-moval and resettlement, described Indian Territory as "the barren plains of the West," a place offering "no other prospect than the degradation, dispersion, and ultimate extinction of our race."[34] Ross's 1832 annual message to the Cherokee Nation contained his most damning description of Indian Territory. The country was not a dream but a nightmare. The lands offered for native re-settlement stretched over "an extensive prairie badly watered and only skirted on the margin of water courses and poor ridges with copses of wood." The demographic character of the proposed settlements also drew Ross's fire. Proud of the social and economic changes made in Cherokee life, Ross re-sented the presence of what he considered to be less "civilized" Indians. The tribal districts "assigned and occupied by some fifteen or twenty different tribes, and all speaking different languages, and cherishing a variety of habits and customs, a portion civilized, another half civilized, and others uncivi-lized" could only produce a country filled with violence and misunderstand-ing. And Ross went one step further. In order to keep peace in this inevitably factious country, the "congregated tribes" would end up "regulated under one General Government; by no doubt, white rulers."[35]

John Ross did not finally acknowledge the necessity of emigration to Indian Territory until April 1838. But even after accepting the inevitability of removal, he continued to characterize the new homeland as "the wilderness of the West."[36] But the language of "wilderness" and "barren waste," so useful in opposing resettlement, made little sense as Cherokees and other emigrants struggled to fashion new lives on the frontier. Indian Territory had to be reinvented, domesticated by its new native homeowners.

In September 1841, while in Washington lobbying for Cherokee claims, Ross began to change the way he described Indian Territory. Now it was a homeland, a place where native people had once again "lit their fires, built their camps, erected log cabins, and opened farms, under the fond hope of being there permanently established in a *new home*." Indian Territory was not only transformed into part of the American rural dream but Ross also boasted that the first steps had been taken for "the erection of *Schools* and *Churches*, in order, that the arts of Civilization and Christianization might follow in their wake and there flourish."[37] Ross's annual messages and addresses throughout the 1840s and 1850s expanded on that home-building theme. Indian Territory was the good country, the Indian Eden blessed with bountiful harvests and peaceful communities. Here Cherokees and others could find "respectability" of the sort James Brewer Stewart describes in his essay for this collection. Of course that respectability required separation and what Stewart aptly calls "modern racial essentialism." In the summer of 1857, having just toured the Cherokee Nation, Ross presented a redefined Indian Territory. The landscape held "well-cultivated farms, which have yielded abundant crops of grain, and thus affording a full supply for the wants of the people; well filled public schools, large and orderly assemblages, and quiet neighborhoods."[38]

This vision of Indian Territory was a dramatic revision, a reimagining of space into place. But the boundaries of those "quiet neighborhoods" were established by more than the spoken or written word. Having first been invented by white politicians, Indian Territory was now reinvented by Native American settlers. That reinvention involved not only the pronouncements of public figures like John Ross but the fashioning of laws that set physical and cultural borders. Here again race proved to be at the heart of the creation of place.

In the 1830s, as the rhetoric of race and racial identity grew more intense, some of the most prominent and influential southern Indian leaders embraced the notion of a separate "red race." As historian Theda Perdue observes, "the southern Indians who went west took with them . . . institutions, lifestyles, and attitudes developed in the South that they had shared with a white slaveholding society for over two hundred years."[39] John Ross repeatedly insisted that removal and resettlement would spell the "ultimate extinction of our race."[40] A Cherokee delegation addressing Congress described themselves as "the descendants of the Indian race."[41] And the Choctaw Constitution was explicit in its definition of racial identity: "No person shall be principal chief, or subordinate chief, senator, or representative, unless he be a free male citizen of the Choctaw Nation, and lineal descendant of the Choctaw or Chickasaw race."[42]

As Native Americans sought to define their own versions of Indian Territory, race became fundamental in establishing three kinds of boundaries. The first of those boundaries was citizenship. The Cherokee Constitution of 1839 made it plain that national citizenship was based on kinship, that is, blood relations racially defined. The language is so revealing that it deserves full quotation. Citizens were "the descendents of Cherokee men by all free women, except the African race, whose parents may have been living together as man and wife, according to the Customs and laws of this Nation, as well as the posterity of Cherokee women by all free men. No person who is of negro or mulatto parentage, whether by the father's or the mother's side, shall be eligible to hold any office of profit, honor, or trust under this government."[43]

The notion of racial separation was essential to the white invention of Indian Territory. Indians and whites had to be kept apart for the presumed good of both. Defining Indian Territory in terms of white exclusion was the counterpart to imagining American states without Native Americans. Virtually all the removal and resettlement treaties contained provisions excluding whites, with the exception of federal officials and missionaries. But the native nations themselves went beyond the treaties, enacting laws that clearly defined whites not married into native families as intruders. The Cherokee national government was increasingly explicit about the presence of white males. In 1839, just a year after the completion of Cherokee migration to Indian Territory, white males seeking to enter the nation to marry Indian women were required first to obtain a license from the national clerk.[44] When that modest effort failed to stem the tide of whites eager to settle on Cherokee lands, the tribal government drafted a comprehensive statute addressing kinship and racial boundaries in marriage. Insisting that "the peace and prosperity of the Cherokee people" required careful control over those "who may from time to time be privileged to reside within the territorial limits of this nation," the Cherokee National Committee established an elaborate set of guidelines for any white male seeking Cherokee citizenship by marriage. This boundary was not an impenetrable barrier but more like a semipermeable membrane. Whites could become Cherokee citizens by renouncing their whiteness. Those who refused to apply for the required license and take an oath of loyalty to the Cherokee Nation were to be labelled as intruders and expelled from the nation.[45]

Indian nations reestablishing themselves in the West found conceptions of race and racial difference a convenient category both in identifying themselves and keeping whites out of tribal lands. Exclusion of whites was a powerful way to affirm Indian national sovereignty. Becoming much like the immigrants in Jon Gjerde's essay, Cherokees and their neighbors accepted the lessons of an American education in race. But those same native nations, bent on keeping whites at arms length, were equally determined to control their own resident black populations. As William McLoughlin explains, "after removal to the West, Cherokees who owned slaves found it far easier to resettle than those who had no slaves."[46] Having set themselves apart from whites, Indians in Indian Territory sought boundaries to define relations with Africans, whether slave or free.

Throughout the 1840s native governments in Indian Territory introduced a series of laws aimed at separating native people and African Americans. As the American Republic increasingly defined itself as a "white man's country," the native nations in Indian Territory identified themselves as part of a "red man's country."[47] Intermarriage between a Cherokee citizen and "any slave or person of color" was prohibited under pain of corporal punishment.[48] Free blacks, "not of Cherokee blood," were forbidden to own property within the nation.[49] Slaves could not own livestock or firearms, and district sheriffs were empowered to seize such possession for sale at public auctions.[50] Following the practice in the southern states, the Cherokee Nation made it a crime to "teach any free negro or negroes not of Cherokee blood, or any slave to read or write." After 1848 those found teaching slaves to read or write were expelled from the nation.[51]

The presence of free blacks in the nations of Indian Territory posed what many Native Americans saw as a threat to cultural and genetic survival. Indian Territory had been defined by whites in exclusionary terms and was now redefined by native people in similar language. The presence of free black men and women challenged the Indian definition of homeland and sovereignty. At the end of 1842 the Cherokee government addressed this thorny issue in a comprehensive act regarding free blacks. Exclusion and expulsion were the ideological cornerstones of this legislation. Free blacks not originally manumitted by Cherokee owners were ordered to leave the nation no later than January 1843. Those refusing to leave would be reported to the federal Indian agent as intruders liable for "immediate expulsion." Cherokees who freed their slaves would now become personally and financially responsible for the actions of those freed. If those owners were dead or not located, the free black person was required to post a security bond to ensure "good conduct." The law assumed that no free black person could raise the necessary funds for the bond and would promptly leave the nation.[52]

The laws and constitutions of the native nations in Indian Territory were hardly unique given the wider southern experience. That legislation grew out of a period of hardening racial categories. Just as states such as Georgia or Alabama drew boundaries based on race, so did native nations. Nation-building in Indian Territory meant racial separation, notions about "blood purity," and the power of race in the making of place.

Nearly a century after the invention of Indian Territory, the native nations were in eclipse. Allotment under the Dawes Act, rampant land fraud, and the creation of the state of Oklahoma in 1907 all worked to unravel Indian Territory. But ideas about race and racial separation persisted. In the 1920s the town of Muskogee, Oklahoma—capital of the Creek Nation—was a place filled with the racial complexities born of removal and resettlement. The people of Muskogee were white, Creek, African American, Afro-Creek, and many other identities as well. But the racial separations remained. One newspaper advertisement from the period captures the enduring power of race in defining place and places apart. The Right Way Laundry proclaimed itself "the white people's laundry." To reassure its customers that their clothing would not touch that of Indians or blacks, the proprietors promised "we work for white people only."[53] Indian Territory, invented for the purposes of exclusion and separation, continued long after the name vanished from the map.

NOTES

1. John Ross, Annual Message, Oct. 3, 1859, in Gary E. Moulton, ed., *The Papers of Chief John Ross* (2 vols., Norman, 1985), II, 421.

2. Cherokee Delegation to the Senate and the House of Representatives, Feb. 28, 1840, *ibid*, 7.

3. Cherokee Delegation to the Senate and the House of Representatives, Apr. 15, 1824, *ibid.*, I, 77.

4. Jefferson to William Henry Harrison, Feb. 27, 1803, Thomas Jefferson Papers (Library of Congress, Washington, DC), microfilm edition. The complexities and ambiguities of Jefferson's views of Indians are discussed in Bernard Sheehan, *Seeds of Extinction: Jeffersonian Philanthropy and the American Indian* (Chapel Hill, 1973).

5. *Annals of Congress*, 8th Cong., 1st sess., 33–34.

6. Jefferson to Horatio Gates, July 11, 1803, Jefferson Papers.

7. Report of the Committee on Public Lands, Jan. 9, 1817, in Walter Lowrie, Walter S.

Franklin, and Matthew St. Clair Clark, eds., *American State Papers: Indian Affairs* (2 vols., Washington, DC, 1832–34), II, 123–24.

8. Calhoun to the House of Representatives, Jan. 15, 1820, *ibid.*, 473–74.

9. Calhoun to the Cherokee Delegation, Jan. 30, 1824, *ibid.*, 473–74.

10. James Monroe, Message on Indian Removal, Jan. 27, 1825, in Francis Paul Prucha, ed., *Documents of United States Indian Policy* (1975; 2d ed., Lincoln, 1990), 39–40.

11. James Barbour to John Cocke, Feb. 3, 1826, *American State Papers: Indian Affairs*, II, 647–48. See also Allan Nevins, ed., *The Diary of John Quincy Adams* (New York, 1951), 355.

12. D. W. Meinig, *The Shaping of America*, Vol. II, *Continental America, 1800–1867* (New Haven, 1993), 99–100.

13. *The Speech of Mr. Forsyth, of Georgia, on the Bill Providing for Removal of the Indians* (Washington, DC, 1830), 7.

14. Andrew Jackson, First Annual Message, Dec. 8, 1829, in James D. Richardson, comp., *A Compilation of Message and Papers of the Presidents* (10 vols., New York, 1896–99), III, 1021–22.

15. Andrew Jackson, Second Annual Message, Dec. 6, 1830, *ibid.*, 1082–86 (quotation at 1083).

16. Andrew Jackson, Fifth Annual Message, Dec. 3, 1833, *ibid.*, 1252.

17. Report of the Committee on Indian Affairs, Mar. 15, 1836, Senate Document 246, 24th Cong., 1st sess., 1.

18. *Ibid.*, 2–4, 6.

19. *Ibid.*, 5.

20. Meinig, *Shaping of America*, 92. The emergence of Indian Territory as a cartographic expression can be followed in: "Map of the Western Territory," [1834] in Regulating the Indian Department, House Report 474, 23d Cong., 1st sess., 132ff; "Map Showing the Lands Assigned to the Emigrant Indians West of Arkansas and Missouri," [1836] in "Colonel Dodge's Journal," House Document 181, 24th Cong., 1st sess., 36ff.

21. Isaac McCoy, *Remarks on the Practibility of Indian Reform, embracing their colonization* (New York, 1827), in David A. White, ed., *News of the Plains and Rockies, 1803–1865* (5 vols., Spokane, 1995–98), III, 299–300.

22. McCoy, *Remarks*, quoted in *Missionary Herald*, 2 (Feb. 1828), 104–05.

23. McCoy, *Country for the Indians West of the Mississippi* (1832), in White, ed., *News of the Plains and Rockies*, 302–15.

24. McCoy, *Annual Register of Indian Affairs* (1837), 81.

25. Donald Jackson, ed., *The Journals of Zebulon Montgomery Pike, with Letters and Related Documents* (2 vols., Norman, 1966), I, 314 (Sept. 5, 1806).

26. *Ibid.*, II, 10. Wilkinson's journal was published as part of Pike's 1810 *Account*.

27. Edwin James, comp., *Account of an Expedition from Pittsburgh to the Rocky Mountains* (2 vols., Philadelphia, 1823), II, 361. See also George J. Goodman and Cheryl A. Lawson, *Retracing Major Stephen H. Long's 1820 Expedition: The Itinerary and the Botany* (Norman, 1995), 100–120.

28. Thomas Nuttall, *A Journal of Travels into the Arkansas Territory During the Year 1819*, ed. Savoie Lottinville (1819; rep., Norman, 1980), 157.

29. *Ibid.*, 229.

30. *Ibid.*, 232.

31. Washington Irving, *A Tour on the Prairies* (London, UK, 1835), 39.

32. *Ibid.* Not all members of the expedition shared Irving's enthusiastic evaluation of the Indian Territory landscape. Charles J. Latrobe reported that the land set aside for Indians was "in fact a desert, with an ungrateful soil and stinted vegetation." Latrobe, *The Rambler in North America* (2 vols., London, UK, 1835), I, 243.

33. Cherokee Delegation to the Senate and the House of Representatives, Apr. 15, 1824, in Moulton, ed., *Ross Papers*, I, 77.

34. John Ross and George Lowrey, Annual Message, Oct. 14, 1829, *ibid.*, 172; John Ross, Annual Message, Oct. 24, 1831, *ibid.*, 230.

35. John Ross, Annual Message, Oct. 10, 1832, *ibid.*, 254.

36. Cherokee Delegation to the Senate and the House of Representatives, Feb. 28, 1840, *ibid.*, II, 7.

37. John Ross to Elizabeth Milligan, Sept. 5, 1841, *ibid.*, 101.

38. John Ross, Annual Message, Oct. 5, 1857, *ibid.*, 404.

39. Theda Perdue, "Indians in Southern History," in Frederick Hoxie and Peter Iverson, eds., *Indians in American History: An Introduction* (1988; 2d ed., Wheeling, WV, 1998), 132–33.

40. John Ross, Annual Message, Oct. 24, 1831, in Moulton, ed., *Ross Papers*, I, 230.

41. Cherokee Delegation to the Senate and the House of Representatives, Feb. 27, 1829, *ibid.*, 155.

42. Joseph P. Folsom, comp., *Constitution and Laws of the Choctaw Nation* (New York, 1869), 19.

43. *Laws of the Cherokee Nation adopted by the Council at Various Periods* (Tahlequah, 1852), 7.

44. *Ibid.*, 32–33.

45. *Ibid.*, 92–94.

46. William G. McLoughlin, *After the Trail of Tears: The Cherokees' Struggle for Sovereignty 1839–1880* (Chapel Hill, 1993), 125.

47. *Ibid.*, 128.

48. *Laws of the Cherokee Nation*, 19.

49. *Ibid.*, 44.

50. *Ibid.*

51. *Ibid.*, 55–56.

52. *Ibid.*, 71.

53. Muskogee *Times-Democrat*, Mar. 3, 1926.

BIBLIOGRAPHY

McLoughlin, William G. *Cherokee Renascence in the New Republic*. Princeton: Princeton University Press, 1987.

———. *After the Trail of Tears: The Cherokees' Struggle for Sovereignty 1839–1880*. Chapel Hill: University of North Carolina Press, 1993.

Meinig, D. W. *The Shaping of America*. Vol. 2: *Continental America, 1800–1867*. New Haven: Yale University Press, 1993.

Moulton, Gary E. *John Ross, Cherokee Chief*. Athens: University of Georgia Press, 1978.

Nobles, Gregory H. *American Frontiers: Cultural Encounters and Continental Conquest.* New York: Hill & Wang, 1997.

Perdue, Theda. "Indians in Southern History." In *Indians in American History: An Introduction*, 2nd edition, ed. Frederick Hoxie and Peter Iverson. Wheeling, Ill.: Harlan Davidson, 1998.

Prucha, Francis Paul. *The Great Father: The United States Government and the American Indians*, 2 vols. Lincoln: University of Nebraska Press, 1984.

Schulz, George A. *An Indian Canaan: Isaac McCoy and the Vision of an Indian State.* Norman: University of Oklahoma Press, 1972.

Thacker, Robert. *The Great Prairie Fact and Literary Imagination.* Albuquerque: University of New Mexico Press, 1989.

9

The Culmination of Racial Polarities and Prejudice

David Brion Davis

The classic, authoritative Eleventh Edition (1910–11) of *The Encyclopaedia Britannica* can well be seen as a great compendium of the knowledge and wisdom of the nineteenth century, updated in final form for the twentieth century.[1] The authors of the essays, many of which are often long and beautifully written, include many of the most famous writers and scientists of the time. The subject "Indians, North American," commands thirty double-columned pages of fine print, covering nearly two hundred tribes, fifty-five "stocks," much technical information on Indian languages, and a sober assessment of the Indians' then present "condition" and "progress."

The subject "Negro" warrants less than five double-columned pages, but in the second part, "Negroes in the United States," Walter Francis Willcox, a Cornell professor of social science and statistics and the chief statistician of the United States Census Bureau, presents a cautiously optimistic and highly statistical view of the post-Reconstruction condition of African Americans, and cites three works each by Booker T. Washington and W. E. B. Du Bois.[2] The first and more generalized essay, by Thomas A. Joyce, an anthropologist at the British Museum's Department of Ethnography, draws on a far more international scholarly literature and conveys the impression of cautious objectivity. For example, Joyce states at one point that "the negro is largely the creature of his environment, and it is not fair to judge his mental capacity by tests taken directly from the environment of the white man, as for instance tests in mental arithmetic." Yet Joyce shows no hesitation on the key issue:

Mentally the negro is inferior to the white. The remark of F. Manetta [in *La Razza Negra nel suo stato selvaggio* (Turin, 1864), p. 20], made after a long study of the negro in America, may be taken as generally true of the whole race: "the negro

children were sharp, intelligent and full of vivacity, but on approaching the adult period a gradual change set in. The intellect seemed to become clouded, animation giving place to a sort of lethargy, briskness yielding to indolence. . . ." The arrest or even
deterioration in mental development is no doubt very largely due to the fact that after puberty sexual matters take the first place in the negro's life and thoughts.

This basic white consensus, embodied in such influential and "progressive" works as Ulrich Bonnell Phillips's *American Negro Slavery* (1918) and
W. E. Woodward's popular *A New American History* (1936), was in many
ways the product of the historical changes described in the preceding eight essays on "Racial Consciousness and Nation-Building in the Early Republic."
As the essays vividly suggest, the ways in which slaves were freed in the
North, together with the "removal" of the Indians from the Southeastern
states and the expansion and defense of racial slavery in the South, exerted a
profound influence on the meaning of emancipation in the Civil War and the
ultimate abandonment of Reconstruction. The resulting white consensus on
Negro inferiority, greatly reinforced by Euro-American pseudoscience and
popular media such as film, became a massive blight or ideological pathogen
against which generations of black and white scholars and activists have
struggled.

In the antebellum period a few white radicals, such as Gerrit Smith and
John Brown, emerged from the racist Platonic cave of misperception and succeeded in viewing the world through African-American eyes.[3] Yet as Smith
and Brown discovered, the truth of equality was too overwhelming to bear. If
Africans and people of African descent were truly equal and capable of all the
mental achievements of whites, then the whites' recognition of guilt should
resemble Michelangelo's faces of the Damned in the Sistine Chapel's
"Last Judgment."[4] This vision of guilt would include not only the four centuries of the ghastly Atlantic slave trade and New World slavery, the many
decades of Jim Crow and the thousands of lynchings, but also the long-term
effects of what the black abolitionist Theodore S. Wright termed in 1836 "the
spirit of prejudice," which

> like the atmosphere everywhere felt by [the colored man] . . . wither[s] all our hopes,
> and oft times causes the colored parent as he looks upon his child, to wish he had
> never been born. . . . This *influence* cuts us off from everything; it follows us up from
> childhood to manhood; it excludes us from all stations of profit, usefulness, and
> honor; takes away from us all motive for pressing forward in enterprises, useful and
> important to the world and to ourselves.[5]

As Wright and other black writers emphasized, this humiliating and dehumanizing prejudice could be self-reinforcing in the sense that white contempt
and denial of hope could lead to despair and patterns of behavior that pro-

voked more prejudice. Given the genuine progress made since World War II, it is extremely difficult for today's historians to imagine the psychological effects of enslavement and rabid racism on black aspirations and behavior in the nineteenth and early twentieth centuries.[6] Even in the 1930s and 1940s, at the time of Stepinfetchit and Native Son, the number of African-American college graduates, doctors, lawyers, generals, and business executives in the year 2000 would have seemed incredible.[7] Of course we still have a long way to go in freeing ourselves from the heritage of the white racist consensus symbolized by the 1911 *Encyclopaedia Britannica* article. But meanwhile, the moral shock of facing the realities of our past can easily oversimplify history by moralistically dividing its actors into "the children of light and the children of darkness."

For many years there has been a strong tendency to write history in the constant shadow of "what should have happened," from the perspective of the late twentieth century. Precisely because both masters and slaves were complex human beings, their relationships often defy easy formulas and expectations. The fashionable and continuing emphasis on slave resistance, while correcting the "Gone With the Wind" mythology, makes it virtually impossible to explain why slavery could be so economically productive and successful over long periods of time, why slave prices in the South continued to rise through the 1850s and well into the Civil War, and how two or three adult white males could control one hundred or two hundred slaves on an isolated Caribbean or Southern plantation. It is also easy to forget that negrophobia has sometimes been closely related to negrophilia, much as anti-Semitism and philo-Semitism have "bled over into each other," as the historian Harold Brackman puts it.[8] But above all, if we are to understand the workings of historical evil, we must strive to *understand* (which must always be distinguished from exoneration) the minds not only of slaves and free blacks but of masters, blackface minstrels, colonizationists, antiabolitionists, and leaders of lynch mobs (how can one understand the Second World War without seeing the world through the eyes of Hitler, SS troops, and their commanders?).

The eight excellent essays in this collection point to the 1830s as a time of critical change for African and Native Americans, a transformation that led, I would conclude, to a "culmination of racial polarities" during the century that followed. Of course no matter when a historian begins a particular inquiry or narrative, there is always a "before." Without questioning the centrality of the 1830s (and some of the essays do move back into the eighteenth century), I think it is important to take note of a number of recent discoveries regarding the much earlier Euro-American "construction of race," particularly a 1996 seminar that met in colonial Williamsburg and then produced a special issue of *The William and Mary Quarterly*.[9] Thus before discussing a few of the issues raised in the preceding essays, I would like to summarize some of the antecedents and preconditions that help to put early or mid-nineteenth-century racial developments in broader perspective.

As the medievalist Paul Freedman has recently shown, "whiteness studies" should turn first to the symbolism of social class in medieval Europe. For many centuries the aristocracy, clergy, and commercial classes looked upon serfs and peasants with contempt, derision, and sometimes fear. Unlike Jews, Muslims, heretics, and lepers, who were also degraded and dehumanized, the servile peasants constituted a large majority of the population and furnished the physical labor on which the elites depended. Therefore, as Freedman emphasizes, the images of the medieval peasant could combine a mockery of filth, stupidity, and bestiality with occasional tributes to the peasants' simplicity, piety, and closeness to God. Yet the need to justify vast inequality and subjugation led to the conclusion that the lower classes were the progeny of Cain or Ham (as Freedman points out, it was in the Islamic world, with its heavy traffic in African slaves, that Noah's curse of Ham's son Canaan was first widely used to link blackness with slavery).[10] Medieval Europeans also elaborated Aristotle's argument that many humans are simply born and constructed to do heavy toil. And especially in France, serfs and peasants were "often depicted as dark-skinned or 'black,' either by reason of their labor in the sun and their proximity to the earth, or as a sign of their overall hideousness."[11]

The discovery that medieval European peasants were often perceived as "black" by whites who stayed out of the sun and never handled dirt and manure fits in with Peter Kolchin's report that some nineteenth-century Russian nobles "actually claimed that whereas they had white bones peasants had black bones." And according to Kolchin, "Russian noblemen saw the peasants as inherently different from themselves, possessing the same lazy, childlike character that American slaveholders ascribed to blacks."[12]

Despite some ambiguity over the meaning of dark skin color—exemplified in medieval Europe by the statues and paintings of the noble African knight, Saint Maurice, and the black king or Magus in depictions of the Nativity Scene—European Christian culture was already receptive to negative views of "black."[13] As the distinguished medievalist William Chester Jordan has put it: "[A]llegorically the words 'Jew' and 'Blackness' conjured the Devil; morally they denoted evil; and mystically they evoked the Day of Judgment."[14] Since medieval Europeans hardly ever viewed sub-Saharan Africans in person, their first impressions of dark-skinned humans would probably have come from religious paintings of the devil, his torturers, or a black or swarthy crucifier of Christ.[15]

Despite these predispositions, there can be no doubt that slavery produced racism, in the sense that the negative stereotypes that had been applied to

slaves and serfs since antiquity, regardless of ethnicity, were ultimately trans-
ferred to black slaves and then to most people of African descent after
bondage became almost exclusively confined to blacks. On the other hand,
there is a sense in which people of dark skin were "made to order" for Europeans who had struggled for centuries to find markers that would help to justify class polarities and also identify, even at some distance outdoors, people
who could be classified as "natural slaves." This is not to say that European
maritime nations consciously planned to found New World colonies based on
African slave labor. Black slavery was almost always a delayed and unexpected choice. Yet when Columbus sailed from Spain in 1492, African slaves
were already producing much of Europe's sugar on the Portuguese plantation
colonies of Madeira and Sâo Tomé. And there is much evidence to support
James H. Sweet's conclusion that "the Muslims created a plethora of racist
ideas, but it was the Iberians who, in conjunction with a rising demand for
slave labor, turned these ideas into a coherent ideology. . . . Iberian racism
was a necessary precondition for the system of human bondage that would
develop in the Americas during the sixteenth century and beyond."[16]

The Muslim societies from Spain and North Africa to the Mideast never
developed racism in a judicial or institutional way, but as they increasingly
drew on sub-Saharan supplies of slave labor, Arabic and Persian literature
conveyed most of the antiblack stereotypes adopted by Euro-Americans in
the eighteenth and nineteenth centuries. Ibn Khaldun (1332–1406), one of the
greatest historians and social thinkers of the Middle Ages, drew a significant
line between white slaves and black slaves and concluded that "the Negro nations are, as a rule submissive to slavery, because [Negroes] have little [that
is essentially] human and have attributes that are quite similar to those of
dumb animals." Khaldun added that "most of the Negroes of the first zone
[the tropics] dwell in caves and thickets, eat herbs, live in savage isolation
and do not congregate, and eat each other."[17] In other medieval Arab and Iran-
ian works the black "appears as a kind of monster or bogeyman," "ugly and
misshapen," "naked and licentious." According to a thirteenth-century Persian writer, the east African "Zanj differ from animals only in that 'their two
hands are lifted above the ground' . . . . Many have observed that the ape is
more teachable and more intelligent than the Zanji."[18]

The frequent likening of blacks to animals is especially significant in view
of the theory that slavery was originally modeled on the domestication of animals (Aristotle remarked that the ox was "the poor man's slave"), as well as
the common use of bestialization as a way of dehumanizing humans and depriving them of all respect, honor, and dignity.[19] In a sense, enslavement has
been the most extreme expression of this all-too human desire for individual
or group supremacy, achieved by subjugating "the Other."

The widespread existence of Islamic antiblack racism from the tenth century onward is confirmed by the response of black and colored writers, who cried out, for example, "If my color were pink, women would love me/ But the Lord has marred me with blackness"; "though my hair is woolly and my skin coal-black/ My hand is open and my honor bright." "I am a black man," a famous singer and musician wrote on seeking lodging in Damascus: "Some of you may find me offensive. I shall therefore sit and eat apart."[20]

There has been little study of the transmission of racist ideas from Muslims to Christians (or Jews) in the Iberian Peninsula. Gomes Eannes de Azurara, the Portuguese royal chronicler who in the mid-fifteenth century described the capture and sale of the first African slaves shipped to Portugal, referred ambiguously to the blacks who had already been enslaved by the Moorish prisoners "in accordance with ancient custom, which I believe to have been because of the curse which, after the Deluge, Noah laid upon his son Cain ["Caim," a Latin word in the original text], cursing him in this way:—that his race should be subject to all the other races in the world."[21] In 1625 the English Reverend Samuel Purchas also drew upon an account of Muslim slavery to make a more explicit linkage between Noah's curse, blackness of skin, and slavery.[22] Nevertheless, as Benjamin Braude makes clear, Europeans long associated Ham with Asia, and the Noachic curse was more of an *ex post facto* justification than an original motive for enslaving black Africans.

But the centuries of warfare between Christians and Muslims, culminating in the Christian Reconquest of Portugal and Spain, certainly did nourish the image of white Christians overcoming dark-skinned Moors—an impression reinforced by the fact that Berber armies included thousands of black slaves. James Sweet affirms that "the Portuguese were undoubtedly influenced by the attitudes of their Muslim trading partners along the Saharan littoral," and by the fact that many black slaves toiled in salt mines and fields on the Saharan frontier.[23] Whatever the sources of influence, the African slaves shipped to Lisbon in the fifteenth and sixteenth centuries were stripped naked and marketed and priced exactly like livestock. A. C. de C. M. Saunders and other scholars have documented the grim plight of slaves and free blacks in Portugal from the 1440s to the 1550s. Since protective laws were not enforced, the main curb on racism was the fraternization and occasional marriage with members of the lowest classes of whites—a situation that in some ways anticipated social relations in parts of Latin America and in what Ira Berlin has termed "the charter generation" period of slavery in North America.[24] For many centuries the interaction between blacks and whites of the lowest servile orders prevented racial polarization in the most rigid and modern sense.

One can only speculate on possible Portuguese lines of influence in England. From the Treaty of Windsor in 1386, England was strongly allied with the nation that initiated and long dominated the African slave trade (English ships, like African slaves, were a common sight in Portuguese Madeira). Although the English long showed little interest in Africa and became heavily involved in the slave trade only in the late seventeenth century, they seemed especially prone to racist views of Africans as early as the 1550s. According to the early voyager Robert Gainsh, the Negroes were "a people of beastly lyvyng, without a God, lawe, religion, or common wealth." African women, Gainsh continued, "are common: for they contracte no matrimonie, neyther have respecte to chastitie." Images of "blacke beasts" and "brutish blacke people" recur throughout the Elizabethan traveler descriptions that Emily C. Bartels and Alden T. Vaughan and Virginia Mason Vaughan have examined.[25] In effect, this new research confirms the judgment Winthrop D. Jordan made nearly thirty years ago:

> They [English commentators] knew perfectly well that Negroes were men, yet they frequently described the Africans as "brutish" or "bestial" or "beastly." The hideous tortures, the cannibalism, the rapacious warfare, the revolting diet . . . seemed somehow to place the Negro among the beasts. . . . Slave traders in Africa handled Negroes the same way men in England handled beasts, herding and examining and buying.[26]

In view of the much later American colonization movement, it is important to note that Queen Elizabeth, in the waning years of her reign, "called repeatedly, though unsuccessfully, for the expulsion from the realm of 'the great numbers of negars and Blackamoores' who had become a 'great annoyance of hir owne leige people.'"[27] Two centuries later, when London received numerous blacks who had been freed by the British during the American War of Independence, Granville Sharp and other philanthropists founded Sierra Leone as a refuge for a people who were generally prevented from finding jobs or becoming integrated into English society.[28]

The essays in the "Constructing Race" collection point to an extraordinary contrast between the first English representations of Africans and those of Native Americans, who were often perceived as the descendants of the ten Lost Tribes of Israel, whose conversion would thus bring on the millennium. If the beastly, "black" European peasant personified the human Id and became a template for the later depictions of the Negro slave, English observers marveled over the aristocratic bearing and posture of Native Americans, who were said to be "borne white" and who seemed to share no characteristics with the English lower classes. Indeed, because Indians were associated with Nature, the "modesty" of their women and their sensitivity to status appeared to legitimate England's vast hierarchical social structure. According to Karen Ordahl Kupperman, English writers actually looked to the Indians' customs and culture for solutions to what they perceived as the growing social problems of their own homeland.[29]

Of course English settlers, like other Europeans, would soon look upon some Indians as unredeemable "savages" who could be slaughtered or enslaved and sold to the West Indies. Still, the Englishmen's initial conviction of commonality, reinforced by a continuing dependence on Indians for trade and military alliance, worked against the kind of racist separation and degradation associated with Africans. A further theme of pragmatism can be seen in the fact that white settlers in frontier South Carolina used Indian scouts to hunt down fugitive black slaves but also relied on armed slaves to ward off repeated attacks by Native Americans.[30]

As we have seen, then, one can trace a continuity of negative and dehumanizing images of black Africans from medieval Muslims to fifteenth- and sixteenth-century Iberians and on to sixteenth- and seventeenth-century northern Europeans and Euro-Americans. Yet racism was clearly nourished by the haphazard and somewhat fortuitous spread of black slavery from Portugal, the Mediterranean, and Atlantic Islands to the Spanish New World colonies, Brazil, Barbados, Virginia, and then most of the Western Hemisphere (it is difficult to imagine an eighteenth-century European monarch, after the New World slave system was solidly in place, following the example of Portugal's Manuel I, who in 1491 helped to persuade the ruler of the Kongo to be baptised as Joâo I, and who even accepted an embassy in 1513 from the Empress of Ethiopia).[31] Though the continuities of negative imagery are important as preconditions, I think it is a mistake to imagine a teleological picture of racism developing in a linear or inevitable progression.

The complexity and fortuity of racial attitudes can be illustrated by a number of random examples: the decision of a seventeenth-century Massachusetts court to return kidnapped captives to Africa;[32] the highly dignified and individualized portraits of blacks by a galaxy of great Renaissance and early modern painters; the alliances of various kinds between American indentured servants, sailors, and black slaves; the popularity among London's poor in the early nineteenth century of the ultra-radical Spencean preacher, Robert Wedderburn, a mulatto son of a Jamaican slave who was inspired by the Haitian Revolution and edited the periodical *Axe Laid to the Root*;[33] and finally, the international fame of Olaudah Equiano and Phillis Wheatley, to say nothing of Toussaint L'ouverture and Frederick Douglass.

Above all, until the late eighteenth century, antiblack racism seldom permeated entire white populations or became a tool for political manipulation. It was not until the mass emancipation of slaves became *thinkable*—starting with the judicial decisions and cautious legislation of the northern states in the early 1780s and culminating with the Haitian Revolution and the French emancipation decree of 1794—that race took on new and highly explosive popular meanings.

As Lois Horton and Joanne Pope Melish make clear, the consequences of gradual emancipation in the North coincided with the ending of white indentures and with a white democratization that increasingly separated the white working class from a competitive population of former slaves who, in the words of one early mulatto preacher, "have been taught to view themselves as a rank of beings far below others," a people whom whites thought of as "despised, ignorant, and licentious."[34] As northerners repressed and effaced their own historical experience with slavery in an effort to claim the distinction of "free soil," they converted the free blacks, as Melish perceptively shows, into a "marooned" population of "unaccountable strangers." Even black abolitionists could not agree on a confusing question: were white prejudice and black degradation the result of their own ancestors' bondage? Or of the continuing existence and expansion of black slavery in the South? The former answer, concerning slavery in the North, might well alienate white abolitionists, since they wanted to think of the North as historically "free," and even more important, northern abolition would then underscore the long-term complexity and difficulties of emancipating slaves. In striking contrast to the British abolitionists like Thomas Clarkson, who never had to live with the consequences of emancipation and who narrated a succession of triumphs that gave the illusion of continuity from outlawing the slave trade in 1808 to the ending of slavery and apprenticeship in 1834 and 1838, American abolitionists failed to honor or celebrate their preceding generations' truly difficult struggles to abolish slavery in the North. From the time English Quakers posed embarrassing questions to Pennsylvania Quakers about the consequences of emancipation in the 1780s, American abolitionists were deeply perplexed by the issue of the free African Americans' "condition."[35]

Even the most radical French abolitionists could first assert that no society could legitimate the crime of slavery and that "the restoration of a slave's freedom is not a gift or an act of charity . . . [but rather] a compelling duty, an act of justice, which simply affirms an existing truth," and then quickly add that "since our greed has reduced the blacks to a degraded and impotent state, [an immediate emancipation] would be equivalent to abandoning and refusing aid to infants in their cradles or to helpless cripples."[36] Though some modern historians are inclined to view such statements as examples of blatant hypocrisy, even former slaves often agreed that the institution was psychologically "degrading" and debilitating, and entailed serious problems of self-confidence, self-perception, and aspiration. The notion that slaves needed "preparation" for freedom became discredited—despite the biblical model of the Israelites' forty years of preparation in the wilderness—by measures like Britain's "apprenticeship," which merely prolonged the exploitation of black labor. Yet given the deprivations of bondage, it was hardly unreasonable to think of some kind of rehabilitation, as opposed to abandoning freedpeople in the midst of an increasingly racist and competitive society. In view of the efforts of missionaries to "civilize" the Cherokees, for example, it is remarkable how little thought abolitionists and liberal legislators gave to the issue of providing freed slaves with the skills, education, and self-confidence needed to become truly "free" in the dominant white and capitalist culture.

Nevertheless, as James Brewer Stewart makes clear, from the beginning of northern emancipation African-American leaders hammered away at the crucial need for uplift, self-improvement, and the achievement of "respectability." White abolitionists then repeated similar appeals, which echoed much of the rhetoric concerning the "civilizing" of Southeastern Indians (and as Daniel K. Richter shows, the misguided efforts of Quakers to "civilize" the Miamis and other Northwestern tribes). To put matters in perspective, we should remember that the 1820s was a decade of unprecedented urbanization, when white workers were still consuming extraordinary quantities of alcohol and were only beginning to adjust to the clock-determined regimen of factory discipline. Indeed, the powerful temperance movement was in part directed by the goal of making workers more responsible and productive.

The 1820s also witnessed the birth of the Second Great Awakening, which led converts like Theodore Dwight Weld to campaign for schools that combined intellectual study with manual labor, before he became a radical abolitionist who reached out to and worked with the black community in Cincinnati. The movement for black uplift, upward mobility, and respectability was thus part of a much broader effort to democratize the onset of modernity and to create a more unified and socially responsible citizenry.

Such words jar or even anger some modern historians brought up in an antibourgeois, antielitist tradition. Though they take pride in their own status and usually try to train their own children to be courteous, neat, considerate, well-mannered, highly skilled, and well-informed, such historians and other writers tend to romanticize the supposedly communal, anti-individualistic behavior of a vaguely pre-modern, pre-"Market Revolution" era.[37] With respect to American race relations, this means the mixing of blacks, both slave and free, with mostly lower-class whites in grog houses, cellar bistros, oyster houses, lottery stalls, and houses of prostitution. If a dominant theme of American history has been upward mobility into an increasingly diverse middle class, one of the tragic costs of this dramatic improvement in education and standard of living has been a widespread disdain and contempt for those left behind, at least temporarily—for those who still lived as our ancestors did: the ancestral indentured servants, criminals, and steerage-traveling immigrants from whom most white Americans are descended. Yet even the harshest critics must admit that no nation in history has attracted so many millions of immigrants (and would-be immigrants) from all parts of the world. Nor has any other nation given such newcomers, at least over a number of generations, such a range of opportunities.[38]

But the most serious consequence of downgrading the importance of the black quest for uplift and self-respect is the way it minimizes and detracts attention from the truly central point: the racist white backlash against every form of black elevation, upward mobility, and "self-improvement." As Stewart, Melish, David R. Roediger, and Lois Horton all show, the freeing of slaves in the North led to a concerted movement—which in effect lasted at least until the 1940s—to keep the Negro "in his place." White mobs repeatedly attacked black schools, churches, fraternal societies, abolitionist printing presses, and other symbols of African-American elevation and integration into white American society. Despite such pressures, some antebellum blacks did become prosperous or achieve higher education, sometimes abroad, but their lives were filled with insult and peril.

This vehement and continuing hostility to black uplift and self-improvement, to the specter of blacks becoming more like middle-class whites, is difficult to explain. I can think of a number of possible causes. One can point to the enduring stigma of slavery, which has been a handicap in various cultures including parts of Africa. The cultural gap that separated African Americans from Anglo-Americans was probably even wider than that experienced by Irish, German, Polish, Italian, and eastern European Jewish immigrants. And as Jon Gjerde and David Roediger make clear, many immigrants found that antiblack racism was the easiest route to assimilation and winning acceptance as "white," respectable Americans. As Gjerde puts it: "By becoming white, they were able to etch out a niche amid the uncertainties of the early national era. In an effort to make certain that the larger society differentiated them from the non-white, the unfree, and disempowered, these immigrants became among the most vociferous advocates of a *herrenvolk* republic" (96). In a now classic work, Edmund S. Morgan argued years ago that lower-class white southern farmers made a similar discovery by the early eighteenth century.[39] If free blacks no longer served as what Senator James Henry Hammond termed "the mud-sills of society" and began climbing to the highest floors, the entire edifice of American democratic society might collapse as if struck by an earthquake of 9.8 on the Richter scale.

Building on the work of William G. McLoughlin, Theda Perdue, and other historians, James P. Ronda shows that even the Southeastern Indians who were in effect deported to the West took with them many black slaves and the racist standards and values of the white slaveholding society. Thus the Cherokee Constitution of 1839 barred anyone "of negro or mulatto parentage" from holding "any office of profit, honor, or trust under this government." Like most of the southern states, the Cherokee nation severely restricted slave manumissions and made it a crime to teach any slave or free Negro (not of Cherokee blood) to read or write. Efforts to exclude and expel free blacks take on added meaning when we read of the prohibitions of intermarriage with "any slave or person of color" "under pain of corporal punishment." If Cherokees and Choctaws could not become white, they could at least take pride in being "red" and try to prevent their tribes from becoming black.[40]

There is a mountain of evidence suggesting that at the very core of opposition to black upward mobility lay a frantic, obsessive fear of what antebellum Americans termed "amalgamation" ("miscegenation" was a product of the Civil War years). In other words, white (and even many Native) Americans assumed that the growth of genuine social equality would inevitably lead to racial intermixture, including intermarriage. In retrospect, this deep apprehension seems wholly irrational, since blacks were supposedly ugly and physically repulsive, and as matters developed there has been so little black-white intermarriage between emancipation in 1865 and 1999 that the incidence today is still well below one percent of all marriages (this is especially remarkable when compared with the intermarriage rate between Jews and Gentiles [about fifty-two percent of marriages involving Jews]).[41] Yet the antebellum white obsession seems to have been based on four factors: (1) the actual high incidence of sexual intermixture in the South, where white men continued to exploit slave women; (2) the visible blending of races in the Luso-Hispanic world, a point driven home by news reports and debates over annexation during the Mexican War; (3) a long popular tradition regarding the blacks' superior sexuality; (4) and probably most important, the whispered awe regarding the grossly misunderstood meaning of certain semi-additive genes. Thus although we now know that African ethnic groups embody far more genetic diversity than that found between, let us say, a given African group and Chinese or Europeans, whites were dumbfounded for many centuries by the observation that even grandchildren of single black grandparents could share many of the somatic features of a "Negro."

When Fray Prudencio de Sandoval wanted to make the same point in 1604 about the Christian descendants of Jews (*Conversos* or *Marranos*), he took it for granted that everyone knew that if Negro men "should unite themselves a thousand times with white women, the children are born with the dark color of the father. Similarly, it is not enough for the Jew to be three parts aristocrat of Old Christian for one family line [i.e., one Jewish ancestor] alone defiles and corrupts him."[42] This Spanish obsession with "purity of blood" (*limpieza da sangre*) was clearly one of the sources of modern racism and rested to a large extent on the generational dominance of dark skin and kinky hair, which had little if anything to do with other, more "internal" genetic traits.[43] But for many white Americans, at least vaguely aware of the rapid natural increase of the slave population in the South, it appeared that if slavery were abolished and racial intermixture spread to the North, the United States would soon become "a nation of Negroes."

Nevertheless, despite the general white hostility to black upward mobility, despite the number of leaders from Jefferson, Madison, and Monroe to Clay and Lincoln who favored the "colonization" of free blacks outside the United States, despite the notorious Fugitive Slave Law and *Dred Scott* decision, there were more moments of toleration and openness than one might expect. In 1843, for example, abolitionists succeeded in repealing the Massachusetts law forbidding racial intermarriage—a revolutionary step that the nation as a whole would not take until *1967*, with the landmark Supreme Court decision of *Loving* v. *Virginia*.[44]

Even the white crowd that responded to the Lincoln-Douglas debate in Freeport, Illinois, was more open to racial social equality than David Roediger's highly insightful essay suggests. He astutely points to a revealing moment when Stephen Douglas's backers "chanted over and over" "White men, white men." Actually, they voiced these words only once (but did repeat "white, white"), and the sexual context is crucial for an understanding of the wholly opposing viewpoints. In an effort to besmirch Lincoln and "the Black Republicans," Senator Douglas accused Lincoln of relying on Frederick Douglass, the famous former slave, as one of his three advisers (Frederick Douglass later made sport of this in a speech in Poughkeepsie, New York).[45] Douglas then asserted that he had earlier seen the black leader in Freeport, riding in a magnificent carriage: "a beautiful young lady was sitting on the box seat, whilst Fred Douglass and her mother reclined inside, and the owner of the carriage acted as driver." This image of a former slave cavorting as an equal with two seemingly prosperous white women evoked an amazing response: "Laughter, cheers, cries of 'right, what have you to say against it,'&c." When Douglas angrily replied, "I saw this in your own town," someone shouted, "'What of it[?]'. There were further cries of 'Good, good,' and cheers, mingled with hooting and cries of 'white, white.'" It was only after Douglas added that "another rich black negro" was campaigning in the state "for his friend Lincoln as the champion of black men," that someone yelled, "White men, white men." Yet other voices chimed in: "what have you got to say against it," "that's right, &c."[46]

We need to learn more about such diverse points of view within the general public, especially since historians are far too inclined to generalize on the basis of region, class, religion, and ethnicity. James Stewart is surely right when he points to a profound shift in the abolitionists' perception when they realized that "moral suasion" had failed and that the growing nationalism of the Jacksonian period demanded an acceptance of the racial status quo—an agreement never to question the South's controversial and now "peculiar" institution that undergirded the system of racial control in the North. As abolitionists saw the necessity of somehow regenerating the entire society, perhaps by endorsing slave violence, they became more alienated from the general public. Yet as Lacy K. Ford Jr. brilliantly demonstrates, southerners themselves continued to harbor more reservations about racial slavery than most of us have recognized. Even in the Deep South, where the economic necessity of slave labor could hardly be doubted, legislators feared black majorities and attempted without success to prohibit the commercial influx of slaves for sale or hire; indeed, Louisiana and Mississippi, fearing an insurrection if the states became a dumping ground for rebellious blacks, even developed "character tests" for imported slaves!

Daniel K. Richter's insightful essay on the way well-meaning Quakers misinterpreted "Indianness" provides a theme that unites the preceding eight articles. During the once-celebrated era of "Jacksonian democracy," white Americans became increasingly entangled in a web of misjudgments and contradictions as they generally abandoned efforts to uplift, include, and assimilate Indians and blacks. Jackson himself dissociated the westward removal of Indians from any ideal of a civilizing process and eventual integration. The parallel hope of removing African Americans from a hopelessly prejudiced society failed, largely because leaders in the Deep South saw the project as an abolitionist Trojan horse (despite the vehement attacks on colonization by free blacks and Garrisonians). Yet in the end many blacks and Indians were doomed for a prolonged period to a kind of colonization—the first group in urban ghettos, the second in often arid and ambition-stifling reservations.

NOTES

1. The first edition, published in three volumes, appeared in 1768–71; the eleventh has twenty-nine volumes.

2. Professor Willcox is the only scholar whom I have met and talked with who was well over the age of 100. In the mid-1950s, when I was still in my twenties, he honored me with a request to write his biography, a project I felt incapable of doing.

3. John Stauffer, "The Black Hearts of Men: Race, Religion, and Radical Reform in Nineteenth-Century America" (Ph.D. diss., Yale University, 1999).

4. It is interesting to note that Michelangelo included the face of a black man among the Elect, in the Last Judgment; *The Complete Work of Michelangelo* (New York, n.d.), 250.

5. Theodore S. Wright, in *Friend of Man*, Oct. 27, 1836, reprinted in *The Black Abolitionist Papers*, ed. C. Peter Ripley (5 vols., Chapel Hill, 1991), III, 184.

6. One of the most successful recent attempts to deal with this issue is Bertram Wyatt-Brown, "The Mask of Obedience: Slave Psychology in the Old South," found on the internet, http://www.clas.ufl.edu/users/bwyattb/sambo2.htm.

7. Even more mind-boggling, for someone living in 1940, would have been the black "Dionysian" males recently discussed by Orlando Patterson—i.e., Michael Jordan, O.J. Simpson, Michael Jackson, Dennis Rodman, and others to say nothing of General Colin Powell, who might well have been elected president of the United States. Orlando Patterson, *Rituals of Blood: Consequences of Slavery in Two American Centuries* (Washington, DC, 1998), 235–82.

8. Harold Brackman, personal e-mail to the author, Aug. 16, 1999.

9. "Constructing Race," *William and Mary Quarterly*, 54 (Jan. 1997). Though I did not attend the seminar, I wrote the introduction to the published papers, "Constructing Race: A Reflection," 7–18.

10. Freedman, *Images of the Medieval Peasant* (Stanford, 1999), 89. However, as Bernard Lewis points out, the Hamitic story "was by no means generally accepted by Muslim authors," though "for the sellers and buyers if black slaves, the curse of Ham provided both an explanation and a justification." Bernard Lewis, *Race and Slavery in the Middle East: An Historical Enquiry* (New York, 1990), 125. Freedman notes that the Hamitic justification for serfdom was especially prevalent in Germany but not in Italy. Benjamin Braude, in his invaluable essay, "The Sons of Noah and the Construction of Ethnic and Geographical Identities in the Medieval and Early Modern Periods," *William and Mary Quarterly*, 54 (Jan. 1997), 103–42, presents a detailed picture of the mistakes, contradictions, and inconsistencies in the European (and historians') interpretations of Noah's biblical curse.

11. Freedman, *Images of the Medieval Peasant,* 139.

12. Kolchin, *Unfree Labor: American Slavery and Russian Serfdom* (Cambridge, MA, 1987), 170, 186.

13. *The Image of the Black in Western Art,* II: *From the Early Christian Era to "The Age of Discovery,"* ed. Jean Devisse and Michel Mollat (2 vols., New York, 1979).

14. William Chester Jordan, "The Medieval Background," in *Struggles in the Promised Land: toward a History of Black-Jewish Relations in the United States*, ed. Jack Salzman and Cornel West (New York, 1997), 53.

15. *Ibid.*, 58.

16. Sweet, "The Iberian Roots of American Racist Thought," *William and Mary Quarterly*, 54 (Jan. 1997), 162, 166.

17. *Ibid.,* 147–48; Lewis, *Race and Slavery in the Middle East*, 53, 122. Lewis provides French as well as English translations of Ibn Khaldun's remarks on blacks being an inferior kind of humanity, much closer to the "animaux stupides." In parts of the Arab world the word for slave, "abd," became limited to black slaves and was even extended to free blacks.

18. Lewis, *Race and Slavery in the Middle East*, 46–48, 96; Bernard Lewis, *Race and Color in Islam* (New York, 1971). The term "Zanj" referred generally to the kind of East African blacks who for many centuries had been shipped as slaves to the Persian Gulf, where, in the Tigris-Euphrates delta they rose in revolt from 869 to 883 C.E. For many other racist passages, see Gernot Rotter, *Die Stellung des Negers in der islamisch-arabischen Geselschaft bis zum XVI Jahrhundert* (Bonn, 1967).

19. David Brion Davis, "At the Heart of Slavery," *The New York Review of Books*, Oct. 17, 1996, 51–54; Davis, "Introduction: The Problem of Slavery," *A Historical Guide to World Slavery*, ed. Seymour Drescher and Stanley L. Engerman (New York, 1998), ix-xviii.

20. Lewis, *Race and Slavery in the Middle East*, 28–30.

21. Gomes Eannes de Azurara, *The Chronicle of the Discovery and Conquest of Guinea . . . Now First Done into English by Charles Raymond Beazley, M.A., F.R.G.S., and Edgar Prestage, B.A. Oxon* (2 vols., London, UK, 1886–87), I, 54; Braude, "Sons of Noah," 127–28. The captives included light-skinned Muslims, who appealed for ansom in the form of five or six Black Moors who would be traded, once they were returned to Africa, for each of the three men who had apparently been free when captured. Since the above translation may be open to doubt, the original text reads as follows: "E aquy avees de notar que estes negros postoque sejam Mouros como os outros, som porem servos daquelles, per antiigo costume, o qual creo que seja por causa da maldicom, que despois do deluvyo lancou Noe sobre seu fillho Caym, pella qual o maldisse, que a sua geeracom fosse sogeita a todallas outras geeracooes do mundo, da qual estes descendem. . . ." Gomes Eannes de Azurara, *Chronica do Descobrimento e Conquista de Guiné* (Paris, 1841), 93. Azurara later speaks contemptuously of the blacks, who lived "like beasts," and "in a bestial sloth," and may well have been referring to a Muslim interpretation of Noah's curse, though as Braude points out, he inaccurately referred to Josephus's *Antiquity of the Jews*. Cain was often confused with Canaan, and there were also difficulties in translating the Hebrew and Latin words for Canaan and Cain.

22. Braude, "Sons of Noah," 137–38. Drawing on George Sandys's description of a Muslim slave caravan, Purchas's book six of *Hakluytus Posthumus, or Purchas His Pilgrimes* (1625–26) is all the more revealing since in the earlier editions he had celebrated the unity of all humankind, "without any more distinction of colour, Nation, language, sexe, condition, all may bee One in him that is ONE." As Braude observes, the growth of New World slavery was beginning by 1625 to bring a change in English attitudes toward the Curse of Ham. Braude, "Sons of Noah," 138.

23. Sweet, "The Iberian Roots of American Racist Thought," 162.

24. Saunders, *A Social History of Black Slaves and Freedmen in Portugal, 1441–1555* (Cambridge, UK, 1982); Berlin, *Many Thousand Gone: The First Two Centuries of Slavery in North America* (Cambridge, MA, 1998).

25. Alden T. Vaughan and Virginia Mason Vaughan, "Before *Othello*: Elizabethan Representation of Sub-Saharan Africans"; Emily C. Bartels, "*Othello* and Africa: Postcolonialism Reconsidered," both in *William and Mary Quarterly*, 54, (Jan. 1997), 19–64. The Vaughans conclude that the few exceptions only prove the rule: "Elizabethan images of Africa featured an unbalanced, sometimes ambiguous, but overwhelmingly derogatory picture of a segment of the world's population that the English had theretofore scarcely known at all" (44).

26. Jordan, *White Over Black: American Attitudes Toward the Negro, 1550–1812* (Chapel Hill, 1969), 28.

27. Vaughan and Vaughan, "Before *Othello*," 42.

28. For one of the several studies of blacks in Britain, see James Walvin, *Black and White: The Negro and English Society, 1555–1945* (London, 1973).

29. Kupperman, "Presentment of Civility: English Reading of American Self-Presentation in the Early Years of Colonization," *William and Mary Quarterly*, 54 (Jan.

1997), 226. For French Canadian and other efforts to idealize Native Americans, in contrast to blacks, see David Brion Davis, *The Problem of Slavery in Western Culture* (New York, 1988), 165–81.

30. Berlin, *Many Thousands Gone*, 66, 69; James H. Merrell, "The Racial Education of the Catawba Indians," *Journal of Southern History*, 50 (Aug. 1984), 363–84; Philip D. Morgan, *Slave Counterpoint: Black Culture in the Eighteenth-Century Chesapeake and Lowcountry* (Chapel Hill, 1998), 477–83.

31. Robin Blackburn, *The Making of New World Slavery: From the Baroque to the Modern, 1492–1800* (London, 1997), 117–18. "Ethiopian envoys reached Venice in 1402. Ethiopian pilgrims made their way perhaps as far as Rome in 1408. An Italian, Pietro Rombulo, was in Ethiopian service for most of the first half of the fifteenth century. The Ethiopian community in Jerusalem sent regular missions to Rome." Braude, "Sons of Noah," 126.

32. Elizabeth Donnan, ed., *Documents Illustrative of the History of the Slave Trade to America* (Washington, DC, 1930–35), 3, 4–9; John Winthrop, *Winthrop's Journal "History of New England," 1630–1649*, ed. James K. Hosmer (2 vols., New York, 1908), II, 251–53.

33. Iain McCalman, ed., *The Horrors of Slavery and Other Writings by Robert Wedderburn* (New York, 1991).

34. Lois E. Horton, "From Class to Race in Early America: Northern Post-Emancipation Racial Construction," and Joanne Pope Melish, "The 'Condition' Debate and Racial Discourse in the Antebellum North," both in this collection.

35. The letters between London and Philadelphia Quaker Meetings in the 1780s show that "the Philadelphia Quakers were extremely reluctant to send London detailed information on the condition of emancipated blacks, arguing that the cause of emancipation must be defended on its higher grounds, not on a possibly misleading study of the consequences. When London Meeting for Sufferings finally received the information they sought, early in 1788, they rejoiced over the progress made by certain free blacks, and indicated that the heart-warming stories sent from Philadelphia had resolved various doubts." Quoted from David Brion Davis, *The Problem of Slavery in the Age of Revolution, 1770–1823* (1975; reprint edition with a new preface, New York, 1999), 232–33, n28.

36. *Adresse de la Société des Amis des Noirs, á l'assemblée nationale, á toutes les villes de commerce, á toutes les manufactures, aux colonies, á toutes les sociétés des amis de la constitution* (1st ed., Paris, 1791), 76; (2d ed., Paris, 1791), 107–08.

37. For a brilliant questioning of the "market revolution" concept, see Richard Lyman Bushman, "Markets and Composite Farms in Early America," *William and Mary Quarterly*, 55 (July 1988), 351–74.

38. I once suggested that this "continuing desire of millions of people to immigrate to the United States from all quarters of the world [could be seen] as a kind of uncelebrated revolution in slow motion." Davis, *Revolutions: Reflections on American Equality and Foreign Liberations* (Cambridge, MA, 1990), 3.

39. Morgan, *American Slavery, American Freedom: The Ordeal of Colonial Virginia* (New York, 1975), esp. 316–87.

40. *The Constitution and Laws of the Cherokee Nation: Passed at Tah-le-quah, Cherokee Nation, 1839* (Washington, DC, 1840), 24, 26. Although the Indians tried to exclude whites, other than missionaries and government officials, it is highly significant that

whites could *become* Cherokees by renouncing their whiteness—an option not open to blacks (except for those who already had some Cherokee ancestry).

41. In 1960 marriages between blacks and whites constituted about 0.125 percent of all marriages in the United States; in 1997, 0.568 percent. *The New York Times World Almanac and Book of Facts, 1999* (Mahwah, NJ, 1999), 877. My statement is also based on a private discussion with the Harvard sociologist Orlando Patterson.

42. Fray Prudencio de Sandoval, *Historia de la vida y hechos del emperador Carlos V.* Vol. 82 of *Biblioteca de autores españoles* (Madrid, 1956), 319.

43. Despite this Spanish desire for "purity of blood," which seems to have arisen from the mass conversion of Jews and subsequent intermarriages, I have already mentioned the wider acceptance of black-white intermixture in the Spanish colonies. This was partly the result of a drastic shortage of white Spanish women, coupled with the unifying influence of the Catholic Church. The Luso-Hispanic cultures also placed a great premium on marrying a lighter-skinned spouse and producing as light-skinned children as possible.

44. James Oliver Horton and Lois E. Horton, *Black Bostonians: Family Life and Community Struggle in the Antebellum North* (New York, 1979), 70; *Loving v. Virginia,* 338 U.S. 1 (1967). As the Hortons point out, free blacks did not actively participate in the repeal of the law against interracial marriage; they were far more interested in the successful integration of Boston's schools. In 1843 white abolitionists and other advocates of repeal tried to assure the public that legalizing black-white marriages would result in less, not more, racial intermixture.

45. John W. Blassingame, ed., *The Frederick Douglass Papers:* Series One: *Speeches, Debates, and Interviews* (6 vols., New Haven, 1985), III, 233–37. At one point Douglass said, "It seems to me that the white Douglas should occasionally meet his desserts at the hands of the black one. Once I thought he was about to make the name respectable, but now I despair of him, and must do the best I can for it myself. (Laughter.) I now leave him in the hands of Mr. Lincoln. . . ." (237).

46. Paul M. Angle, ed., *Created Equal? The Complete Lincoln-Douglas Debates of 1858* (Chicago, 1958), 156.

BIBLIOGRAPHY

Allen, Theodore W. *The Invention of the White Race: Racial Oppression and Social Control.* Verso, 1994.

Bugner, Ladislas, ed. *The Image of the Black in Wesern Art.* 4 vols. Cambridge: Harvard University Press, 1976–1989.

"Constructing Race." *William and Mary Quarterly,* special issue, LIV, 1 (January 1997).

Gossett, Thomas F. *Race: The History of an Idea in America.* Dallas: Southern Methodist University Press, 1963.

Hannaford, Ivan. *Race: The History of an Idea in the West.* Baltimore: Johns Hopkins University Press, 1996.

Jordan, Winthrop D. *Black Over White: American Attitudes Toward the Negro, 1550–1812.* Chapel Hill: University of North Carolina Press, 1969.

Lewis, Bernard. "The Historical Roots of Racism." *American Scholar* 67 (Winter 1998): 17–25.

Morgan, Edmund. *American Slavery, American Freedom: The Ordeal of Colonial Virginia.* New York: Norton, 1975.

Ruchames, Louis, ed. *Racial Thought in America: From the Puritans to Abraham Lincoln,* vol. 1. Amherst: University of Massachusetts Press, 1969.

Index

About the Contributors

David Brion Davis, Sterling Professor Emeritus, Yale University, and Director of Yale's Gilder Lehrman Center for the Study of Slavery, Resistance, and Abolition. He is author of *The Problem of Slavery in Western Culture* (1966; rep. 1988), winner of the 1967 Pulitzer Prize for Nonfiction; *The Problem of Slavery in the Age of Revolution 1770–1823* (1975; 2d ed. 1999), winner of the National Book Award, the Albert J. Beveridge Award, and the Bancroft Prize; and *Slavery and Human Progress* (1986). His most recent publication is *In the Image of God: Religion, Moral Values, and our Heritage of Slavery* (2001).

Lacy K. Ford Jr. is professor of history at the University of South Carolina and is author of *Origins of Southern Radicalism: The South Carolina Upcountry, 1800–1860* (1991). His current research interests focus on antebellum political culture, and he is currently at work *on Making Southern Conservatism: Political Thought in the Jacksonian South* (forthcoming).

Jon Gjerde is professor of history at the University of California, Berkeley. He is author of *From Peasants to Farmers: The Migration from Balestrand, Norway to the Upper Middle West* (1985) and *The Minds of the West: Ethnocultural Evolution in the Rural Middle West, 1830–1917* (1997). He is editor of *Major Problems in American Immigration and Ethnic History* (1998) and *Major Problems in American History* (2002). He is currently at work on a study of anti-Catholicism in the antebellum United States.

Lois E. Horton is professor of sociology at George Mason University. She has taught at Howard University, has been a visiting scholar at the National

Museum of American History of the Smithsonian Institution, and has been a visiting professor at the University of Hawaii and at Fredrick Maximilian University in Munich, Germany. Her books include the coauthored *Black Bostonians: Family Life and Community Struggle in the Antebellum North* (1979; rep. 1999); *In Hope of Liberty: Culture, Community and Protest Among Northern Free Blacks 1700–1865* (1997); and *Hard Road to Freedom: The Story of African America* (2001).

Joanne Pope Melish is associate professor of history at the University of Kentucky, where her research and teaching focus on the production and deployment of racial ideologies in the nineteenth-century United States. She is the author of *Disowning Slavery: Gradual Emancipation and "Race" in New England, 1780–1860* (1998).

Michael A. Morrison is associate professor of history at Purdue University and coeditor of the *Journal of the Early Republic*. He is author of *Slavery and the American West: The Eclipse of Manifest Destiny and the Coming of the Civil War* (1997), *The Human Tradition in Antebellum America* (2000), and coeditor with Ralph D. Gray of *New Perspectives on the Early Republic: Essays from the* Journal of the Early Republic, *1981–1991* (1994). In 1998 the Carnegie Foundation for the Advancement of Teaching named him Indiana Professor of the Year.

Daniel K. Richter is the Richard S. Dunn Director of the McNeil Center for Early American Studies and professor of history at the University of Pennsylvania. His research and teaching focus on colonial North America and on Native American history prior to 1800. Before joining the Penn faculty, he taught at Dickinson College and the University of East Anglia, and he has been a visiting professor at Columbia University. Richter is author of *Facing East from Indian Country: A Native History of Early America* (2001) and *The Ordeal of the Longhouse: The Peoples of the Iroquois League in the Era of European Colonization* (1992), and coeditor, with James H. Merrell, of *Beyond the Covenant Chain: The Iroquois and Their Neighbors in Indian North America, 1600–1800* (1987).

David R. Roediger teaches in history and in the Afro-American Studies and Research Program at University of Illinois—Urbana, where he holds the Babcock Chair. He has previously taught at Northwestern University, University of Missouri, and University of Minnesota. His books include *Our Own Time* (1989, with Philip S. Foner); *The Wages of Whiteness* (1991); *Towards the Abolition of Whiteness* (1994); and *Colored White* (2002). His current writing is on southern and eastern European immigrants and race in early twentieth-century United States.

James P. Ronda holds the H. G. Barnard Chair in Western American History at the University of Tulsa and is a past president of the Western History Association. A specialist in the history of the exploration of the American West, his books include *Lewis and Clark among the Indians* (1984); *Astoria and Empire* (1990); *Revealing America: Image and Imagination in the Exploration of North America* (1996); *Voyages of Discovery: Essays on the Lewis and Clark Expedition* (1998); *Jefferson's West: A Journey with Lewis and Clark* (2001); and *Finding the West: Explorations with Lewis and Clark* (2001). Professor Ronda has been a consultant and had on-camera roles in a number of television documentaries including those for PBS, C-SPAN, A&E, and the BBC. He is currently writing one of the catalogue essays for the National Lewis and Clark Bicentennial Exhibition.

James Brewer Stewart is the James Wallace Professor of history at Macalester College. His many published works include *Joshua R. Giddings and the Tactics of Radical Politics* (1970); *Holy Warriors: The Abolitionists and American Slavery* (1976); and *Wendell Phillips: Liberty's Hero*. His most recent publication is *To Heal the Scourge of Prejudice: The Life and Writings of Hosea Easton*, which he edited with George R. Price.